Canadian Miss
the Death Railway

From the records of Dr. Walter G. Anderson,

Missionary, Physician, and Prisoner of War

Compiled and annotated by his niece,

Ann Louise Smith

Dedication

I dedicate this book to the memory of my Uncle Walter, who had my respect and love for all his tenderness and love of knowledge. I also dedicate this volume to my dear Mum, who passed away suddenly just as the book was being finalized for print. I admired her spirit and love for keeping her hands busy. "Busy hands are happy hands," she would say. I love you, Mum.

Ann Louise Smith

It should be noted, for those who do not remember the days of the Forties and Fifties of the last century, that some of the expressions used in these texts may sound offensive, in terms of what is acceptable language today. In common usage back then, words like "Japs", "Nips", " coolies", etc., may sound inappropriate to today's more sensitive ears. These expressions appear in the actual documents that comprise this book because they are consistent with the flavour of their time.

Smith, Ann Louise
Canadian Missionary POW on the Death Railway

ISBN 978-0-557-04502-0

Table of Contents

Lt. W.G. Anderson, M.D. -- I.M.S. 1941

Introduction

This book covers the wartime years of missionary physician Captain Walter G. Anderson, M.D., I.M.S. (*1907 +2002), from his own records, as compiled and selected by me, Ann Louise Smith, his niece, with the support of many people, including Kaca Henley, the editor.

My Uncle Walter was born in India on January 29th, 1907, the son of Canadian missionary parents who also gave their full life service there from 1901 to 1946. Hindi was his mother tongue. India was his home and his country.

Walter had his early schooling at Clifton Grange in Ootacamund, Central India, and his high school education also in Ootacamund, at Breek's Memorial Boarding School for Boys, where exams were set by Cambridge University of England. His life style and upbringing were conservative as compared to ours here in North America as he was raised by missionaries and among the Indian people and their ways of life.

He came to Canada for his medical education. His quick mind and high standards gained him entrance into the University of Toronto in 1924 (at the age of 17), where he proceeded to receive his B.A., M.D. and D.P.H. His internships at St. Michael's Hospital and the old Hospital for Sick Children prepared him well. He was appointed to the Medical Ministry in India in 1937 by the United Church of Canada.

During his years in India, he served on the Central India Mission Field as Staff Doctor, then Medical Superintendent at Ratlam, Indore, Banswara, and Dhar.

Before leaving India for Singapore in 1941, the newly conscripted Lt. Anderson with the two family Jack Russell terriers, Quintie and Punch.

At the beginning of the war, Walter was conscripted into the Indian Army Medical Service, as Lieutenant W. G. Anderson, later to become Captain. He arrived in Singapore on the S.S. Devonshire just nine days before the fall of the city on February 15, 1942 and he was taken and held prisoner by the Japanese the following day.

His internment was in the environs of the Thailand-Burma Railway Line, built along the River Kwai by POWs and conscripted labourers – clearing, levelling, carrying bamboo through jungles, mud and monsoon weather. Although a physician who tended to the needs of all around him, Walter was not spared manual labour on the railway line and bridges, or digging latrines and graves. He persisted in his medical work; the skill of his hands and the care of his heart were often his only supplies. Intense heat and the work demands and harsh conditions imposed by his Japanese captors made for desperate situations.

Surreptitiously, Walter kept a little diary, using two-inch pencil stubs to write with, as they were easier to hide from his Japanese captors. When his writings were found and confiscated, he managed to obtain another notebook and recorded what he could remember of his original entries, now and then leaving gaps to be filled in as memory returned.

Much of the time, he was the only doctor in the Dutch POW camps and he said they were the worst. I imagine there were some horrible memories he just wanted to block out (something of an indication of this is to be found in the *War Crimes* section of the Appendices, p. 251) Almost without medicine or instruments, he helped fellow prisoners, coolies and Japanese with their medical issues. Sometimes he felt that his request for leniency for other prisoners instead brought on more severe treatment by those in charge. He was well liked by the coolies (the simple folk who did all the small jobs for the Japanese officers). On his birthday one year, they cooked him a birthday cake by wrapping it in banana leaves and burying it in the ground to cook.

In September 1942, while in the Changi POW camp, the prisoners were told they had to sign a form stating they would not try to escape. They refused, and in retaliation the Japanese began shooting prisoner after prisoner until finally Lt. Col. Holmes (who was in command of the prisoners) decided that it was best to sign it, under duress, to avoid more prisoners being shot. Later, in 1945, Walter happened on to documents justifying this decision. In fact, we were moved by a quote that he penciled lightly on a copy of the form they were to sign: " *'It is great sin to swear unto a sin, but greater sin to keep a sinful oath.' Shakespeare*". He saved the documents about this "Selerang" incident and they are included here on pages 69-73.

These are only a few of the riveting contents of the doctor's prison diaries. We have interspersed them with the chatty and heartbreaking letters from his parents, faithfully written to him despite an absolute minimum of information as to their son's whereabouts and conditions.

After the War, Walter was very quiet about his days as a POW; he never spoke of those times until he was in his eighties and, in his words, had forgiven the Japanese. It was then that Walter decided to try to find the sole three postcards he had been allowed to send home.

Over a period of several years Uncle Walter would ask me repeatedly to help him go through his old trunks looking for those postcards. He was very anxious to locate them, and not one of us realized that they would not have been in his trunks but rather in his parents' trunks. Of course, that's exactly where we finally found them in 2002. It was going through the materials at that time that sparked my determination to make his experiences available to those interested in his amazing history.

I had the excitement and joy of discovering all the material included in this book while cleaning out our family home in Toronto, Ontario after Walter's passing on September 2nd, 2002. He was very methodical and kept records of everything, a trait I'm sure he inherited from his parents. Among the treasures we found (and have reproduced samples of in this book) were his Nippon-English and Malay-English vocabularies, handwritten in a tiny notebook (p.158), and the calendars he created to track the days and months of his internment as a prisoner of war by the Japanese (p. 174).

All this and so much more was contained in the 21 trunks of materials saved in my grandparents' basement, covering their entire lifetimes, including their many years of missionary work in India. Grandma Mabel Anderson never threw out any written material and much to our amazement we found letters, photos, testimonials and documents that had been stored dating back to 1901 when my grandparents first went to India for the United Church of Canada.

So complete was this treasure-trove, and so fascinating was the history it told, that it seemed logical to begin compiling and preserving it for posterity in a book, to honour the memory of this extraordinary man. For the most part, this book contains the writings of my Uncle Walter and my grandparents, Rev. and Mrs. Frederick Anderson, and some relevant documentation, covering the period of World War II and immediately following the war.

We decided to combine letters and diary entries chronologically to show, in parallel with his experiences, what was transpiring in his parents' lives. It is interesting to realize that while Walter was imprisoned in POW camps in the dense jungles of Burma and Thailand, his parents were also living in missionary camps, in the jungles of India.

We are sure Walter had no intention for his diaries to be published, clearly the frequently cryptic and fragmentary notes were for his own record. The small handwritten pages, many the worse for wear and the passage of time, often fragile and virtually indecipherable, have been copied as far as possible verbatim, maintaining his own short forms and quotes, without attention to proper grammar as he tried to conserve as much paper as possible.

Any misspellings or inconsistencies in names of places and persons may be due to problems with legibility, although we have checked everything possible. We have, in a number of places, inserted explanatory notes in square brackets, where we were able to explain abbreviations or specific uncommon terms, or give some background. We have also spelled out those abbreviations and acronyms that we were able to track down, and placed them in square brackets for easier reading.

It should be noted that the materials in this volume have been compiled without a lot of background in military and medical matters and terminology on my part, although I have done my utmost to obtain the relevant definitions and explanations. I ask the reader`s patience and forbearance with errors or misinterpretations.

We have also included reproductions of the only three post cards he was allowed to send home (his only chance in 3½ years to send word to his parents) and his wonderful letters written after his release, as well as documentation around his journey back home to Dhar, India.

Ann Louise Smith

Prologues

Message from the Author

I am Walter G. Anderson's very proud niece. When I was in school, all my essays were about my Uncle Walter and his life in India as a missionary doctor. He always had pleasant stories to tell us about various operations and situations during his years in India. We had the job of clearing the house out after he died, and what excitement when we found all the letters and documents. It is sad to think that they had been down there for over 50 years.

I have had the idea of creating this book ever since his passing and spent several months just putting everything in chronological order and into binders. My mother and a good friend of hers helped to decipher Walter's journal and I deciphered the handwriting of my grandparents' letters, then did the typing. I felt that if my grandparents took special care in storing and protecting these special memoirs, then it was important to share them with all our family members and friends across Canada, United States and India.

I have tried to include as much as I felt important regarding the war years, and have researched many web sites to find explanations and correct spellings. With the help of my editor, we decided to combine the parents' letters and his journal pages chronologically, to show what each were doing during the same time period. Walter did not receive the letters until a year and a half later, so one can see how stressful it was for both son and parents not knowing what was happening to each other during those time periods.

My grandmother wrote her letters to her son on stationery with some lovely little drawings from life in India. I was charmed by them, and decided to place a few of them here and there throughout the book, to brighten it up and help create a mood for the reader.

I want my children, grandchildren, niece and nephews and descendants to know how important their great uncle was during the war and after.

All the hard times and horrific sights he saw and endured during the period of 1942 – 1945 did not change his gentle, caring personality. I have tried to give a little detail to his earlier years to help the reader understand him and his quiet life style in India. Also, I have touched on his return to his missionary duties as a doctor in Ratlam and many other cities in India from 1946 – 1976.

I hope one day I can manage to write a story about his parents, my grandparents and Uncle Walter's mission work. I do hope you enjoy reading about Walter's part in WW II in Burma and of his parents heartfelt letters, not knowing whether Walter was receiving their letters or not. Grandma used to cut the Casualty reports out of the papers to check for her son.

In all my research I have not found anything that mentions that there were any other Canadian missionary doctors in Burma. A Canadian in India as a missionary doctor and in the British Indian Army I imagine was not recognized as a Canadian but rather as a British subject.

Ann Louise Smith
Lindsay, Ontario, Autumn 2008

Walter and his sister Marion, 1937, before his departure to India.

Message from Walter's sister

Walter Gilray Anderson was my big brother, he was seven years older than me and I was so very proud of him. In my younger days, he made a doll cradle and even knit a doll's sweater for me. As I grew older, he accompanied me on the train from Ratlam to Hebron School in Conoor, situated on the tea plantation hills. He was on the "Metagama" in 1924 with our parents and me on our way to Canada when the ship was hit by a grain ship. He kept a diary for 1924 and so has quite the story about the collision.

Later years, when he was a prisoner under the Japanese, he even thought of me and mentioned me in one of his three cards he was allowed to send home with very few words to our parents. I don't think, at that time, I realized the conditions and stress he was suffering as a prisoner, until the war was over and he related some of the situations he had to endure. Thank goodness he was able to come home safely to India and relate some of his experiences, although he was very quiet about the war for many years.

He was held up high by the Indian folk on a level with Mother Theresa. To me and all his friends he was the perfect gentleman. While he was still working in India the Mission named a Village after him called the "Walter Villa", that's how much they admired him and his work. Yes, I'm very proud of my brother.

Marion Louise Anderson/Goodchild
Lindsay, Ontario, Autumn 2008

Marion Louise Goodchild, Dec.12,1913 - Jan.7, 2009.

Message from the Editor

When my friend Ann Louise Smith asked me to help her with a book honouring the story of her missionary doctor uncle, compiling his wartime journals and letters, I expected something dry, and – forgive me – a little boring.

I could not have been more wrong. I had no idea of Walter G. Anderson himself, a man of conviction, dedicated to his dual vocation, steel-strong and feather-gentle, human, moral and caring. Nor did I count on Ann's enthusiasm, diligence and persistence in preparing this volume, the years she had already spent examining and sorting uncountable boxes of papers, yellow with time and crumbling to the touch. And the mind-numbing and vision-destroying task of typing out miles and miles of minuscule text, word by word, to make it accessible.

This volume is indeed a labour of love and devotion on her part, sharing with the world this man she so admired and, indeed, making him available to enthusiasts of the history of World War Two. I am amazed at her insight into just what would help a reader see the man`s true nature, the breadth of his knowledge, and the respect he evoked in all who knew him.

My contribution to this volume was my knowledge of language, my abilities with desktop publishing, and some experience with graphic design. We planned the structure of the book to entertain and inform, as clearly and evocatively as possible. We decided to include a variety of materials, letters (often detailed and personal) in italics, with journal entries in regular type, with explanatory notes in bold face. For visual interest, we interspersed the writings with a broad range of illustrations, photos, copies of documents, newspaper clippings and more. Helping Ann with the selection of what to include, and where to place it, was the hardest – and the most exciting – part of the task

This book immortalizes the man in this world, and it is to be hoped that, from the other world, where he and his sister are surely watching over his devoted niece, he can overcome his self-effacing modesty, and be at least a little pleased with our efforts.

Kaca Polackova Henley
Lindsay, Ontario

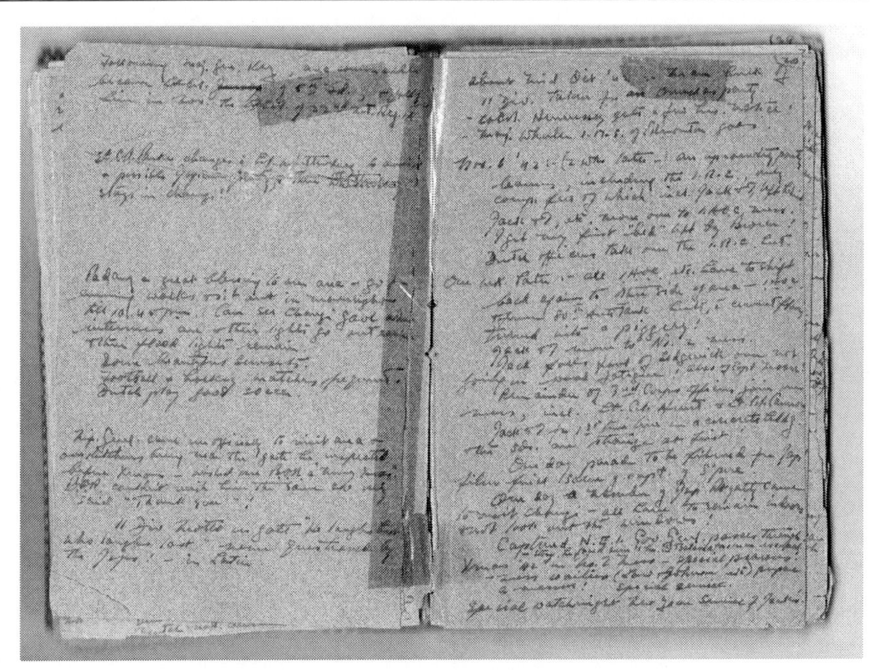

Pages from Walter's POW Diary/Journal, 1941-44.

1941

True Copy
From – The Director General,
Indian Medical Service.

To – The General Secretary,
United Church of Canada Mission,
Central India, Indore.
New Delhi, dated the 27th Feb. 1941

Dear Sir,

*Will you kindly refer to Colonel Huban's letter No. 4-6/41-*R *dated 15th January 1941 intimating that Dr. Anderson was not to be called up for some time to come. It is regretted that owing to the urgent needs of the army it has been necessary to review his case and it has now been decided to call him up on 15th March 1941. The Commander, Bombay District, has been requested to issue a calling up notice accordingly.*

Yours faithfully,
(Sd.) **[Signature illegible]**
Major, I.M.S.
For Director General, I.M.S.

[Walter's first journal entry]
MARCH 13th, 1941
Left United Church of Canada Mission Hospital, Ratlam, Central India, for Poona

MARCH 15th, 1941

Reported to Indian Medical Corps Depot, Poona. Commissioned Lieutenant in Indian Medical Service. Lived first few days at Napier Hotel. Then at 6 Stanley Road, Mrs. James. Early morning – drove two hours. After breakfast to lunch – lectures, gas mask drill, revolver practice etc. Afternoon drill period. One night route march. Uniform outfit made and fitted. All Indian Officers sent after two weeks to Officers training course, Mhow. Major Johnson posted in Poona and I go to Jubbulpore.

Staff of Indian Military Hospital, Jubbulpore, 1941

APRIL 1st, 1941

Arrive in Jubbulpore. Put up at Nubudda Club. Indian Military Hospital. Commanding Officer, Lieutenant Colonel Loganadan. Posted to take early morning sick parade along with Captain Palmit Kan at Indian Army Officer Cadet Training Corps – also Medical Officer for Indian Army Europeans and Officer's families. Indian Military Hospital had 700 to 800 beds.

AIR MAIL

Office of the Contr. of Mily. Accounts, Southern Command.
Station, Poona, the 18th April 1941
The Under Secretary of State for India,
Accountant General's Department, India Office, London.
Lieut. W.G. ANDERSON, I.M.S., I.M. Hospital, Jubbulpore.

Sir,

I have the honour to state that the above named officer, who has been granted an Emergency Commission in the Indian Medical Service under the terms of the Government of India, Defence Department letter No. 336/Med/D-1 dated 28.9.1940, reported for duty at the I.H.C. Depot, Poona on 15th March 1941 (F.N.) and became entitled to sterling overseas pay of L.15/- p.m. with effect from that date. It is therefore, requested that with effect from 15th March 1941, sterling overseas pay may please be paid to the officer's nominee; The American Express Company, Inc. 52, Cornhill, London, E.C.3

The above payment will be included in the confirmatory statement to be rendered by this office for the quarter ending 31st March 1941.

The favour of an acknowledgment of this communication is requested.

I have the honour to be, Sir,
Your most obedient servant,
(Sd.) N.V. Gokhaley,
Dy. Asst. Contr. of Mily. Accounts, South Command.
Copy forwarded to Lt. W.G. Anderson, I.M.S. (E.C.)
Indian Military Hospital, Jubbulpore

About MAY 9th, 1941

Went to Sangor, Central Province as officer. Commanding Officer of Central India Medical Hospital for a month for Captain Addison. Bus trip from Jubbulpore to Sangor, the hottest I've ever had. Took over Addison's room and bearer. Fed at Staff mess of Sangor Hospital Service. Sangor Hospital, old style, coal, with domed ceilings and thick wall arches – same in mess of old equitation school. Commandant: Colonel Williams who went with His Highness of Ratlam to U.S.A. on India polo team – he conducts a better Church of England service than the Chaplain.

Had charge of Central India Military Hospital, Cantonese Hospital, British and Indian Families Hospitals and visited Indian Wing, child center twice a week with the Colonel's wife. Was member of Cantonese Board – required to make out the Sangor Sanitary and Health report for previous year. Cantonese and Sanitary rounds.

Maternity case two weeks after arrival – reported four weeks overdue! Called at night. Bearer **[watchman]** away with my bicycle! Walked home next morning. Case came off okay at 11 a.m.

Sunday drives with Mr. Rowe, Indian Medical Doctor, visited city, fort, etc. Interesting old cemetery! Hot weather S.P. closed, station nearly empty for a wait, not unpleasant.

About JUNE 10th, 1941– Back in Jubbulpore.

Living at Royal Signals Mess, became Medical Officer to the Indian Army Ordinance Corps Training Command – a small city over whole race course area. Two **[officers]** to battalions and Headquarters Corp. and Depot. I take sick parade of one T. Battalion and a civilian Doctor takes the other. Sanitary rounds about twice a week. Again have Indian Army families and officers on courses. Later also became Medical Teacher recruiting officers, and through lack of the Medical Officers at times have oversight of Surgery, Venereal Disease, and skin wards at Indian Military Hospital.

Captain Devine F.R.C.S. **[Fellow of the Royal College of Surgeons]** on leave. Left me his private cases to watch! Became also examiner for Prudential Life Insurance Co. Received Rs.16/ **[Rupees]** a time.

JULY 1941
Indian Military Hospital,
Juppulpore, dated 13/7/41

To,
The Officers Commanding,
" " I.A.O.C., Trg. Centre,
" " S.T.C.(I).
" " 13 A.T.Coy.
" " 35 Rest Camp.

Owing to the withdrawal of I.M.S. Officers by the Southern Command resulting in an acute shortage, the following provisional medical arrangements are made with effect from 15th July 1941.

Lt. W.G. Anderson, I.M.S… In medical charge of I.A.O.C., T.C.
Jem. K.M.E. Hassan, I.M.D..In medical charge of S.T.C.(I).
Jem. Baij Nath, I.M.D... In medical charge of 13 A.T.C. and 35 Rest Camp.
Lt. Col. A.D. Loganadan I.M.S.

Copy to:- Commanding, I.M.H., Juppulpore
Lt. W.G. Anderson, I.M.S.
Jem. K.M.E. Hassan I.M.D.
Jem. Baij Nath I.M.D.

OCTOBER 1941

Building a new Medical Inspection Room and Detention ward at the Indian Army Ordinance Corps Training Command I take 10 days casual leave to Dhar, move into new Medical Inspection Room on return. Lieutenant Colonel Loganadan posted to Malaya. Succeeded by Lieutenant Colonel Admiral Chand, Colonel Harry Cohendt of Indian Army Ordinance Corps Training Command, Brigadier Hind and District Commander. I move back to live at club on return from leave. Good tennis courts at club. Mr. Walsh, Club Secretary. First Aid PM instruction classes at hospital.

Each Medical Officer takes his turn being Orderly Medical officer on duty at Indian Military Hospital from 1 o'clock on and sleep there all night. Sometimes dark and very cold going and coming at night and early A.M. on bicycle! Play hockey, soccer, volleyball etc. with the orderly staff with Medical Officer posting changes. These night duties come around often. I was the only European at the Indian Military Hospital. For a time Major O'Neil and later Major Tennant was 2nd in command. Evidence of some very ardent recruiting officers – new recruits arrived at the Indian Army Ordinance Corps Training Command – one with marked visual defect, others with huge varices and cystoceles etc!

NOVEMBER 1941

Get a posting to Malaya but date not fixed – 1st December, 7th December, 3rd January all postponed.

DECEMBER 7th – 8th, 1941

Japs invade Malaya and Eastern war begins. Few days after landing at Kota Baru Japs sink "Prince of Wales" and "Repulse" by bombing. Daily papers show Japs always infiltrating southwards down Malaya and coming down the West coast, getting behind our lines.

DECEMBER 21st, 1941

I get 10 days overseas leave to Dhar. 31st return to Jubbulpore instead of Madras.

Walter Anderson with his parents, Rev. Frederick & Mabel Anderson, Dec. 1941.

1942

JANUARY 18, 1942
[From father]

United Church of Canada Mission
Central India
Rev. F. J. Anderson
Mission Treasurer

Dear Walter

Received your letter yesterday and we look for another day when the mail arrives. Perhaps this will have to be forwarded to catch you but it is not important anyway.

You may have heard from some of your M.E. friends of Miss Pearson's left turn from Jubbulpore. The telegram to the Jub. Stn. Master worked. Miss P. was informed and allowed herself to be transferred to the train for Bombay. But she was a good girl guide and got things done. She saw that her luggage was transferred with her and was able to get in touch with Mr. Davis and others who were at some board meeting and they collected Rs. 198 / s and cashed Miss P's. Rs. 200/ - cheque which she got from me via Miss Stevenson when the trains crossed at Dolanda Station north of Jaora. So Miss P. got to Bombay and must wait there for her ship which, she says, is still somewhere near Calcutta. Her adventures have begun and she has cleared her first hurdle.

Tomorrow I go to Ratlam and hope to return Tuesday evening. On Thursday we hope to get our carts off to Amjhira for a first camp and go out ourselves Friday by which time the carts will be there. 2nd camp may be Mangod or near it and 3rd at Nalcha. Perhaps that is all we will do as Holi **[Hindi Spring Festival]** *comes about March 1st and there is little use being out at that time unless it be in a village where Christians are.*

We had our Leper Home Service conducted this morning by Rev. Bala out of **[?]** *in front of their church. Miss Stevenson was out with us. She is quite willing to go to Neemuch (Sunda Ghar) for a few months if the Commission agrees to lend her. If travel should get more difficult Miss Martin may not go to Canada this Spring. But I hope the near future may be brighter. Was glad to hear of Churchill's safe return to England.*

And so we wish for you a skilful handling of your 'cases' in the relief of suffering. Safety for yourself and a speedy return which I suppose will be when the Japs have been conquered and some of them driven back home. War is beastly but our cause is just and in the interest of humanity and freedom we can enter the struggle and pray for victory. Be strong and of good courage.

Yours lovingly
Father

JANUARY 19th, 1942

Left Jubbulpore, along with Munton and Stephenson of Royal Army Ordinance Corps. – 4 pm. changed to troop train special at Itarsi. Found copy of secret train orders lying open on Itarsi Assistant Station Master's desk that night and all sorts of people in office! Had night dinner in Reference Room at table next to Pundit Nehru and family. Italian P.O.W. **[Prisoner of War]** troop train came through while we waited. Coming events cast shadows before them. Difficulty getting railway coaches for the draft, Munton took over and we all finally got 3rd class compartment after midnight.

JANUARY 20th, 1942

Breakfast at Khandwa. Felt like clipping up to Mhow and Dhar instead of going on to diminishing Malaya. Long tiresome day on the train!

JANUARY 21st, 1942

Arrive Bombay. One Indian Other Rank **[means any rank below commissioned officer]** taken to hospital sick with sheer funk **[complete panic]**. I could not get steel hat or water purifying tablets. March to Calaba transit camp. Tablets.

JANUARY 22nd, 1942

Registered at Embarkation and knocked about Bombay – movies – supper at Grunis **[?]** Hotel – Lunch at the Taj.

[All letters written to Walter between January 22, 1942 and November 1st, 1942 were not received by him until April 4th, 1943.]

JANUARY 22, 1942

[From Mother, note attached stating: *First letter from India to Singapore. Contact lost! Returned D.L.O.* **[dead letter office]** *Aug. 28th,1942*]

Dhar, Central India

My dear Walter

It seems very unreal to be writing to you where I suppose we must be as contented as possible for this is a state of affairs which will continue for some time. The first message that acknowledges the receipt of a home letter will perhaps establish some regularity.

This is Thurs. night – we go out to camp tomorrow afternoon where we receive the mail. This morning we rec'd your keys by Reg. letter. This afternoon we rec'd the suitcase in good condition. It doesn't even look too dusty! Grey shirt, blanket, racquet, press, shoes, white pants, 2 white elephants & brass plate – (I think that is all.) The last mentioned – plate is a beauty. I thank you for the lovely thing – but it is going to be ours only until you come. The elephants too are so quaint and cute I have left them in their cases in the suitcase because we are to be away about 3 weeks this trip. We have arranged to get our mail forwarded also the paper and shall get the papers at 4:30 instead of 2 o'clock. The other mail will reach us at 5 to 5:30 daily.

Father got back after rather sometime – he went on Monday – got home Wed. tea time – 4:30. Such are some of the delays – in bus travel! Committee meeting at 8:30 Tues. and took the whole day except mealtimes and cinema time – mailings after the picture again.

Father went to the bus Wed. a.m., but couldn't get a seat so had to wait till 1:30 p.m. so he got home last evening. The camp – left for Amjhira this morning. After the heavy work of getting things ready for those carts – always leaves me feeling I would like to think it was finished but next comes the last bits of food to take, leave house in order and servants with directions etc. – no knitting being done! The Evangelist Committee allowed Miss Stevenson to take the education appointment in Neemuch till spring. She left on the 3 o'clock bus today. I took her to the bus and Margaret and I saw her off to Ratlam where she stays overnight.

I was sorry that my last letter to you in Central India did not make as good time as some lately – that would happen to the last one! Thanks for all the letters you have kindly sent since we were able to write you. Note with Keys, Itarsi – Bhusanal – to date. What a night you had on train, how tired you must have been to start out with! I do hope you can get some enjoyment once you embark and a good rest. (We are going into Gwalior territory so their stamps will have to be used,) I send this now – we are in Dhar State.

A comedian is on radio and he has just said – "well, where did he go? He went to sea, and he saw and came back." 'had sore eyes from winking at the mermaids'. Eastern news is no joke – now we shall have to depend on Times of India for what we get and have [**these next few lines were written all around the edges of the letter**] *and the neighbours report any outstanding items. I can't begin to say what's in my heart or would say. Do take care of yourself dear boy. Card and note from Miss Greer today. Shall quote and enclose small sheet.*

Best love from
Mother

[**enclosed on a tiny paper:**]

May you go out in Gods protecting care, with His love shining over you. May you have courage and consciousness of this, and return, safely, in good time. I shall not cease to pray for you. Many people love you dearly, don't forget that and take good care of yourself, Walter ji. **[ji is a term of endearment in India]**

First Letter from India
To Singapore written Jan. 22 '42
Contact Lost!
Returned D.L.O. Aug. 28 '42

Mabel Anderson's handwriting around the edges of her letter. Notice also the picture on the letter paper. We include other examples below and throughout this book.

[Note: The 'camp' mentioned throughout is where Rev. Fred and Mabel Anderson would set up to work, usually in various locations in the jungle with tents; they would teach and preach the word of God, also teach the people life skills, in fact, helping them to help themselves with things like personal hygiene, caring for their babies, cooking and gardening.]

In Camp, Rev. and Mrs. Anderson on the right.

JANUARY 23rd, 1942

Embarked and sailed about noon on S.S. "Devonshire". Still on her maiden voyage. Officers and families accommodations very good. Troops quarters not so good! Many Jowans **[young soldiers]** sick and not keeping themselves clean.

One Indian Medical Service Lieutenant and I in a cabin. Captain Markby (Vermoni) Royal Army Medical Corps from Jubbulpore made himself troops surgeon. Treated the Indian Medical Corps Indians rather roughly – dress parades and exercise each morning and he put them through it! He wanted to hold morning inspection before landing and have Indian troops parade on the foredeck naked! We discouraged it.

Air raid drills – Medical Officers all in ships Hospital. I gave daily lectures in First Aid in Hindustani on deck each afternoon. Food quite good! I am teased for having curry and rice each day – getting used to a rice diet!

SS Devonshire

On board A.M.: – All reinforcements – Indian Army: – 10th Baluchi Regiment including Lieutenant Burhanudin, brother of His Highness of Chitral (?) and Lieutenant Lee who later was decapitated by Japs. See following list:

Reinforcements:
10th Baluchi Regiment
Bombay Sap. & Minus…
I.A.O.C. [Indian Army Ordinance Corps]
Postal Services
I.M.C. [Indian Medical Corp]
Accounts Dept.
Officers – Baluchi Regiment
Royal Signals.
I.M.O.C. – [Indian Medical Ordinance Corp]
B.S.M. [British Sergeant Major]
I.M.S. [Indian Medical Service] and
I.M.D. [Indian Medical Dept.]
2 Rajisthan Rifles (2nd Battalion rifles)
Hyderabad State Forces
Mostly non-combatants.

Kept out of sight of land all the way to Sunda Straits. Thus crossed the Equator twice going to Singapore **[see map on p. 36].**

Joined a Brigade in Indian Ocean going to Batavia from England – so greatly enlarged our convoy. Originally from Bombay, our convoy was four ships and destroyer escort. Empress of Asia, Felix Roussel, a Dutch steamer Plancius and S.S. Devonshire. New convoy contained Empress of Australia. Markby one night did an appendix operation on an Indian Other Rank – old ships doctor said this. "The only time he knew of when the doctor did not ask to stop the ship." Empress of Asia an old three-funnel coal burner with plenty of black smoke and slowest in convoy – a good target for any enemy vessel!

Inside Sunda Strait – danger area.

SS Empress of Asia (above) and SS Felix Roussel (below) were also part of the convoy.

JANUARY 28th, '42
[From Mother]
In Camp Amjhira, Gwalior State

Dear Walter

It seems so unreal to be writing to you – I don't know where! but writing will be done, just the same. We count days, you may be sure, and our coming out to camp may coincide with your departure! The last letters to you in Central Province were returned, as luck would have it, and have been sent to your Base Postal Depot. Hoping they will reach you some day. I intend to number my letters but made a rather forgetful beginning!

Just after sending on that letter, we came out here, and are camped under a large banyan tree (seven tents). I don't know whether you will remember a nice big talao **[pond]** *at Amjhira. One has to drive half way round it before getting to the village. Well, we didn't go round it but have struck camp almost at the point where the road comes along-side. The morning view is what looks like a lake, with banana and palm trees etc. on opposite bank and village houses, with two superior ones about four stories high. It's rather an interesting view.*

We have with us Sam, Daud Bala, David Kuria, (Sam's servant boy) Bhura and Daniel. Tomorrow forenoon Pastor Abraham will be out for a few days. Sat. Peter Maoji will join the camp. Mangal Prasad lives in the village, that is, when he is not in our camp! He comes about four times a day, his wife comes twice and son Joseph comes roughly a dozen times! Today is Maharram **[a celebration]**, *in Dhar, and tonight is the time it is celebrated here.*

Right here I better retrace my steps a little, ere I forget, to say – the suitcase came, not even looking dusty. It looks nice. I opened it and put your racquet into its press and put it, then into your tin trunk. The collar of the grey shirt is not even crushed! That blanket is certainly much lighter, since washed! "Thanks a lot" for the lovely plate it contained! It will be ours till you come back. I love the colours as the light strikes on it just right to show them. Yours of 22nd and postcard of 23rd both received. How I wish we could have answered them right there and then! So glad that the dhobi **[person who did laundry]** *turned up in time, that the picture was good, hope your watch keeps going well, that you got advice from Amexico, and Canada Life. Quintie got your Salaams, but not Punch yet* **[their dogs]** *! Sent Mission Christian Hospital a note but yours was not in – since our bright postmaster at Dhar sent two days mail to a place beyond here – Manawar. It came back, in time so only last evening I received your post card. The bus driver brings out the newspaper and drops it off here every day. Mrs. Harcourt and Mrs. Y. Masih were at Dhar* *where we left, in fact they just stepped out of our drawing room in time to let us lock the front door. Word came yesterday, Air Mail from New Zealand, from Miss Hilliard, signed also by Dr. Jean Whittier, Miss McLeod and Miss Buckholtz to Father asking him to have money to meet them at port, and to let the stations concerned know of their news. The letter was posted at Wellington. Jan. 9th.*

We were quite excited to get this news. Today we got news that a cable had come to Ratlam of Mrs. Menzies and Miss Stewart's safe arrival in Los Angeles. So we won't worry any more about them.

I had a letter from Moir yesterday saying thanks for the prospect of coming to Dhar for a fortnight, in Spring, and that they had heard from you. Margaret and Jimmie went to camp for about a week. They will not go out again! Moir will go out on Sat. again. Margaret takes Jimmie to the hills at Easter time and Moir comes right to us. Did I tell you I had written to two Ladies in charge of two boarding houses of Mussoorie? One of those houses is 'Sylverton' where Dr. and Mrs. Hana, of the Irish Mission were stopping the summer you and I were in Landour.

It is very central. The other is that 'Airyland' you wrote about from C.P. **[Central Province].** *I had a nice little letter from Miss Boyd, two days ago. I quote. – "all of us on the Ratlam Medical staff will be remembering him daily in our morning prayer service. We have had two minutes silent prayer every day for many months, just before the Lord's Prayer, when we have remembered those in trouble through the war, and I will be adding, from now on a prayer for Mothers of sons. There is so little one can say to help, and just nothing one can do but my sympathy is all with you." She began by saying she only heard you had gone from Father when he was there for committee.*

Father had a very lame back yesterday and couldn't go out with the men. I gave him aspirin and "P.D." rubbed on his back seemed to help. Today he went nearby. He has now been in bed for some time so I had better stop my typing. He went to bed just as I started, at 8:30!

We had a storm last night and some sides of our old tent leaked! Hope for better night tonight. Margaret writes asking how we managed through all the rainy nights – they had had three rainy nights in Dhar!

Shall call off till morning. Must describe our walk last Sunday.

Next morning – sunny though clouds about. Not quite so cold, so far. No more rain last night. Gave Father my camp bed because his back is lame, so the result, after two nights, is I am sending to the village for long tacks, and the canvas will be loosened, at center.

Sunday morning we were invited by Mangal to go for a walk! To see a place about two miles from here called "Amka Jamka". One passes over a small ruffet **[small waterfall]**, *among trees, and to the left in the beginning of a ravine are temples. It seems to contain a temple or two on every ledge, as the ravine deepens. On investigation one finds not only temples but a 'bawri'* **[a shady place near a canal]** *from which water flows from one smaller tank to another, so that every temple has a small tank or 'hawd' beside it. The path goes on down and follows what is left of a little stream, among bushy coverings, including fruit trees like Staphal, Nimbo, etc. It might be in a glade of Coonoor! It's a lovely spot! How I wished you were there! Farther down is a cave. Not made up like Bagh, but open at fronts except for a six foot wall some Sadhu had built to shelter himself while he sleeps. Inside – about 15 ft. deep – the rock ceiling comes down to within 12 ft. of the floor, and all along the farthest wall are little shrines built, and some of them containing the more sacred idols are caged in like little lions. At one end of this, perhaps 50 ft. cave, goes a dark passage which is said to go to Mandu! It has to go to some more or less renowned places so Mandu will be the nearest! When one goes down the lovely path through the trees the cave is up several wide steps (as though approaching a church), to the left. After this we were taken to some fields where it looked from a short distance as though the fields were covered with slimy racks on which lay a certain amount of dry grass. The poles stuck up through it in regular rows. On a close up we found the patch so covered was also enclosed within a wall of matting all round, and on one side there were four doors. We finally gained admission and found ourselves in what is called a 'Panwari' where the panleaf vines are cultivated. They are about eight feet high, trained up on grass stocks from a swamp, and are laid out in the most regular rows only three feet or less apart. The patch is going up over a knoll, so that the watering is simple from the top. These vines; so beautifully cared for, is something in a much finer art of cultivation than anything I have seen in India. There are four owners to this patch, so the four doors. At the beginning of each, or inside each door is a stone well covered, the god which will call forth snakes to bite the thief who ventures to steal their Pan leaves. Nearly a hundred coolies work in these patches here, of which there may be six. The vine and leaf looks something like that of the Vanilla vine. Every market day, in Dhar, for instance, is catered to, and on Wed. (yesterday) the coolies* **[poor, unskilled, uneducated people]** *were seen going in numbers to break leaves to pack for market. This is your Birthday – we are well aware. Now the mail must be sent to village. Animal marks were made, half a mile away.*

Deepest love and remembrance.
Mother

JANUARY 29, 1942
[From Father]

United Church of Canada Mission
Central India
Rev. F. J. Anderson, Mission Treasurer

Dear Walter,

Received all your mail, I think, including your "last letter" and later post card. The letter from Sun Life Co. arrived before we left Dhar and I left it there unopened. Glad you got the small refund on account early payment of premium. Will return the paper to Sun Life when I get a chance to do so. Mother will have informed you that your suitcase and contents arrived in good shape.

Since coming to camp I received an Air Mail letter from Miss Hilliard. It was posted in Wellington, New Zealand on Jan. 9th but may not have left N.Z. on that date. Miss Hilliard used "Java Pacific Line" note paper so we can understand that the party including the Misses Hilliard, Munns, McLeod, Whittier and Buckholtz are now somewhere between N.Z. and Bombay but very likely much nearer Bombay. We may look for them anytime now. With the arrival of Dr. Jean Whittier, Dr. Smith will be able to go to Indore, and Miss Scott will officiate the return of Miss Hilliard. Miss McLeod will be welcomed to the Ratlam – Bamnia Bhil area and Miss Munns to the Ujjain Balaki area.

The airmail letter contained a letter from D. Armstrong to Dr. Scott which I have sent on to him. It was interesting to read in it Armstrong's remark that "the Mission Council must know that it is Dr. W. H. Russell's opinion that if he returned to India he would be called up for military medical service as Dr. W. Anderson was called". That apparently is the reason given by Welford, or one of the reasons, for enlisting in the Royal Canadian Army Medical Corp. Apparently he did not inform the Board that he had tried to enlist in the Indian Medical Service.

Miss Boyd has received word from Miss Stewart (doubtless by cable) that she and Mrs. Menzies have landed in Los Angeles. So, so far the voyages are safe. I have not heard yet whether Miss Pearson has sailed from Bombay. We were hoping that you would see her there but apparently you did not meet. Glad you enjoyed the day or two in Bombay and that the Dhabi did not disappoint you.

Margaret Harcourt writes that they had heavy showers of rain the last three nights in succession, but we have had only one shower night before last and it was not heavy enough to hurt anyone or anything, much to our surprise and pleasure.

We are nicely situated just a short distance from a large talao **[pond]** *which we enjoy looking at from the camp. It would be lovely to have a boat but also there are none except a few leaky ones used by Singooa gatherers in the season. The water looks fresh and clean and very inviting but I have not seen anyone in swimming. We have one big tree for our camp so the helpers' tents are pretty close to ours but they are not a nuisance at all. Mangal comes daily but sleeps at home in the village so we are spared his loud chatter at night. He will likely be with us in our next camp. I am not sure yet where it will be, but not further away from Dhar. Holi comes on March 1st or 2nd which means our return to Dhar by the end of Feb.*

Our draw back to our present camp is that Amjhira village is on the other side of the talao and we have no callers for night meetings. That gives us quiet nights and lots of sleep but the camp is less profitable than we would wish. Our work is not strenuous in consequence. I seem to have had an attack of something like Lumbago but am better today and hope to be free from it tomorrow.

Just a mile beyond Amjhira is an interesting place called Amka Jamka – a very miniature Bagh Cave. We wish you had seen it, we did not know about it before. It is worth a visit. And not far from it there is a Pan leaf industry in operation. It too is well worth seeing. I leave it to Mother to describe both places in her letter.

The Amjhira State Dispensary doctor is on leave so we have not met him but the Compounder seems to be a nice competent chap. There is also a graduate nurse attached to the institution.

Our thoughts are with you as you journey to where duty calls and especially on this your birthday anniversary. We wish you many happy returns of your birthday and a safe return and soon to the land of the lotus. Bring back a few Japanese scalps as souvenirs but keep your own safely.

With love and all good wishes.
Father

JANUARY 29, 1942
[To parents]
En Route, "somewhere at sea"

Dear Mother & Father

I should probably write something today's date, not that it really feels any different! It is certainly one nice way of celebrating by having an "enjoyable" sea voyage because so far it has been quite quiet and really most enjoyable. It is a pity there has to be a war on to spoil it at the other end! But I suppose if that were not the case one would not get a free passage with all the benefits of 1st class as far as it is possible to alleviate the expenses of tropic seas and climate. One thing new at least is to be writing for the time being from a different hemisphere. I believe I have been completely around the globe three times, but always in the same hemisphere; so there is always something new to happen anyways – like going back to go under Niagara Falls, or to climb the hill at Songarh!

It is a bit difficult to write a letter under present circumstances – what to say, what to leave out etc. etc. **[because of censors]**. *I hope you got my card which someone was going to post for me. That was the last I wrote before leaving. We went down and came aboard right after that, having a bite to eat first, and did not lose much time in getting under way. Have seen nothing but clear blue water since there, except our personified female travelling companions. I suppose the difference between this and the cold grey-blue dull Atlantic water is really in the sun and degree of roughness at the time. Certainly it has been remarkably calm, with a bright moon at night. Last night was the calmest I think I have ever seen an ocean surface out at sea. Complete blackout on the outside makes everything at night seem ghostlike. This has one main disadvantage in that all outside communicating openings have to be kept shut, and being where we are it is not exactly cold! However there is an inside blower or ventilator system which seems to work fairly well if you can get the blast of it right on you. So on the whole things are not too bad considering. I have an Indian room-mate, same as I am, on his first trip but apart from the one moderately rough day he has not felt too bad. Quite a number felt that day a bit too much, but it was really nothing to speak of!*

Usually we see at best some porpoises, but so far there has been nothing except flying fish. Perhaps that is what we are, and poor at that! Have exercise daily in speaking Hindi (hope I'm understood) in giving talks. One chap today didn't know where his heart was, or what it was for, let alone his lungs. Again others seem quite bright.

I wonder how soon I shall run across Jack Leech. According to reports in the paper a little while ago his department must have been having a bit of work to do. Quite sultry tonight and it makes me feel sleepy. Advancing watches, we lose a bit of sleep too. So if you will excuse me I'll go below where it is even warmer, but will get under a blower. Food is quite good. I hope everything in Dhar is OK you will be out in camp I expect by now. I hope Quintie is not too lonesome without Punch **[the family's Jack Russell terriers]**.

Love Walter

JANUARY 31st, 1942
Information that Johore causeway was blown up and our troops retired on to Singapore Island!

MONDAY, FEBRUARY 2nd, 1942
[To parents]
"Somewhere at Sea"

Dear Mother and Father

Here is another brief letter following my one of Jan. 29th if they reach you they should both arrive the same day. I wrote one to Marion **[Marion is Walter's younger sister and mother to Ann Louise, the author],** *and also briefly answered a letter to Lacomb Presbytery in Alberta but addressed to Mr. K.J. Beaton of Toronto. I have been going through a number of letters myself in a censoring sort of way – remarks by some never before at sea with regards to sea life and food are quite amusing! Still so far this has been a really good voyage and nothing unpleasant happened! It has been showery for the last two days and a more bit rolly, to the discomfort of a few, but at the same time a bit cooler. The cabin blowers have never since the one occasion been shut off, so the night is cool enough under it. I find the bunk too soft! All the furniture, fittings etc. on this ship appear to be new. Dining room upholstery in green bright leather looks nice (if you don't already feel green!) The food is quite good, neither are we alone. Our crowd is quite congenial too. (There goes the tea bell and my pen is going dry – more later.)*

You remember the story of the old lady who was leaning over the rail looking through the field glasses and the officer picked a hair off her shoulder and held it in front of her glasses so that she thought she saw what she was looking for! (Came another "raval" **[complicated]** *part of the story!) Unlike the lady we did not know when to look but were only told on asking afterwards. I remember about the time though it was beautiful calm moonlight and of course there was nothing like what the hair in front of the glasses represented!*

As time goes on we begin to speculate and wonder whither to! There is a daily bulletin on board and it is not exactly uplifting. It may be that I shall have no occasion to look for Jack Leech, or look up the address Miss Clinton gave me, and again I might. I am also beginning to feel that I have brought far too much stuff along with me. In the uncertainties of the moment it may become a nuisance. I am wondering again if there is any chance of running into Miss Stewart and Mrs. Menzies. This is probably unlikely but I have in mind where they were. It certainly would be odd to

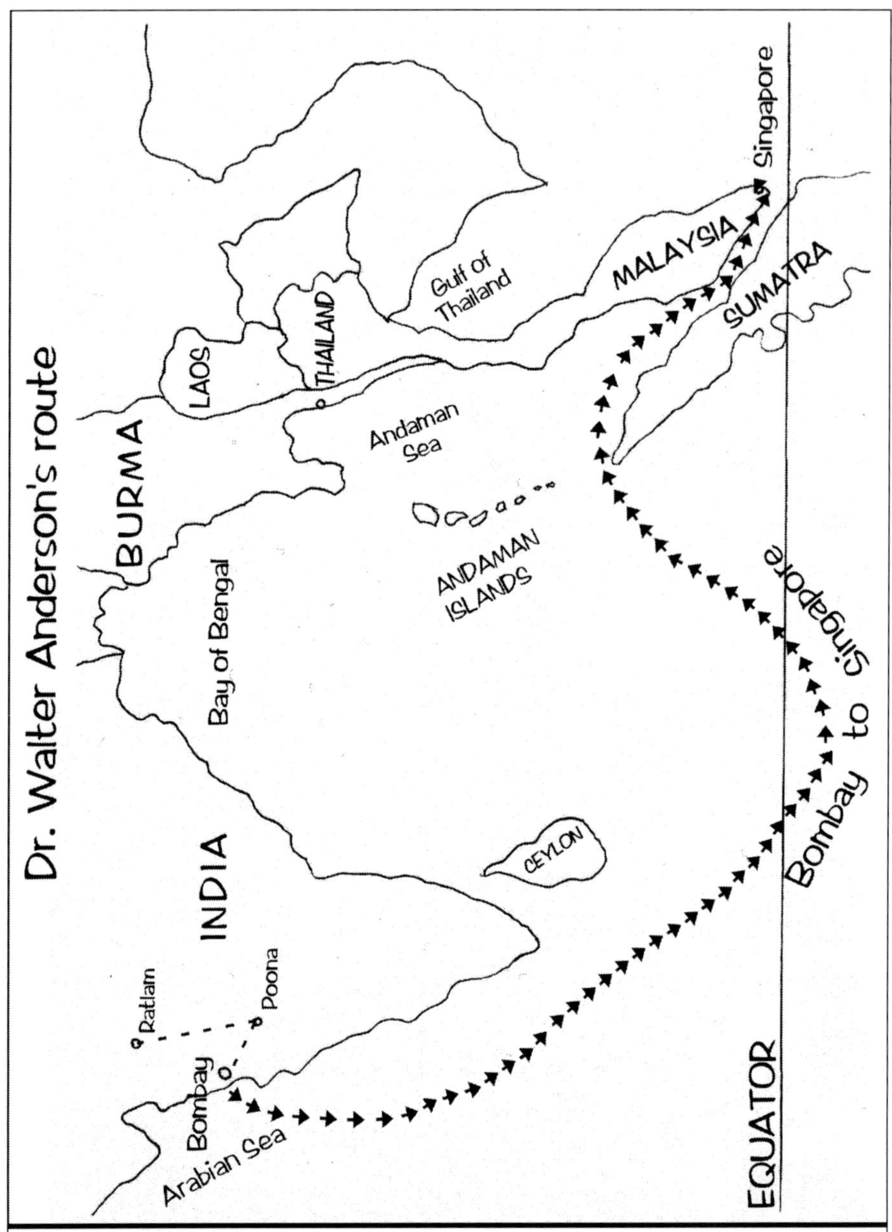

This map illustrates the route taken by Dr. Walter Anderson from Ratlam to Poona, and by the convoy that transported him, twice crossing the equator, to Singapore.

see them. The moon is covered over with cloud tonight which is a help in a way. This is after today's rain.

Now I must get to bed and try not to lose any sleep. I hope in my next to be able to give some other sort of address.

With Lots of Love
Walter

[The next few words added before letter was mailed from ship]

"All serene and still wondering" **[apparently meaning "all quiet on the sea, no bombs etc. and still wondering what is in store for us when we land"]**

FEBRUARY 3rd (?), 1942

Majority of convoy put off for Batavia. We original four plus small City of Canterbury came in for Singapore – feeling we were going into the trap!

FEBRUARY 4th, 1942

About mid A.M. going in file through Banka Strait, led in escort by His Majesty Ship "Exeter", our first air raid from Jap planes flying high from Banka over to Sumatra. No hits.

After this we broke convoy and each made fast for Singapore. Devonshire fastest. Great danger of submarine among group of 7 islands **[Andaman Islands]**, made one very nervous the last night – did not fully undress. Packed kit in packs etc. So would have some necessaries in whatever I could save if the rest was lost.

FEBRUARY 6, 1942
[From Father]

United Church of Canada Mission
Central India
Camp Sultanpur

Dear Walter

As you see from the heading on Camp address we have moved from Amjhira. Our camp was really closer to the village Rajapura *which is right up against Amjhira. Sultanpur is only between four and five miles from* Rajapura *so we had not far to come. The road for a motor was bad in places but on the whole it was not too bad and our excellent driver navigated the course with skill and courage. Sometimes we had to get out and cut the top off high spots in the middle of the road or fill in the ruts.*

Sultanpur is a small village five miles from Tirla, which now is our nearest post office. Our campsite is a small hilltop with two or three old banyan trees, which give us plenty of shade. The men are camped about half a furlong away and on a lower level. Their tents are pitched among a mango tree. There is water in abundance about twenty five yards away and we have a man to carry it and cut wood.

Clouds were gathering the morning we moved and actually a few drops fell but it cleared up and all looked bright until our carts came. Then clouds again gathered and the rumble of thunder was heard. The tents were hustled up and our saman **[possessions]** *was rushed under cover any old way just in time to be sheltered from a rain and hail storm. And so we spent the night. All our tents were wet in the morning and the ground too wet for the men to use their cycles. The sun shone and all was nice and dry again in the afternoon and it has been lovely since.*

The Catechist **[assistant teacher]** *and I have visited some of the neighbouring villages and found the people all friendly enough as usual but so far none have come to our camp. So we have quiet enough evenings and nights. Just now it is so quiet that we heard the 9 pm gun all the way from Dhar!*

Quite close to us are the ruins of an old town named Sultanabad but I have not yet explored the ruins. Will try and do so tomorrow. Nearly a mile away is an interesting under rock cavern something like the Bagh caves but there are no supporting pillars and there is no built up front wall. It is quite a spacious chamber. A Sadhu **[holy man]** *sits there in charge of a Mahadur shrine. There is a deep pool of water and quite large enough to swim in, just in front of the semicircular cave. It is fed by a stream which falls into the pool – quite a nice little Niagara. The rock ceiling of the cave had a good many rags hanging from it and I was told that people* *who go there – and there is a mela* **[celebration]** *every year – attach a rag to a bit of wet earth and throw it up to the ceiling. If it sticks the person is proved to be a legitimate son of the father. If it falls he is said to have two fathers! I threw one up and it stuck. So all is well! The mela day this year is next Friday but we shall move on towards Nalcha before then.*

We heard Miss Pearson was due to sail on the 4th but do not know whether she has actually sailed. Nor have we heard anything more of the party coming from New Zealand. The last word from Andy Taylor was written from Maymyo wherever that is in Burma.

The bad news that Malaya had been taken by the Japs and Singapore invested before you could have arrived then makes us conclude that your party must have been redirected to Rangoon and we are hoping to hear from you in due time from there. We look for word of your arrival any time now though it may not come for several days yet. We think of you as you journey in peril by the way and in peril when you land and pray for your safety.

And now I must get to bed. Will send this letter off to Tirla post office in the morning. All well with us. Be careful of yourself.

Lovingly,
Father

Enclosed find American Express Co. Credit notice and balance statement I have not received any remittance but it may come. Will let you know later if it does.

FEBRUARY 7th, 1942
All on deck by 4 A.M.

Friday, FEBRUARY 1942

Arrive quietly in Singapore outer harbour 9 am. From out at sea could hear the big guns firing towards Johore, and see two tall smoke columns constant from the Naval Base – no noise from the armed troops on deck. Harbour shoreline seemed dead. About 11 A.M. Japanese air raid. Empress of Asia hit coming in and whole middle part set on fire – grounded in sand bar – 50 killed? One Jap plane brought down. Could see it burning all day. Small boats from shore went out to pick up survivors.

"Felix Roussel" came in front-funnel with black smoke and flag half mast – radio room hit and operator dead and seven others machine gunned. Smoke went out like magic.

Poor "Captain" Punnswamy (Accounts) very frightened! In one days wait—entered channel and docks at dusk. Disembarked at 11 P.M. near and in light of burning godown **[warehouse or storage building at the wharf.]**

Indian Medical Services and Indian Medical Doctor taken in Australian Lorry out to No. 4 Indian Reserve Corps at Paserio near North East shore of island – arrived just after midnight.

New Indian Reserve Corps camp from the day before, an old rubber estate all wet from rain. Told we could sleep on roof. Found and slept on desks until dawn and used tent-cover bags. Quarter Master Captain Magcock, fire not put out – no hose pressure where Irish stokers refused to stay on the job – so reported!

Later reports of Senior Medical Officer being last one off the Ship's Hospital porthole; getting a Military Cross.

[large empty space left here]

Magcock thought we had messed up his office and slept on his desk! First night in rubber and coconut grove. 4 A.M. Jap planes going over to Singapore and the City siren alarm – near equator- Camp Dawn Patrol picket seen hiding by the trees. Came again at dusk.

During the day we got new tents up in allocated company areas in the rubber. Am attached to Hyderabad State Force Regiment. Major Wahid Khan, Officer in Command of party. Camp officers were in a Chinese house. Indian Medical Services and Indian Medical Doctors tend to congregate at Medical Inspection Room and Whittenburg orders to stay with the men in our own tents! Hyderabads go out on a special night job, risky – carry up rice store.

FEBRUARY 8th, 1942

Last night – papers report Japs landed in Force on the Island – in North West sector held by Australian Imperial Force also about 35 Hyderabads again in rice duty at night get fired on – one returns. I held an inspection and find some fresh Nips bomb the shore batteries near us.

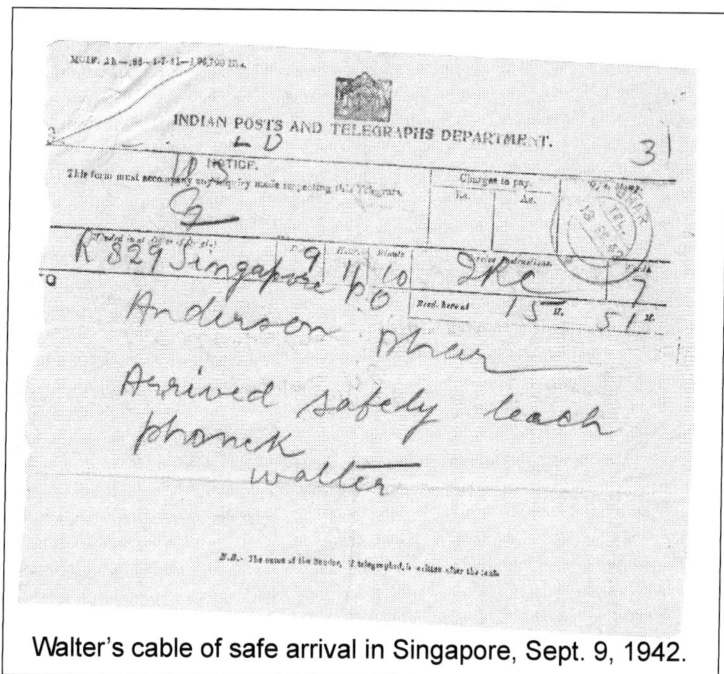
INDIAN POSTS AND TELEGRAPHS DEPARTMENT.

NOTICE.

This form must accompany any enquiry made respecting this Telegram.

Charges to pay.

K 829 Singapore 9 11 10

Anderson P.O. Dhar

Arrived safely leach phonek

Walter

Walter's cable of safe arrival in Singapore, Sept. 9, 1942.

[Telegram to parents]
FEBRUARY 9th/42 [Rec'd Feb.13 1942]

From Singapore
Anderson – Dhar

Arrived safely leach **[sic]** *phoned*
Walter

[Note found in amongst these letters from Walter stated that his last personal letter – see next page – was posted in Singapore 9th February 1942 dated Feb. 8th, 1942, only six days before the fall and surrender of Singapore to the invading Japanese army on February 15th, 1942. His next letter was not written until 3½ years later in August 1945 in liberated P.O.W. camp near Prachai, Thailand.]

FEBRUARY 8th, 1942
[To parents]

Base Postal Depot
Singapore

Dear Father and Mother

Here is the first real opportunity to try and write a bit and even this will likely be not long. I should say that we have landed safely first of all! And that counts for a good deal. The last letter of mine was posted on board on the 3rd Feb., which I hope reaches you along with the other. This I shall send via Air Mail from here but no telling when it will get away. You may get the ship letters first. The last of this journey was not without moments of excitement, some boredom, and a wee bit of wishful thinking! But we were very fortunate on the way for various reasons, and everything turned out well for us. On the whole it was a very fast voyage. I suppose I can say that, because I did not have the work to do that many had in looking after things on hand. Incidentally Capt. Markby from Jubbulpore did an appendix operation one night – I did not hear about till next morning. To see some land and green leaves looked good – even a square inch under your feet of solid earth and one green leaf overhead somehow makes me feel a bit better anyways! So far I have been doing nothing much but just waiting to be appointed somewhere keeping occupied is in a way much more restful! Specially here. Again I am sorry I brought that big black trunk. A slight amplification of those lists instructions would suffice here and be less worry. It is a bit difficult to move about and get things, I mean awkward etc. but I hope tomorrow to be able to get off a cable to you. I have a few stamps for airmail but must get more. Surface mail goes without stamps. I was handed a message this a.m. to say please phone Lt. J. N. Leech etc.! So he knows I am here and I'll try and get in touch with him today. I don't know whether he is near us or far.

Now will close this and get it in. All well, hoping to get busy soon – I mean in any sort of professional way – and a tinge of enjoyable excitement, only it is a pity there is a war on.

Please send regards from this side to Ratlam when writing. Salaams to those in Dhar when you go in from camp!

With heaps of love,
Walter

Walter's friend Jack Leech and his wife Bessie.

FEBRUARY 9th, 1942

Manage a trip to Singapore City and send mine and 4 other cables to India. Difficulty in getting a taxi back by 12 or 1 noon! Mailed a letter in camp on return. (Reached India!) Each night in camp was worse than before. Nips shell Changi from Johore and shells pass overhead.

FEBRUARY 10th, 1942

1:00 AM. – order to strip camp and ready to move off at 5 A.M. Threat of Japs landing on Partar again. 17 miles walk to refugee camp – Alexandra and Ganglia roads.

Major Khan takes us 6 extra wrong miles. He drops out! Struggling, wandering column seen by Wavell, who passed by! Not a good impression! Reported on this visit, he said "Too many in Head Quarters".

C.H.I.R.C. – O.C. Lieutenant Colonel W.G. Whittenberg,
Lieut. Major G. Hyatt,
Q.M. Captain A. Magcock,
Adj. Captain (Maj.) Patrickson
Most of I.R.C. was non-combatants
Medical Officer Captain Das I.M.S. [Indian Medical Service]

[empty space left here]

8 pm. Jack Leech phoned.

[empty space left here]

Hiding on roadside in air raid, some of us were picked up by a lorry and got to camp via 7 Medical Reserve Corps. of Alexandra Hospital. Treated my first war casualty here, - a leg laceration from our own ack-ack **[anti-aircraft guns]!**

FEBRUARY 11th, 1942

All combatants sent up to 2nd line of defence. The rest of us move to part of camp huts across Alexandra Road.

FEBRUARY 12th, 1942

Only plenty of Jap planes in sky, nearly all time – none seem to get hit.

FEBRUARY 13th, 1942

Each night gets worse with artillery firing. Battery set up right beside us in some low bushes. Nips think it is on nearby hill and shell it – One shell killed several (about 12) of our Indian Medical Corp men watching! We dig in slit trenches.

FEBRUARY 13th, 1942
[From Father]

United Church of Canada Mission,
Central India
Camp Sultanpur

Dear Walter,

Your cable from Singapore received here in camp this evening. Margaret received it in Dhar this afternoon and sent it out to us at once by a hostel boy. We were delighted to learn of your safe arrival and our anxiety is relieved to that extent. The Times of India received this morning told us of Japanese landings on the Island and only ten miles from Singapore City so our anxiety for your safety now is very keen. We can only trust and pray that in the midst of great danger you will be preserved and come through whole and well.

Glad you mentioned Leech phoning. He too then was well and knew of your arrival. Mother will write Bessie at once. I suppose you will have all the war news up to date so there is no point in enlarging upon it from this distance. The noise of guns will be continuously in your ears and doubtless some of the havoc wrought will be unpleasant before your eyes. May you skillfully relieve suffering and comfort those who may be beyond human medical skill to save.

We had a visit from Margaret Harcourt and some of her staff early this week. She told us that her driver Benji is going to take a three weeks training course and then serve as a trainer in Rajapura. Margaret is to get a badli **[replacement]** *driver from Mr. Smillie.*

Today we went to the Gunga Din mela. I think I mentioned Gunga Din in my last letter since we came to this camping place. There would be at least a thousand people there and all apparently enjoyed the outing from Dhar and other places round about. P. Abraham came out for the day but he has gone back to Dhar – to get home before dark. We are keeping the badli boy here over night and he will take and mail this letter in Dhar in the morning.

We have decided to move camp to Tirla next Tuesday (17th) and will likely remain there till the 28th. Holi begins March 1st and as the festival continues for at least a week and the weather too warm for tents after that, the 28th will doubtless mark the end of our touring for this season.

Dr. Scott has called a meeting of the College Board for the 24th and I think we will motor in to Indore from Tirla and get back the same night. Mrs. Smith writes that a lot of new building work is being done right in front of her bungalow in Mhow. She does not say what for but no doubt it is quarters for troops. They are likely to be only temporary. There is plenty of room there for a good many buildings.

Miss Pearson sailed I believe on the 6th Feb. bound for New York. After I got the air mail letter from Miss Hilliard from New Zealand, Dr. Catherine Whittier received a cable from her sister Jean from Java but I don't think there was any mention of when they were likely to leave there. If not shut up in Java they will not likely be far from India now.

There was some Canadian mail this week but no letter from or word from Marion. It seems to us that she has no very serious intentions of keeping us informed as to her welfare or we would be hearing from her.

We understand that Dr. & Mrs. Hodge are coming to Ratlam to make a home for Dr. Alice Hodge and will use the so called Welford Russell bungalow. So Dr. Campbell will be alone in his castle till it is time once more to go to the hills.

You will have heard that Marshal and Madame Chiang Kai-Shek have come from China on a visit to India and are now in Delhi. How the General can leave his armies at this critical time I don't know but I am sure he and his wife are welcome guests. And now I seem to be out of news. The hostel boy Marsingh will be leaving early in the morning with this and I hope it will reach you in due time and find you well.

With best wishes for your continued safety.

Lovingly
Father

FEBRUARY 13th, 1942
[From Mother]

In Camp – Sultanpur

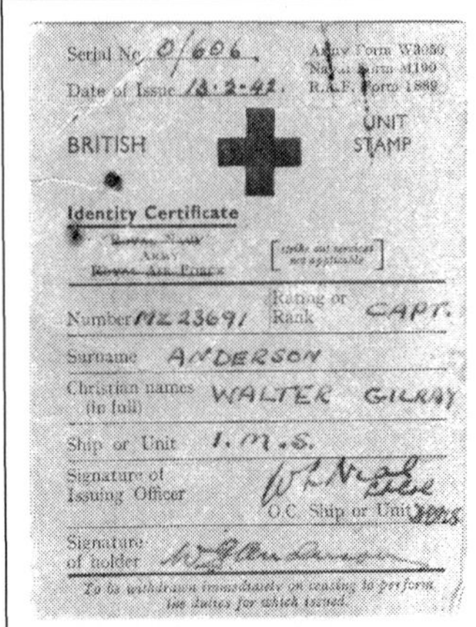
Serial No. 0/606
Date of Issue 13·2·42.
Army Form W3050
R.A.F. Form 1889
UNIT STAMP
BRITISH
Identity Certificate
Army
Number MZ 23691
Rating or Rank CAPT.
Surname ANDERSON
Christian names (in full) WALTER GILRAY
Ship or Unit I.M.S.
Signature of Issuing Officer
O.C. Ship or Unit
Signature of holder

British Red Cross Identity Certificate, Feb. 13, 1942.

My Dear Walter

What a moment it was, at about six o'clock this evening, when a red bicycle and a big boy were suddenly seen approaching our tent! As soon as I saw the Red of the wheel I recognized it, and knew there was a message!

As I have already told you I wrote Margaret to open any wires that came and send on one from you! I was quite sure you would send one when you reached your destination! Anand was to be sent out with it! Mansingh came and he tells us that Nawin went to Indore to train yesterday and his Mother went as far as Rasalpura. Anand could not leave when she was away.

It is such a relief, to know you have landed, even on a besieged island to which the "eyes of the whole world" have turned – as the Times of India said today. Oh, how I hope they have been checked, ere it's too late! They come out of an unseen hole like those (flying) white ants that come out in an evening and just swarm over everything! I must write to Bessie Leech tomorrow! Your message will be good news to her. The latest reports from your parts don't help us to relax – quite the opposite! I have been trying to find a place in the hills. Just yet only a room at 'Zephyr Lodge' (very centrally located, Margaret says) is offered. It is too expensive – being 150 rupees each, including baths and all. The spot is so central that we would like it. She says it's bright and nice, with bath, in a little cottage with a nice veranda, etc. I am writing others. Miss Martin of 'Airyland' says she is full except a place she wants to reserve for Dr. and Mrs. Hume who were in Manila on Dec. 8th. They hope to get back.

Where the hope is I know not! I wrote Mrs. Smith (Her Highness who is Matron at Woodstock). This reminds me I wrote to Charlotte, in Mhow. She was interested. She says she hears the Military are cast eyes at Arch Deacons bungalow! She is expecting to be approached any time. She is taking in two memsahibs, wives of Drs. who have come for training, a Mrs. Thomas (Baptist Mission Orissa) and Mrs. Sloan, of Madras, Scotch Mission). This may, she says, save her residence to her for awhile. In front and beside the road, is a building program of 3 lakhs **[a lakh = 100,000 Rupees]** *being carried out, and the place stacked with timber. She says "gone the peace and quiet, open space and view" A training center.*

The most exciting news related to India, today is that Marshal and Mme. Chiang-Kai-Shek are actually in Delhi – guests who will do more for the Indian mind than anyone I could think of! I hope they will do great things. If they just catch the public – how we hope!

A note with the accounts from Miss Boyd, today says "Samuel Girdharis daughter is just about an hour old". That will have been on the 10th most likely. Did I tell you Mrs. Bacons baby has arrived – "Howard Roland Jan. 27th at Indore." All fine.

Bhura's son Benji (tailor) is sick in Hospital with jaundice. Bhura wanted to go in immediately. He could not get in with Margaret whose car never comes out with less than a load in it! So I said he could go next day a.m. and return the next a.m. He wanted longer, finally, and so now won't go at all – his own choosing! It was really because I gave him a lecture on his sons children being there too when there was no woman in the house.

We shall move to Tirla Tuesday and I have asked Nariya to come out Tues. for six days. Bhura and he can exchange places on 18th. Father is called to College Board and he thinks he will indulge himself with a private car so shall take Nariya back with me. Benji was vomiting a good deal, so Margaret wanted him quiet. Bhura has worn out other housekeepers with his visitors and family! Benji's wife's people, when she went home, would not let her come back, and complained of this.

Margaret's driver Benji is again likely to leave for training. It seems that Mr. Smillie has to have a trainer of Motor Mechanics, or some such, and he has chosen Benji, of whom he is very fond. A substitute driver is being sent by Mr. Smillie. Benji first goes for some training he has not already had, to some other place.

Now Father has been in bed for some time, and this must go with him in the morning. I kept Mansing, who was supposed to return this evening. He went to see the temple in the cave, and is bedding down with the men for the night. An outing for him! He is such a nice boy.

Now Walter dear, I wonder if you have received my last letter to Jubbulpura! Do be just as careful, of my Walterji as you can. We are anxious – you know for your safety, we and many others pray and hope. We can't hope for any letters from you inside a fortnight, at least.

With very best love and the best of luck. I haven't remembered at the right time to get the full text of 'Tiny Tim's Blessing' from Margaret. Shall soon.

Ever Yours
Mother
Our Best Wishes to Jack Leech

FEBRUARY 14th, 1942

Heard Japanese tanks coming firing down the road at night, then turn up another road! Camp Morton – shelled mid AM. – exciting time with a Sikh in a trench! First actual being under continuous shell fire. Also some machine guns from Nip planes. Called to help in Medical Inspection Room. Several casualties including General Roth with compound fracture of leg and one Indian Medical Service Captain with knee injury. Got these evacuated in Commanding Officer's green car to Civilian Hospital. Commanding Officer was terribly nervous. Shells passing over all day and hits dropping around. Shell-shocked young officer of Leicester Regiment didn't like any trench near Medical Indian Reserve, couldn't join up with British Battalion (East-Surreys and Leicesters) due to Japs 5th Column snipers. Last seen, he was hiding under a bridge. (Had been through long firing and exposure on Jap Golf Course).

Order to move off at 6 pm for Raffles Place – shelled on the road. My topi **[hard cork hat]** blown off my head – no casualties. Left at night in a deserted city. Frightened men**…[page damaged here]**….-came to Victoria Memorial**….**

[empty space and more damage]

Japs run through Alexandra Hospital – kill Operating Room Staff and patient (except Captain Smiley, Military Cross), and many other patients and staff – frightful affair. Nip Assistant Director of Medical Services wept and promised punishment.

Two Lieutenants International Red Cross men turned out food and drink for us men in spite of so frequent raids and running for cover in Camp. Bombing several times of hill behind us making the ground shake.

Saw big Red Cross on sheet in front of building and this Raffles Hotel (used as hospital with patients on the lawn outside), then lay down for a bit on waterfront before found the way to Raffles Place. Slept, then lay after midnight in empty offices and shops near new Robinson's Store. Heard shells landing. Odd fires.

FEBRUARY 15th, 1942

Chinese New Year celebrated on the 15th this year.

About 11 P.M. – Jap planes bombed opposite side of Raffles Place where No. 3 International Red Cross is located. Killed 50, 100 wounded. Some casualties brought over to our Medical Infection Room. Got an Australian Imperial Force Ambulance to try and take them to Hospital. Difficulty to find room. Indian Captain Das and I go in Commanding Officer's car to Cathay Building Hospital for supplies, and make enquiries at Victoria Memorial. Our guns firing off all they had at my waterfront –made terrible din. Lorries outside Union Jack Club Hospital. Bombed as ambulance approached it. At 6 P.M. and getting evening, a sudden awing silence. I slept that night alone in Medical Infection Room (shop) more fright by silence than the noise.

FEBRUARY 16th, 1942

[taken prisoner]

Morning wind of surrender of Singapore! All British told to move in to Robinson's Store and Indians separated. We're allowed to take what we need from the store (I got a towel and thread from a Chinese salesman – weeping!) We see the first Japs when they come and collect the arms and ammunition held by our Indian Reserve Corps personnel. I'm amazed at smooth English spoken by the Nip young officer. Couple of Chinese shop looters bayoneted by Japs across the square. Slept night in Robinson's.

FEBRUARY 17th, 1942

Moved off to Changi at noon. One lorry allowed us – put in our unit supplies and stores from shop tin goods. 1 and 2 red panniers fill up back of lorry and Hyatt drove furiously! (All Indian troops grouped and marched off to Farran Park at 8 A.M.) We get a married quarter house on Battery Road cleaned out for the unit to occupy when they got there walking. Share house with No. 3 International Red Cross. Pick up a little red clothing, mattress, mess tin, mosquito net etc. We are packed in tight on the float.

[Large empty space left here]

Had lost all my luggage, trunks, bedding, suitcase, camp bed etc. except pack and hammock when we left Alexandra Road Camp on 14th.

FEBRUARY 18th, 1942

No. 4 and No. 3 International Red Cross merged under Commanding Officer Lieutenant Colonel P. Coffin. Early crowded days on Battery Road. Lived on our tinned stores. I use the Medical panniers **[a basket for carrying a load over a mule].** Acute water shortage – long queues for water bottle fills at one area forming. Latrine-digging fatigues **[dirty jobs]** for all units. British and Australian Imperial Force P.O.W's in Changi – 40,000+ ? Captain Morris Indian Medical Services (Canadian from 12 Indian General Hospital), Major Black etc. and I went twice to help get Roberts Hospital ready for No. 1. Malaya General Hospital etc. to move into, but got no permanent job there: – Could bathe in the big Changi's bathing pagan. Have seen ringworms in the men prevalent. Mrs. Cornelius the only woman in Changi! Royal Engineer put up perimeter barbed wire. Nip guards wander about at night only. An Argyle killed first night trying to get away. Nips shot Chinese boatmen if they tried to come and sell.

Truck load of Chinese machine gunned on the beach in the morning. British Other Ranks find two alive 'Leonard' and another, and smuggle them into Hospital.

Divisions of Southern Area, 18th Division Hospital Area, Australian Imperial Force area, and 11th Division, and Malaya Command. We in South Asia. Parade lining the road one day to be viewed by the Japanese conqueror Lieutenant General Yamashita. Japanese movie men, formed guards ad-lib came by! A week later we paraded again to be seen by the Nip chief Admiral!

New Indian Reserve Corp. Unit

Officer Commanding Lieutenant Colonel P. Coffin

2nd in Command Lieutenant Colonel Hennessey

Adjutant Captain Edwards

Quartermaster Captain Walsh

Morris remarked that a typewriter first seen at Roberts Hospital should be smashed since that's what lost the war!

[empty space left here]

Changi must have been very pretty and a luxury cantonment **[area around hospital for military]** before the war. Pretty badly shelled. Travellers Palms in front of our house.

Morris and Lallias appointed to South Area Hospital in Diet Centre opened up. I get posted as Medical Officer to the Indian Reserve Corps because Major Dew didn't want it. Would have preferred a Hospital job but was not known there and we had to keep an eye out for proper feeding such as with a unit you know!

Strict AM. and PM. unit roll call checking. All go on Tokyo time. 1 hour & 40 min. ahead of Singapore time.

FEBRUARY 21st, 1942
[From Mother]
In Camp Tirla

My dear Walter

I don't know how to start a letter to you now my heart is too full to smile – I can't begin to tell you half that's in my heart for you – and how we are going to get on without you.

.At this stage I don't think there is much use writing but Father insists on writing so I am trying to put in something. The letters I have had in the last few days – such nice letters of kindness and good wishes for you – take up some space in my case! Some home mail came in today and I might mention that the knitted garment I made for Ann Louise were returned to me – what a delivery service! Also one ordinary letter came back. She has not left her address when she moved. Letter came also from Mrs. Williams and Dr. Gilbert Wilson and Flo Gibson. Last week from Marion there came stockings, socks and 2 Khaki hankies for you. No letter enclosed but a snap of Ann Louise at 15 1/2 months. She is running on the grass in some park. Looks strong. Mrs. William's letter today says a good deal about Marion. It says she looks very much better for her two months rest. Dr. Wilson says Dr. Frank H. Russell looks thin and ill and not like his former self. I sent a cable on its way today for Marion to pass on to the families – addressed to Dr. Armstrong. (Thanks for yours, more than I can tell).

I wrote Bessie Leech – I have a reply today and she is with Mr. and Mrs. Ana Kaslam till end of Feb. Then she goes to Hilda Johnson and then to the 'Deodars' for summer from April 15 or May 1st.

I have no arrangement yet for summer – can't think about that – no time! I try to keep my hands busy and wish all the nights were days too! Red Cross is receiving due attention these days. Father is called to College Board and I may have to take him in on Tuesday 24th. I don't feel like going – might only go part way. Have declined Smillie's invitation to lunch enroute. Any spare time must be used for business. I have to drive back here same night.

When I wake and when I work and when I rest or when I retire, I remember you dear boy. Many others are remembering you. Now, I'll try to sleep – Father is sleeping audibly the last hour! I finish tomorrow. Sunday AM. I have to let this go – it's loaded with love!

Will it ever get to you? With loads of love
Mother

Marion with Ann Louise (18 mo).

FEBRUARY 21st, 1942
[From Father]

United Church of Canada Mission
Central India
Camp Tirla

Dear Walter

The fall of Singapore into the hands of the Japanese so soon after your "arrived safely" cable has changed our feelings of relief to real concern; concerning your safety and welfare now. The roar of planes, the screech of shells and the hail of lead over and in the city must have been frightful and the casualty list on both sides must be long ones. The early surrender of the city in face of heavy odds against it was doubtless the only sane thing to do under the unfortunate circumstances and as a result many valuable lives and much property would be saved.

The Japs have already changed the name of the city and doubtless expect to hold it permanently as one of their great possessions together with Hong Kong, Penang etc. etc. but their hopes and ours clash and one day they will surely have to vacate and pay so far as possible for their trespass. We must give the Japanese credit for their courage and skill in conducting the campaign and for accomplishing what we thought impossible.

I suppose the many British, Australian and Indian troops, now prisoners of war, will receive humane treatment and have no serious cause for complaint on that score while still the guests of the Japanese Government. As a doctor you will be able to give your services to those in need whether victims or vanquished.

You see we take for granted that you are still in Singapore and it may be a very considerable time before we can hear from you, but we will rejoice the more if early news should come from you. Meanwhile we here carry on as usual since there is nothing else that we can do and write as usual in the hope that our letters will be forwarded and get through to you wherever you may happen to be and find you well and of good cheer.

Last Saturday's letter was from Camp Sultanpura. Just after writing we received a Christmas present from Marion but there was no letter from her. The parcel contained stockings for Mother, socks for me and Khaki handkerchiefs for you and 'love' for all. And there was also an enlarged snap photo of Ann Louise. Ann was standing alone, has a happy smile on her face and is apparently a strong healthy robust good looking child. We would rather of had a letter from Marion then the gifts but welcome them and the picture. The parcel was posted last Nov. and we remember of course that we heard by cable early in January that she was then well. So we need not worry on that score but it gives us concern that we do not know what financial help she is getting or not getting, though friends will see to it that she does not want.

We had a letter from Dr. Gilbert Wilson a day or two ago, he sends his kind regards to you. One of his married daughters and two children are living with him while the son-in-law is away from home on duty. He keeps himself busy taking anniversary and other services here and there as opportunity offers. He called on Frank Russell recently and found him greatly changed since his return from the west.

The move from Sultanpura to Tirla was a short and comparatively easy one. It took us some time then to decide just where to camp. One place was too far from the village and water supply. The other we selected. We are close beside a well with a plentiful supply of good water. A charas **[a large leather pouch that is lowered into the well to get water]** *is used once a week for irrigating the fields. Our tent is not under but on the shady side of the tree and so in the shade most of the day. It rained a little the day after we came and there have been high strong winds that have left us rather more cold than cool all day.*

I called on the Thakew Ganga Singh and he returned my call next day. He is a young man, a graduate of Daly College and so speaks English very well. He promised to send us some wood for fuel as it is very difficult to buy any here but no wood has come from him. Whether he forgot or decided not to send any, we may never know. We got a little from Bhilo who had a few bundles for sale but that will not see us through. We may get more in a day or two.

Yesterday I had a trip in by bus to Dhar and returned the same afternoon. I saw Punch but he was not very enthusiastic and seems to be reconciled now to hostel life. It may be different when Quintie is back in the bungalow but we want Punch to remain in the hostel.

On Tuesday we are due in Indore for a College Board meeting and will have the day away from camp. On Friday or Saturday we will break or strike camp and return to Dhar as Meli begins on March 1st and there is no advantage in being out there. Miss Martin will be in too about the same time.

So much for this week. "Be of good cheer, be not afraid for lo, I am with you always".

Yours lovingly,
Father

About FEBRUARY 23 – MARCH 8th 1942

Indian Reserve Corps shifted to other quarters on hill near Fairy Point – garage building and two nice huts. Good view up the channel to N. Base. Saw Jap Fleet come in to the base one day, 3 aircraft carriers, several battleships, destroyers. Made myself a small Medical Infection Room. Dig our first bore hole with auger. Got together quite a good library of books. Fatigues, rations, water, firewood, all to be drawn up the hill. Lieutenant Colonel Lincoln Gordon and his pass-a-phone pit!

Just settling in when we're told to move to 11th Division and bring 1st Army. Jack Leech, Major Tilling, etc. join us from No. 7 Medical Reserve Corps and Captain Markby giving me stocks from his Medical Inspection Room at No. 7 that was closing—including a box of M & B's **[sulfa drugs]**.

Jap planes still going overhead in groups of 3's and 9's – 27 – going Java way I suppose. Lots of aerial activity, guarding the harbour and channel. So far we have seen very few Nips. Order to give up our biscuits **[mattresses]** – I keep the linen covers of the mattress I found. **[this section unreadable]**

So far we are all still alive, I can scarcely believe we are POWs. **[Prisoners of War]**. Little spells of depression set in sometimes! Feeling that we will be P.O.W. a very short time only or else a very long time.

Believed In Singapore

DR. WALTER G. ANDERSON, medical missionary of the United Church of Canada from Toronto, who was likely on the Island of Singapore when the Japanese invaded that territory, according to word received at Foreign Mission headquarters here. Dr. Anderson is a graduate of the University of Toronto. He obtained his arts degree in 1928 and medicine in 1934. He had been serving at Rutlam, in Central India, but the word received here indicated that he had gone to Singapore on Feb. 9 as medical officer of the British Indian Army. His father and mother are missionaries of College Street United Church and are serving at Dhar, in Central India.

DR. W. G. ANDERSON SAID IN SINGAPORE

Toronto Medical Missionary Reported Serving With British Army

Dr. Walter G. Anderson, Toronto medical missionuary, is believed to have been on the island of Singapore when the Japanese captured that city, according to advices just received by the United Church of Canada foreign missions department here.

Dr. W. G. Anderson

He arrived in Singapore Feb. 9 and was serving as a medical doctor for the British army, it was reported. Dr. Anderson is unmarried. His father and mother are missionaries of College Street United church, now serving at Dhar, Central India.

A graduate of the University of Toronto in arts in 1928, and in medicine in 1934, Dr. Anderson went to India as a medical missionary in 1937, and served at Rutlam, Central India.

Rev. A. E. Armstrong, associate foreign missions secretary of the United church, said that there was no news as to the fate of Anderson. "He may have been sent away on some ship with wounded people to Australia," he said, "or he may be among the British army officers who surrendered when Singapore fell. We hope to have more news of him soon."

The cable message regarding him was sent to United church headquarters by Dr. Anderson's parents.

"He is a fine fellow," said Dr. Armstrong. "For some time he was on the staff of St. Michael's hospital.

Toronto newspapers reported on what was known of the situation of medical missionary Walter G. Anderson.

The College Street United Church in Toronto, the home church to the Anderson family of missionaries to India.

FEBRUARY 24th, 1942
[From Mr. L.A. Davenport]

College Street United Church
Minister – Rev. C. A. Gowans

Rev. and Mrs. F. J. Anderson
Dhar, Central India

Dear Mr. and Mrs. Anderson:

Dr. Armstrong has telephoned the message that Walter arrived in Singapore on February 9th. This brings the tragedy of that far-away post close to all of us who have had that one word before us in every newspaper, radio program, conversation and thought these past days.

All of us in College Street United Church, as well as those represented by its session in our meeting last night, want you to know we are thinking of you especially just now – and for all of us who knew him, the word "Singapore" will mean "Walter Anderson".

Much comfort and hope comes from the Japanese statement to the Crown Government Exterior Affairs Department that they will agree through the Red Cross to abide by the Geneva Convention for Canadian prisoners, so that Canada will reciprocate toward the thousands of Japanese interned here.

As Dr. Armstrong said, "With his medical knowledge, and that level head of his, Walter should be safer than anyone there."

Our faith and trust – that we have taken often so for granted – is tested and tried daily. Both of you, and Walter have helped many of us hold more firmly to that faith and trust just by your example, by your life here, and as we follow it there in India.

We share with you this new anxiety, and pray more earnestly than ever before for freedom with peace and righteousness for all people, everywhere.

Yours most sincerely,
L. A. Davenport
Clerk of Session

[Large empty area in the journal here]

MARCH 9th, 1942

International Red Cross moved to 11th Division area in Bindwood Camp.

(Fall of Java and N. Dutch East Indies today!) Each move gives us worse quarters than the last! We get one long atap **[palm leaf or thatch]** hut, a bit leaning from blast and with shrapnel holes in it and all are frightfully crowded together on floor, though Lieutenant Colonels must have their space! Kitchen is 100 yards away in a little machine workshop in the wee Penerang Railway and the mess is just a cement floor with a collapsed roof on it. Other huts around us are burnt.

So no end to fatigue now, getting unit area cleaned up. First job to clear mess and build new atap roof and beams – then to build a new hut small size behind the lou **[lavatory]** but where former hut had burned down – a common room hut in front – rice grinding shed, oven, fireplace, shed, etc. All old atap and material to be brought into camp from scrounging parties outside toward the coast. We demolished old

Malay or Chinese huts and brought them in sections. Scrounging became all important. Every moveable bit of furniture and junk from each place we lived in was put on our allotted unit "trailer" and pushed into camp. Lincoln Gordon, the chief of scroungers!

Newspaper "Syonan Times" (Shimbun) later reported capture of 96,000 troops in N. Dutch East Indies.

A few papers brought to camp by Nips – considered bad for morale so not allowed to be read or passed around by Headquarters.

[Large empty area]

Trailers allotted to units from broken vehicles and engines removed – many were converted old car and truck bodies.

MARCH 10th and on –

Organized unit fatigues **[dirty jobs]** – cook house, water, firewood, rations, sanitation, rice grinding, building, gardening – and all units afternoon scrounging parties.

11th Division, and other areas too, rapidly closed in with barbed wire put up by our own Royal Engineers – 2 rows double apron wire with coil of concertina wire between. Cannot now go out of our own area. This wire makes difficulties for our kitchen drainage!

Set up my Medical Inspection Room each morning outside with my pannier stuck under one end of the long hut. Collected some more supplies from Roberts Hospital on our march past to 11th Division Area. Major Tilling digs in under the hut and lives there.

Make our own latrines better than some other units – bring box seats and tenting sides to put around the "battery" of bore holes. Great demand for the auger by all units – can't get enough holes. Early deep trenches for large units near us cause frightful smell and humming with blue bottle flies. 11th Division Asst. Director Medical Services Colonel Mitchell and Assist. Director Medical Service Major Glendenning held daily conference at noon, to hear reports from all units, and give orders for prevention of disease, and medical returns wanted by the Japs. Dysentery (flies) Malaria, Diphtheria and early ordinary Beriberi now the main fears. Major General Key orders unit exam Q **[every]** 2 weeks for signs of deficiency disease, etc. – Old P. C. said feeling his legs for Beriberi was like examining the fetlocks of a horse!

Several British Other Ranks attached to International Red Cross as batmen **[officer's helper]** – but in Indian Red Cross we took turns securing tables at meals. British Other Ranks had their own cookhouse. In many ways they were a nuisance!

I became Medical Officer to the International Red Cross, Provost and I.H.O.C. and made regular inspections inside the main M.I.R.Y.T. area now.

The General inspected different areas each Saturday A.M. Held one dress Division Parade in the area football field, with practice parade before – took the salute – to keep up morale. Only did it once! Drill in uniform for all units each Saturday early A.M. for 15 – 20 minutes too! Some very good gardens came to be developed in time. Edwards grew nice tomatoes. Magcock worked away in garden harder than anyone else.

11th Division Area divided up among Medical Officers for inspection sanitary purposes. An empty tin can lying around for Mitchell was like a red flag to a bull. He made us all most mosquito-breeding conscious!

[empty space here]

Brigadier Stringer director of weekend services, Malaya Command insisted on keeping unit H & D books in Medical Inspection Rooms! A very disagreeable man.

Report the sick examined finally by Japs in all areas. But nothing ever more heard of the matter!

[empty space here]

More sleeping space when we got some small tents and the Lieutenant Colonels move out. Many bed bugs in the huts. Plenty in our unit cane furniture!

No pay or canteen for several months – only way to get anything by officer in charge of Singapore working party, asking Nip guard to buy things, then draw for them out of a hat!

Later received canteen and central library privileges and officers pay, $10.00 or 9.00 in hand, P.M. made great difference. Jack and I like peanut toffee. But before this much black marketing - $3.00 for tin butter. $2.75 for small cheese, $1.25 for small bread rolls etc. Moskovitch slowly gets the racket into his own hands! Sikhs shot one man under wire at night in 18th Division.

Original list of P.O.W. names sent in to Nips in 1st week – they lost. So months later new nominal rolls had ranks for many officers, many down but a few up, like myself after March 15th.

11th Division Units in Camp
No. 1 Mess – Major General Key etc.
No. 2 Mess – Major Lewis etc.
R.I.H.C.C.
I.R.C.
Division Sigs.
3 Corps Sigs.
Provost Unit
I.A.O.C. [Indian Army Ordinance Corps]
5th Field Regiment
155 Field Regiment Lanarkshire Y. Company ?
137 Field Regiment
80th Anti Tank
22nd Anti Regiment

18TH MARCH, 1942
CENTRAL JOINT WAR COMMITTEE OF THE INDIAN RED CROSS SOCIETY & ST. JOHN AMBULANCE ASSOCIATION
20 Talkstora Road, New Delhi,
No.109/PW/33(1)

Rev. F. J. Anderson,
United Church of Canada Mission,
Central India,
Dhar.

As requested in your letter of the 14th March, 1942, inquiry will be made when means of obtaining accurate information have been established.

Direct communication with persons in territory occupied by the Japanese is not possible at present and letters, telegrams and parcels cannot be forwarded.

You will be informed if any definite information is received but it must be understood that there may be long delay and there is no guarantee that inquiries will produce the desired result.

Signed **[not legible]**
Deputy Red Cross Commissioner.

18th March, 1942
No. 14059/ A. G. 16.
GENERAL HEADQUARTERS, INDIA.
Adjutant General's Branch.
NEW DELHI,

Rev. F. J. Anderson,
United Church of Canada Mission,
Dhar, Central India.

Dear Sir,

In reply to your enquiry, it is regretted that no details can be given at present, though this Headquarters is making every effort to obtain information through the International Red Cross and the Protecting Power. If and when such information is received, the next of kin will be informed and a notification of the casualty will appear in the Press.

You will, I feel sure, realize that we are doing all we can in this matter, but until official notification is received; we have no news to give.

Yours faithfully,
Signed **[not legible]**
For ADJUTANT GENERAL IN INDIA.

APRIL 1942

Our condition here in Village too good to last! Just settled in well when April 1942 "F & H" ovld **[overland]** Force parties formed and taken away during the night for Thailand. These long parties mostly emptied

South area + Band! Small "G" Force full, taken to Borneo. "Permanent" "G" & "W" area depleted too! Lots of work for Medical Officer examining and deciding on fit men to go – very unpleasant. Also, giving Small Pox, Plague, Glass Rodding **[method of inoculation],** etc.

First postcard home allowed June 20, 1942.

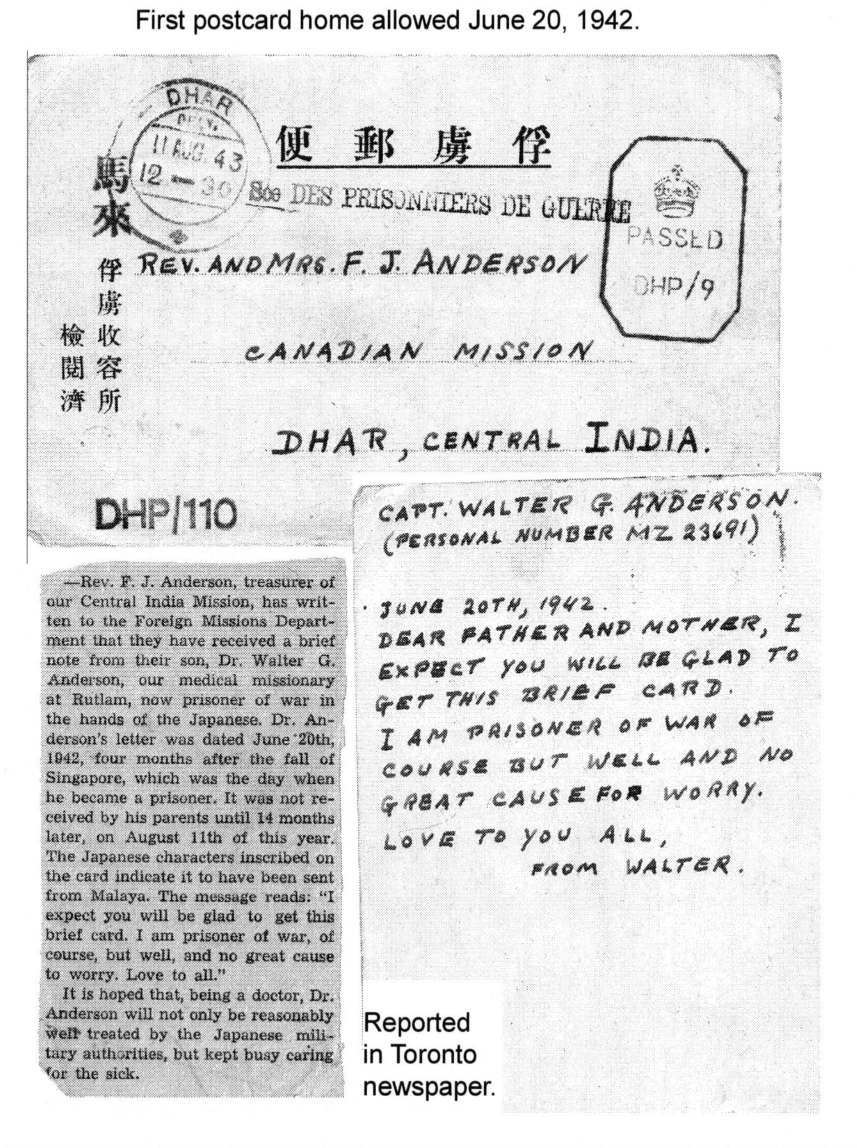

REV. AND MRS. F. J. ANDERSON

CANADIAN MISSION

DHAR, CENTRAL INDIA.

CAPT. WALTER G. ANDERSON.
(PERSONAL NUMBER MZ 23691)

JUNE 20TH, 1942.
DEAR FATHER AND MOTHER, I EXPECT YOU WILL BE GLAD TO GET THIS BRIEF CARD. I AM PRISONER OF WAR OF COURSE BUT WELL AND NO GREAT CAUSE FOR WORRY.
LOVE TO YOU ALL,
FROM WALTER.

—Rev. F. J. Anderson, treasurer of our Central India Mission, has written to the Foreign Missions Department that they have received a brief note from their son, Dr. Walter G. Anderson, our medical missionary at Rutlam, now prisoner of war in the hands of the Japanese. Dr. Anderson's letter was dated June 20th, 1942, four months after the fall of Singapore, which was the day when he became a prisoner. It was not received by his parents until 14 months later, on August 11th of this year. The Japanese characters inscribed on the card indicate it to have been sent from Malaya. The message reads: "I expect you will be glad to get this brief card. I am prisoner of war, of course, but well, and no great cause to worry. Love to all."

It is hoped that, being a doctor, Dr. Anderson will not only be reasonably well treated by the Japanese military authorities, but kept busy caring for the sick.

Reported in Toronto newspaper.

JUNE 1942
First post card **[to home]** allowed us on June 20th, 1942. Also first large up country party leaves for Thailand (Nom Pradok, the beginning of the Bridge Railway).

JUNE 25, 1942
[From Mother]
India

My Dear Walter,

Just now on 23rd by Radio we were notified that we might send you a message. How we miss you, may Heaven give you the message of my heart, every day, and keep you with some professional work.

All your things and your letters received safely on leaving and from on board, and later letter and cable of same date. I cabled Marion. Received a very nice letter from College Street United Church.

All the ladies arrived safely. Marion received your letter. We saw Bessie and children, all well, in hills. We are now returning to work, after six weeks with Mrs. Smillie and Alistair, Oakville.

Hosts of friends send their love and best wishes, and assurance of prayer. More persons then I can name send you messages of love and remembrance. No lists have been published yet, and all the world is weary waiting for them.

I wonder and wonder if you have food, net, and protection from sun, etc. You will be sorry to hear that Mrs. D.F. Smith died during an operation on May 2nd, for Peritonitis. Ruptured Gastric Ulcer. All very sudden.

Mrs. Taylor is coming to stop with us, when she comes down from hills, also her adopted daughter and one dog. One dog sickened and died in hills. Andy Taylor is now in Poona, as patient. Dysentery and Malaria. Much better.

I walked all the way down to Kincraig yesterday, Father had Dandi from bazaar down.

We are both well, except I have cold. Didn't play tennis this summer. I am writing on train. Dust storm on, and its dense.

Do send us a message when you can.

With Deepest love from
Mother

JULY 1942

The General's party leaves for Formosa, including all full Colonels and above and Party "B" (later taken to Marchukus) (General Beckwith Smith of 18th Division dies after Diphtheria in Formosa).

Big Gun 14" from "Queen Elizabeth" revolving, which we blew up after firing into Johore Bahru – a few yards from our kitchen – a great show piece to all Nip visitors and big shots to Singapore.

Great difficulty getting to Roberts Hospital for any meeting etc! By now we had arm bands, ferry flag system this A.M. from area to area. One area ambulance given to take cases to Hospital. Driver a dextrocardia! News given out at the General's unit Commander's conference each A.M. P. C. often made a "ball-up" of giving it out at noon lunch time. E.g. – his amphibian tanks, insanitary bombs red palm olive air, "etc". Couldn't get place names. Several Court Martials held, 5-7 cases of hard labour, Muir-Harding's case! Colonel Mitchell, Major Tilling and I keen on Poultry farming lectures from Captain Rook. Largest of the 3 big guns were fired as it pointed out to sea only! Amazing to look at it – no appearance of damage to it. Area concerts, plays and lectures – seats often rationed. Interesting to hear officers of the "Houston" and about affairs in Java.

Sunday Services allowed. Jack is "Chaplain" to 155 in his regional services – has daily P.M. group meetings – even holds communion services (when lads leave). Slapping incidents, ruptured eardrums etc. on road for not bowing or saluting! Jap cars, or Sikh sentries now – posted throughout Changi with their guard room at Australian Imperial Force gate.

In time less fatigued and we take unit walks to seashore with a flag and these gradually curtailed – no bathing allowed. No knocking down cocoanuts out of the trees allowed. Magcock's early morning trip for the garden – loses one flag!

JULY 8th, 1942
[From Father]
Dhar, C. I.

Dear Walter,

Since returning from Landour Mother and I each sent you a letter addressed to Tokyo. Perhaps this will reach you in the same delivery by courtesy of the Japanese Officials.

There has been no news from Marion for sometime but no doubt she is bravely carrying on and supporting Ann. I sent the money you left for her to Dr. Waters who will see that Marion gets it as needed.

The big item of news is the matrimonial engagement of Margaret Harcourt to a Methodist Missionary named Ginn. She told us last Saturday when she arrived home from Mussoorie. Date of wedding not fixed, so far as we know. We have not seen the man. Margaret says he is not particularly handsome. She met him last summer. I believe he has been in India most of one term.

A Miss Lazarus has now succeeded Miss Caswell as principal of the Girls High School. Miss Caswell is spending July with the Canaras. Andy Taylor was expected home by his parents and he may be there now though I have not heard definitely. Mrs. Tait and Lorna are with us. The College opens next week and Scott expects a record attendance. Miss Baxter is temporarily in charge of the late Mrs. Smith's work as well as her own.

I hear regularly once a month from Poona as per arrangement. This month I am sending your rates to Dean for 2nd half current year. You had made provision for this in advance.

Sam Abraham is off work today with guinea worm. He had trouble with it during the holidays and now it bothers him again. The Monsoon has arrived. It rained heavily most of Sunday night and there have been showers since. The grass is green and wells are filling up.

Many friends keep asking for you. We hope you are well and professionally employed, and that as we are now permitted to send short letters the same privilege may be afforded you.
With best wishes

Yours lovingly,
Father

JULY 9th, 1942
[From Mother]

My Dear Walter

I must take the opportunity to write to you, according to the instructions published. I sincerely hope it reaches you some day. It is from you we should be getting a message, after all these months. You don't know how we miss you and pray for you always. So many friends send you their Best Wishes that I could never name them all. You should not worry about us, we are well, and home again after six weeks with Mrs. Smillie. Having good rains. Bessie and babies are well and brave. Best Wishes to Jack too.

Charlotte Smith died during operation for Gastric Ulcer, from Peritonitis on May 2nd. Mr. Netram passed away a few days later. Miss Clearihue had a successful operation for ulcer of appendix while on holidays in June.

Quintie looks for you at the mention of your name. Your Hospital Staff pray for you every day. I have so many loving enquiries for you. Margaret Harcourt has just announced her engagement to a Methodist missionary. No dates set, we hope for the best. He is a stranger to us all. Una Dobson expects her baby in Oct. Her Father died about March. Arthur likes his trainings. Last news from Marion was in May and she was working hard, was well. She was paying for the care of Ann Louise. Mrs. Tait and Lorna have gone in to dentist for the day.

Walter with Rev. J. Fraser Campbell D.D., 1941.

How we long to know if you are well. I am getting very weary, waiting. Friends at Oakville gave me a Birthday party, and nice gift of a purse. It was all a complete surprise. They did it so nicely, twenty-one of us there. We all thought of you. Tiny Tim says – God Bless every one. Our best wishes to Jack if you see him. I met Mrs. Dye, kind wishes to Bill Dye. His Mother is so nice, we all liked her. Bill is known to our school children, in hills. Now I must post this. It goes with loads of love for you. Try to keep cheerful, and well. Moir and family due home today.

Heaps of Love,
Mother

JULY 10, 1942
[From Rev. Fraser Campbell[1]]
Oakville Lodge,
Landour, Mussoorie, India

My Dear Walter,

I have just learned that the Government arranges to forward letters to prisoners of war; and I immediately write you.

I am sure you will be quietly witnessing by conduct and conversation for the Saviour who "loved us and gave Himself for us". I have been indulging the hope that your professional skill would secure you better treatment than others. Though in my 97th year, I am kept wonderfully well; and in a poor way I try to be of a little use to my fellowmen still. So far as I at present see, it is possible that I may last for some time yet.

Your work in Ratlam is partly being done by a lady doctor.
Now, that is all I venture on at present.

Rev. J. Fraser Campbell

---

1 The Rev. J. Fraser Campbell D.D.: Dr. Campbell was from Cape Breton, Nova Scotia. He was not the first Missionary to India but did arrive the same year as the first in 1877. He spent his first six months in the country in Madras, working among the educated classes. His first station in Central India was Mhow. At the time there were no mission buildings and they had great difficulty in getting living accommodation. Mhow was a crowded military cantonment. They would have to vacate their bungalows if the military needed them. He opened schools, and Sunday schools and had regular services. They opened up work in Ratlam in 1885, one of the largest of the Central Indian States.

When they went on furlough, Walter Anderson's father, Rev. Frederick J. Anderson, took over his duties. Dr. Campbell was first and last a missionary, describing himself as "a servant of Jesus Christ, called to be an apostle, separated unto the Gospel to God". In Central India he found his kingdom and a noble outlet for his exceptional gifts and fine ardors. He influenced the growth of the Church in Central India, and particularly in the Bhil country. He was referred to as the "Father" of the Mission in a very real sense.

Rev. F. J. Anderson was associated with Dr. Campbell in evangelistic work in Ratlam for many years. The Andersons lived with him for some time in Ratlam, in the bungalow which some natives referred to as "the hotel". When other missionaries came to Ratlam, they would stay with him until they were sent to another area. Dr. Campbell baptized both Walter and Marion Anderson. Dr. Walter Anderson knew him for many years before going off to war but was not able to be there when he passed away as he was at that time a Prisoner of War.

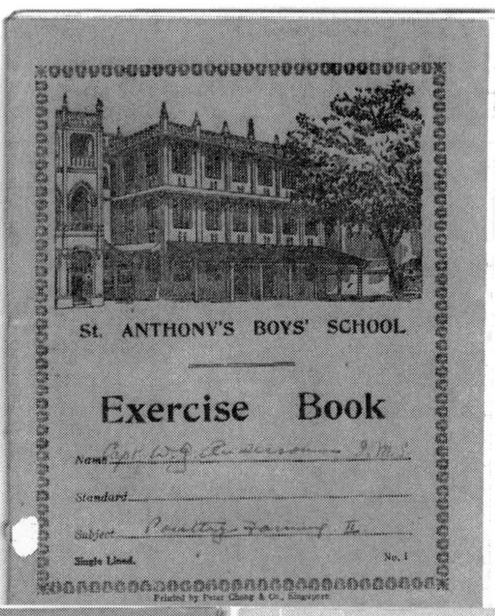

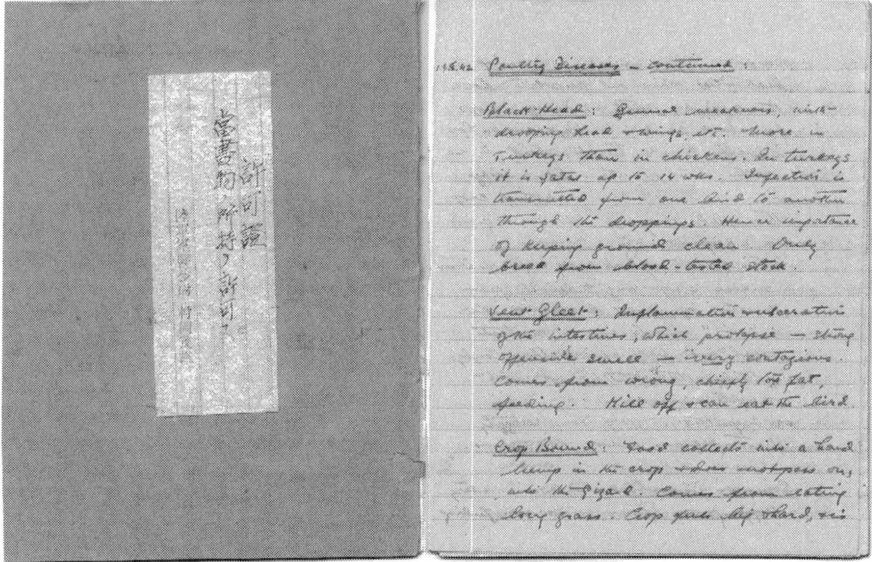

Among Walter's papers was this exercise book with his notes concerning poultry diseases, in amazing detail, one more indication of the breadth of his knowledge and duties during his imprisonment. The chickens in question were apparently for the table of his Japanese captors. The small note on the inside front cover is similar to the one on his log of tropical diseases (see page 74), which he indicates was from the Japanese censor.

AUGUST 1942

A few Red Cross supplies came in August 1942 – The first individual amounts almost nil! All except a few vitamin sweets went into our mess. A supply of South African felt hats were one of the most valued things sent – mine lasted 3 years.

SEPTEMBER 2 – 5, 1942

All Changi except Hospital to be inside Selerang chain boundary by 6 P.M. and order to move received at 3 pm. Everything including firewood taken! International Red Cross has one lawn outside verandah Barrack's square meant for say 700 to 800 men contain say over 30,000. No food or firewood allowed in – 1 well and 1 tap area, no toilets. Dig deep 17 foot trenches in the square. Queues for these! Roach fell into a new one! Perhaps this needed for morale – was wonderful exhibition of spirit. Packed like sardines. Orderliness of International Red Cross mess and serving meals got praise. We ate our pet ducks! Finally got an order to sign non-escape form. So got out at noon on 5th. Diphtheria and Dysentery in the area was serious. 4 escaped and recaptured, one man shot and a 2nd shot as example. Threats to us if we did not sign.

COPY OF SELERANG SPECIAL ORDER NO. 2

1. The requirement by the Imperial Japanese Army, issued under their Order No. 17, dated 31st August, 1942, that all ranks of the P.O.W. Camp, Changi, should be given the opportunity to sign a certificate of promise not to escape, has now been amended in a revised Imperial Japanese Army Order No. 17, dated 2nd September, 1942, to a definite order that all Officers, N.C.O.'s and men of the P.O.W. Camp shall sign this undertaking.
2. I therefore now order that these certificates will be signed by all ranks, and handed by Area Commanders to Command Headquarters by 1100 hrs. on 5th September, 1942.

3. The circumstances in which I have been compelled to issue this order will be made the subject of Selerang Special Order No. 3, which will be issued later.

Sd. E.B. Holmes. Colonel
Selerang
Commanding British and Australian, Troops, Changi

COPY OF SELERANG SPECIAL ORDER No. 3
4 Sept. 42.
1. On 30th August, 1942, I, together with my Area Commanders was summoned to the Conference House, Changi Gaol, where I was informed by the representative of Major General Shimpei Fukuye, G.O.C. Prisoner of War Camps, Malaya, that all Prisoners of War in Changi Camp were to be given forms of promise not to escape, and that all were to be given the opportunity to sign this form.
2. By the Laws and Usages of War a prisoner of war cannot be required by the Power holding him to give him parole, and in our Army those who have become prisoners of war are not permitted to give their parole. I pointed this position to the Japanese Authorities.
3. I informed the representative of Major General Shimpei Fukuye that I was not prepared to sign this form, and that I did not consider that any Officer with the orders of the Japanese Authorities, all prisoners of war were given an opportunity to sign. The result of that opportunity is well known.
4. On the 31st August I was informed by the Japanese Authorities that those personnel who refused to sign the certificate would be subjected to "measures of severity", and that a refusal to sign would be regarded as a direct refusal to obey a regulation which the Imperial Japanese Army considered it necessary to enforce.
5. Later, on the night of 1st/2nd September, I was warned that on the 2nd September all prisoners of war persisting in refusal to sign were to move by 1800 hrs. to Selerang Barrack Square. I confirmed, both on my own behalf and in the name of the prisoners of war, our refusal to sign.

6. The move to Selerang Barrack Square was successfully accomplished on the same afternoon.
7. I and the Area commanders have been in constant conference with the Imperial Japanese Army and have endeavoured by negotiation to have the form either abolished or at least modified. All that I have been able to obtain is that that which was originally a demand, accompanied by threats of "measures of severity" has now been issued as an official order of the Imperial Japanese Government.
8. During the period of the occupation of the Selerang Barrack Square the conditions in which we have been placed have been under my constant consideration. These may be briefly described as such that existence therein will result in a very few days in the outbreak of epidemic and the most serious consequences to those under my Command and the inevitable death to many. Taking into account the low state of health in which many of us now are, and the need to preserve our force intact as long as possible, and in the full conviction that my action, with the approval of His Majesty's Government, I have felt it my Duty to order all personnel to sign the certificate under the duress imposed by the Imperial Japanese Army.
9. I am fully convinced that His Majesty's Government only expects prisoners of war not to give their parole when such parole is to be given voluntarily. This factor can in no circumstance be regarded as applicable to our present condition. The responsibility for this decision rests with me, and with me alone, and I fully accept it in ordering you to sign.
10. I wish to record in this Order my deep appreciation of the excellent spirit and good discipline which all ranks have shown during this trying period. I look to all ranks to continue in good heart, discipline and morale. Thank you all for your loyalty and co-operation.

Sd. E.B. Holmes. Colonel
SELERANG.
Commanding British and Australian Troops, Changi.

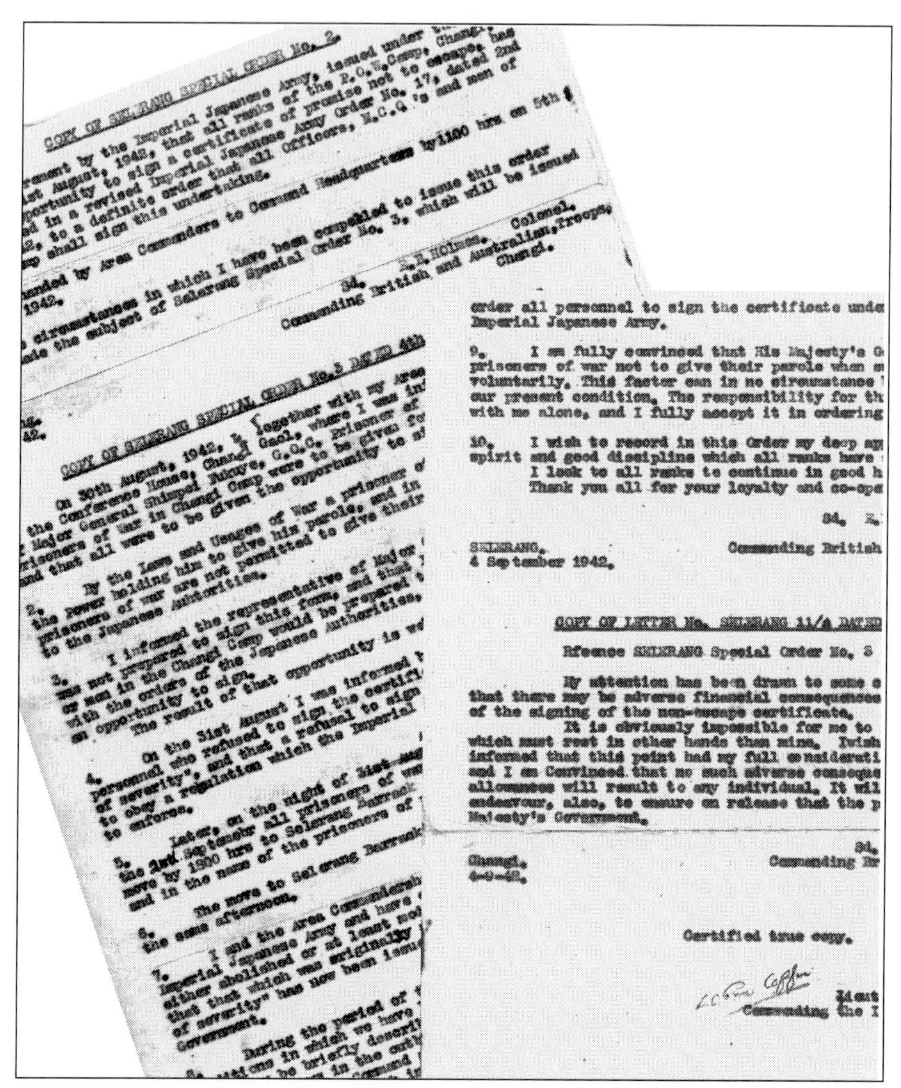

order all personnel to sign the certificate unde
Imperial Japanese Army.

9. I am fully convinced that His Majesty's G
prisoners of war not to give their parole when s
voluntarily. This factor can in no circumstance
our present condition. The responsibility for th
with me alone, and I fully accept it in ordering

10. I wish to record in this Order my deep ap
spirit and good discipline which all ranks have
I look to all ranks to continue in good h
Thank you all for your loyalty and co-ope

Sd. E.

SELERANG. Commanding British
4 September 1942.

COPY OF LETTER No. SELERANG 11/A DATED

Rference SELERANG Special Order No. 3

My attention has been drawn to some c
that there may be adverse financial consequences
of the signing of the non-escape certificate.
It is obviously impossible for me to
which must rest in other hands than mine. Iwish
informed that this point had my full considerati
and I am Convinced that no such adverse conseque
allowances will result to any individual. It wil
endeavour, also, to ensure on release that the p
Majesty's Government.

Sd.
Changi. Commanding Br
4-9-42.

Certified true copy.

Lieut
Commanding the I

This is a carbon copy of the series of Selerang orders. Walter only happened onto them in 1945, when he was walking around the camp in Thailand, in the absence of any of his Japanese captors.

COPY OF LETTER No. SELERANG 11/a
4 September 1942.
Reference SELERANG Special Order No. 3 dated 4 Sept. 42.
My attention has been drawn to some concern which is being felt that there may be adverse financial consequences on individuals as the result of the signing of the non-escape certificate.
It is obviously impossible for me to give a ruling in this matter, which must rest in other hands than mine. I wish, however, all ranks to be informed that this point had my full consideration at the time of decision, and I am Convinced that no such adverse consequences on pay, pension or allowances will result to any individual. It will naturally be my first endeavour, also, to ensure on release that the position is made clear to His Majesty's Government.
Sd. E.B. Holmes, Colonel, Changi.
Commanding British and Australian Troops, Changi.

4-9-42. Certified true copy.
[Signature here] S.C. P. Coffin, Lieut. Colonel,
Commanding the I.R.C.? Changi

SEPTEMBER 2-5, 1942 **[continued]**

Food for a time reduced in International Red Cross to rice and mustard. Little meat twice a week till city ice plant store finished, very poor fish ration. Almost nothing from local unit fishing pagan **[unskilled & uneducatcd]**. Some fish eaten. Stung one day by Stinging Ray Fish! Orders not to wash rice before cooking it! My attempts to make rice wine and yeast drinks – not very successful!

Getting used to rice diet for a long time, at first caused polyuria and nycturia. Always thought of food, of next meal; morning, noon and night conversations of food!

New Nip General Fukuye commanding all P.O.W. camps had before – paraded all Changi in our area padang **[field]** and shouted he would treat us "kindly and generously"! Captain Gulliver Royal Army Medical Corp died of very acute dysentery a few days after he got out. Became ill with enteritis myself. Jack Leech and I had previously treated in unit for dysentery. I take over Division Signals Medical Infection Room. New Deficiency diseases now appear – early pellagra, painful feet. "Changi balls", retrobulbar neuritis, conjunctivitis, calamitis , stomatitis, and glossitis etc. and skin diseases of Tinis, Tropical Pemphigus, scrotal and wound Dip. All areas established daily skin clinics – I take over 11th Division – See some frightful balls and skins. These Medical Officer duties keep one very busy. Great effort to make Tropical Diseases Notes in case of being sent up into jungle. First influx of Dutch from Java soon after Selerang. Difficulties limiting them to areas and not to use our shower and latrines. More and more come to Changi! Occupy buildings in hill cleared by Nip navy as not to see channel! Dutch interpreters suicide in Hospital – cursed by Malay woman – Lieutenant General Heath remained Officer in Command and his wife resided in Singapore – he too came into Selerang, but Colonel Holmes was Commanding Officer. General left towards end of the year.

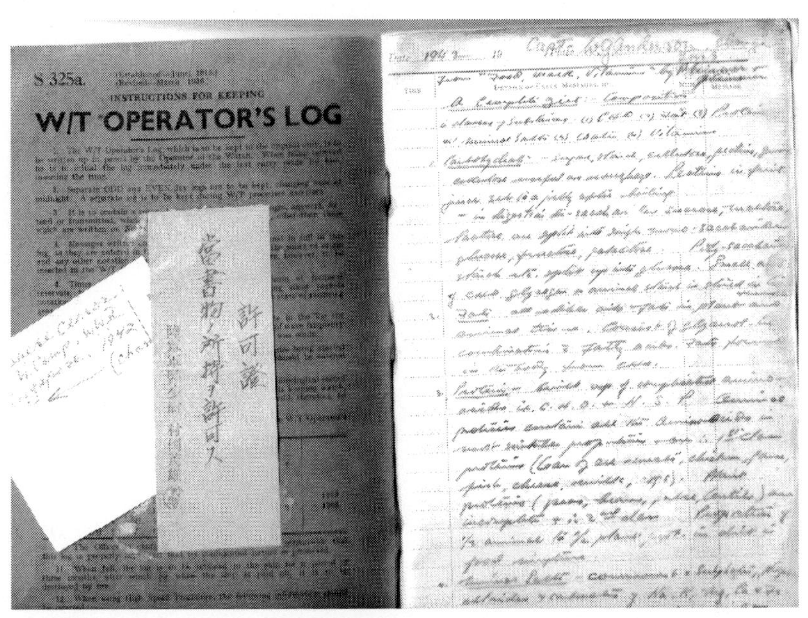

Capt. W.G.Anderson's Operator's log of Nutritional Notes and Tropical Diseases (his tag indicates that the Japanese note pasted into the log is that of a censor).

Jack Leech gives the sermon at a Thanksgiving Service, Church parade held in playing field – a big thing for him, and spoke very well indeed – Australian S.C.F. present. Jack's difficulties with padre of 5th Field Regiment A.C.Q. Colonel Brian Lewis very friendly to Jack – Padre Foster Haig of 15th Division (ncf) a fine tenor, died later with "F & H" Force, also his pianist and young bass – Senior Presbyterian Chaplain Major McLeod took 11th Division communion at first and I and Jack were the elders. Jack's final communion for Indian Army Corp with Fearon, P. C. and others attending before they left Nov. 5th? Allowed to sing "The King" in 11th Division area, so few Nips about, but not in South area!

Incoming Dutch bring articles with them which they sell off – go into a trade and helpful for us! Even their green shorts transfer "crabs" **[pubic lice]** to some of our men! Dutch concert talent something new. Dutch national anthem solemn and pretty.

[Below are the contents of a form that the Prisoners of War were to sign, stating that they would not attempt escape. In pencil on the lower left corner of his copy, Walter wrote the following quote " 'It is great sin to swear unto a sin, but greater sin to keep a sinful oath.' Shakespeare"]

SEPTEMBER 4th, 1942
No……

I, the undersigned, hereby solemnly swear on my honour that I will not, under any circumstances, attempt escape.

Signed

Dated

At

Nationality

Rank or Position

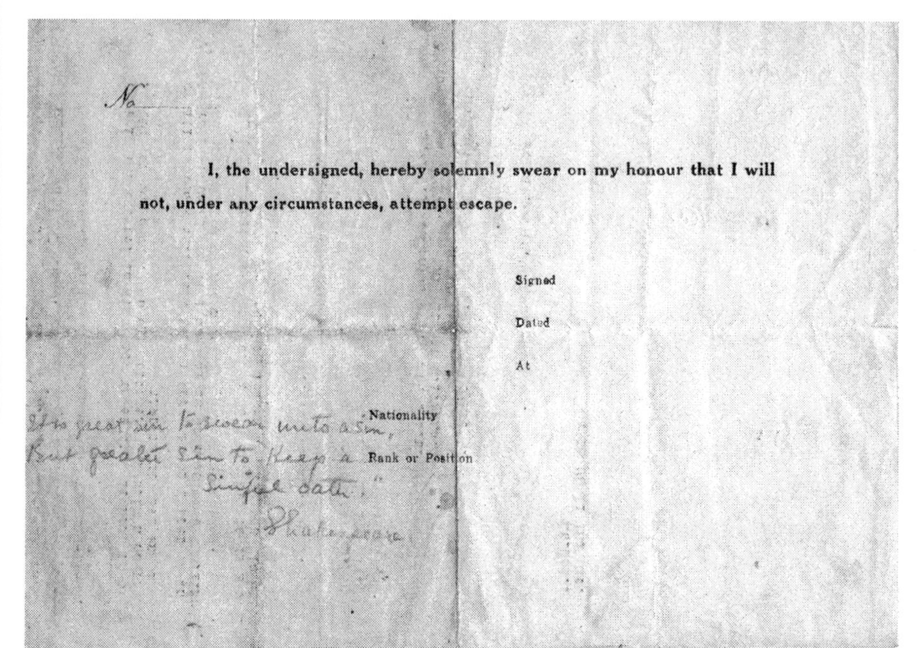

No.

I, the undersigned, hereby solemnly swear on my honour that I will not, under any circumstances, attempt escape.

Signed

Dated

At

Nationality

Rank or Position

"It is great sin to swear unto a sin,
But greater sin to keep a sinful oath."
Shakespeare

This is a copy of the "no escape" form that Walter apparently acquired well after the fact. His Shakespeare quote is pencilled in on the left.

SEPTEMBER 15th, 1942
[From Father]
Dhar, Central India

My Dear Walterji

It is a long time since I wrote you last – for I didn't understand that I could send more. A notice last night said "the International Red Cross state that all letters must be type written". The first, and second letter I sent you were typed so I hope you have received them ere this one gets through. I wrote June 25th and July 9th. I, maybe, should have been writing, as Bessie has done, but I did not understand so.

All are well, and how we and many others are longing for some word from you. Your last letter was from Singapore Feb. 9th.

Andy has been on sick leave and had a good hill holiday, and resumed work. Marion is working at St. Josephs and liking it better. Old Col. Black fell in an elevator from a heart attack, and was killed instantly. Peggy soon went overseas. John Mullin finished with Honours, Gold Medal, Scholarship and a Prize. Isn't that grand! they must be proud of him. We sent him an Airgraph letter to congratulate him. Recent letters from MacKay's, Wallace & Waters. Dr. MacKay is not very well. Mrs. Waters still not fully recovered. MacKay was to officiate at Jean Scott's wedding in May. – Peterborough.

Marion and Ann are well, and still boarding, now moved to where she used to be on Harboard. Ann has grassy, enclosed lawn to play in there, and is cared for while Marion is at Hospital. Several letters sent you in January have come back, naturally. Mrs. T. and Lorna are still with me. Brain tumour resulted in partial eyesight. They may go to Mayo's. Miss Martin has fever today, Margaret injected Quinine. Daniel, David Bala and several others send with Bhabriya's their 'Salaams' with love.

Bhabriya now works here while Mrs. Taylor is here. Nariya is with Dr. Hodge and her parents at R. Bhabriya also sheds tears! Alice Anderson is at Miraj, some trouble on side of tongue – not malignant, but nerve from neck.

Best love from us both.
Father

[Note on edge of letter:]
Council will be at Indore, Crowded out of Rasalpura. If this reaches you for Christmas, remember, we love you dearly and think of you constantly. Many, many dear friends would like to send messages. God's Blessing, and to Jack too.

OCTOBER 12TH, 1942
[Letter from the Waters family, good friends for many years]
Kharna
Via Mehidpur Rd. Station
Central India

Dear Walter,

Your mother has written to say that we can drop a line to you and we are glad to be able to do so.

We all came down for the rainy season and Jimmie stood it very well except for two trips to Ratlam, once with a bad eye that they fixed up for him in a few days.

He is a real boy. He has twelve teeth now and an increasing vocabulary mostly Hindustani words which he learns from his Ayah. He walks all over the place and goes over every day to see Miss Patterson's chickens. He is a great favorite with the Indian people around here and is very friendly with them all.

We hear from my parents in Canada. Mother is not strong after two illnesses and has to be very careful as her heart has been weakened, however, she is resting a good deal and we hope that that will build her up.

We were with the Irwins in Landour last holiday. We expect to return to Landour next summer as I hope to take Kellogg Church services again for six weeks.

I am hoping that I may be able to try my third year Hindi language exams next September and October but that will involve a lot of work in the meantime.

Moir Waters and Walter: lifelong friends (both born in India).

We head out for Church Council and Mission Council the day after tomorrow. It is being held in Indore this year. I am to speak in Hindi at the Christian Temple next Sunday. We hope you are keeping well. We all send our best wishes.

Sincerely,
Moir, Margaret & Jimmy Waters

About mid-OCTOBER 1942

Main bulk of 11th Division taken for an overseas party. Lieutenant Colonel Hennessey gets a few hours notice! Major Wheeler Indian Medical Services of Edmonton goes.

OCTOBER 31st, 1942
[From Mother]

Halloween
Indore, Central India

My Dear Walter

I am sorry that I have no typewriter here with me and I hope this plainly written will be permitted.

I've little doubt you will be thinking of us in Council – as we are. This is Sat. and we shall disperse ere the day is done. We came in here on Tues. 19th and we have been stopping at Miss Baxter's house.

Mr. Smillie was too busy and filled up to have us all there this year. This change has been very interesting and comfortable – lots of walking – but that is good for us – to and from the Seminary Council room. Everyone remembers you lovingly and they wish to send you a resolution of greeting which is very nice.

A letter was posted to you in September. A few days before we came in here Dr. Campbell, on his birthday fell down the first flight of stairs and got rather bruised. They have had him in the ward ever since. Last evening a telephone message came from the doctor Alice H. that he might not last through the night but he rallied. Mr. and Mrs. Boyd have gone home. This accident happened on the first night at home. Bessie and the children were there and it was fortunate Bessie lives down stairs. She is going to help in Hospital work this winter. This is Margaret's last council meeting here. Everyone is so disappointed with her arrangements. She is taking a big risk for she does not know Mrs. Ginn well yet.

Her Mother is thought to be the strong influence. Mrs. H. is greatly upset by lack of enthusiasm all through the Mission. Just announced that Dr. Campbell rallied from another spell at midnight. We shall go home from here. Miss Boyd and Eva Hala come to Dhar. All quite well. So many enquiries for you.

Fondest Love from
Mother

NOVEMBER 6th, 1942 (2 weeks later)

An up country party leaves, including the International Red Cross only comparatively few of which, including Jack and I, left behind. Jack and I etc. move over to Indian Army Ordinance Corps mess. I got my first "bed" left by Brown! Dutch officers take over the International Red Cross hut.

One week later: all Indian Army Ordinance Corps etc. have to shift back again to other side of area – Indian Army Ordinance Corps and former 80th Anti tank huts with cement flooring turned into piggery! Jack and I move to No. 2 mess. Jack falls foul of Sedgwick over not going on wood fatigues! Also of Captain Moore! Remainder of 3rd Corps officers join our mess, including Lieutenant Colonel Hunt and Lieutenant Colonel Cannon. Jack and I for first time live in a concrete building and the beds are strange at first! Our day parade to be filmed for Japanese film final scene of capture of Singapore.

One day a member of Japanese Royalty came to visit Changi – all have to remain indoors and not look out the windows! Captured N. Dutch East Indies Governor General passes through – story, he faced the sun one hour in Batavia, for 1 man (escaped).

Xmas 1942 in No. 2 mess – special process – mess waiters (Law and Johnson etc.) prepare a menu. Special service. Special watch night New Years Service of Jack's. Lieutenant Colonel Parker changes: Lieutenant Whittenberg to arrange a possible Japanese party, and then Whittenberg stays in Changi.

Padang a great blessing to our area – go on evening walks and sit out in moonlight till 10:45 pm. Can see Changi Gaol where interns are and their lights go out early and their flood lights remain. Some beautiful sunsets. Football and hockey matches frequent. Dutch play good soccer.

Nips General came in unofficially to visit area and our kitchens being near the gate he inspected before Xmas – wished one British Other Rank "Merry Xmas". British Other Rank couldn't wish him the same so easily – said "Thank You"!

11th Division Motto in gate "He laughs best who laughs last" never questioned by the Japs in Latin.

[The following letters, mailed to Walter between December 1942 and March 7th, 1944 were only received in December 1944.]

DECEMBER 25, 1942
[From Mother]

Dhar, Central India

My Dear Walter

I should have written you earlier, I am afraid I haven't enough confidence that the letters are going through to you. I wrote last at Indore, and I told you that Dr. Campbell had fallen part way down stairs and was in Hospital. He passed away after a fortnight (of very good care) from Pneumonia on Sun. Nov. 1st at 3 pm. They sent us an urgent wire and we took an hour to be ready and I drove in, so we were there before seven in the evening. The Buchanan's were very glad to see us come. The funeral was at 10 am. Mon. Nov.2nd. I got to work and was till midnight preparing with the help of Mr. Irwin and others, like Miss Drummond. The casket was ready in time. The carpenters always hold one up. Dr. C. was quite rational till noon on Sun. and said he was very tired. One day previous he said that he remarked that he was sore, as though he had had a fall. He was bright in the mornings and dazed in the afternoons.

Mrs. Buchanan, Dr. J. T. Taylor, Father, Pastor Singh & Dr. Scott were on the platform. At the Grave Mr. B., Moir and Dr. Hodge officiated. His Highness Maharaja sent Gun-carriage and buglers who sounded the 'Last Post'.

There were not as many persons there as in pre-war times. Grahams, and Bill Taylor came also. We got home from Council just Sat. night! I worked for some hours, with Mrs. Buchanan clearing out Dr. Campbell's desk and sorting papers for his Biographer, Moir will likely be that. Everything about it was so triumphant. He was 97 years and two weeks old. Father now has most of the business with his Will to attend to. Well he has an office man. I sent Marion an 'Airgraph letter'; also four others, for Christmas. I seemed to feel you thinking of me on Nov. 14th dinner time. Malaya is two hours ahead of our time here.

We were notified that we are to address you 'Captain' last month.

Dr. Eva Hala and Miss Boyd are well started in their work here. We went to Margaret's wedding in Mhow on 18th. Not very large attendance. It was in old Kirk where her Mother's was. No enthusiasm outside her family! They now have a Gill and a Ginn **[surnames]** *in their family. They are stationed near Bareilly. People amazed and disappointed at her choice! We gave her some S.I.* **[Sterling Inlaid]** *spoons and forks. I put your name also on the card. Mandu had them for Honeymoon. They returned via Dhar last Wed. 23rd and we were invited to lunch with them. Will leave Mhow 30th. Had several teas and dinners to farewell Margaret here and there, also at the Palace – a ladies dinner. Mixed crowd at Diwan's dinner.*

Capt. A. Dobson is happy about his wee daughter. Letter from Marion a few days ago – Ann had Mumps – since that letter was written. Moir gave me word from his Air letter. Marion still at St. Joseph's Hospital. She boards on Harbord St.

It is a comparatively quiet day. My dining table holds two big trays of bags with sweets, guavas, kelas and peanuts for children – to be given at 4:30. Miss Boyd is on a little picnic to Natnagra with the Nurses just now. We shall have dinner with them tonight at other bungalow. How lonely this day has been, better not be described. Not unlike other days, particularly Sundays. A host of people remembering you; so lovely. Try to keep cheerful, it helps.

Father had posted a letter to you today, I saw it in the out-going mail. Father had Flu a fortnight ago. Quite over it now. How we long and wait for one word of you! Prolonged suspense bows one down. One has to struggle so hard to be patient. Una Dobson has gone to Delhi, with the baby. Cousin Lorna was married in May. We just heard two days ago. They took their time to write – wrote mid-Oct. We sent Marion cheque for winter coat, for Christmas. She got it but paid more than the thirty for the coat. She still won't look ahead.

Bessie has the house now to herself. She is working about four hours a day at the Hospital and receiving half pay for it. The children are bonnie. Miss Gruchy will be glad of her help. Irene Netram was married, very quiet wedding (considering her Father's death) four days ago. Mr. Graham married them. Groom some Railway man from Delhi.

With deepest love
Mother

DECEMBER 25th, 1942
[From Father]

Dhar, Central India

Dear Walter

We remember you of course every day but, if possibly more especially today when we should be all out happy and glad for all that Christmas stands for and means to them who love our Lord. As usual some of the young men were around very early this morning singing Christmas Carols. Then we opened up our gift packages. The Church was gaily decorated and well filled for the 9:30 a.m. service conducted by Pastor Gokhi. There was quite a good program and the Pastor gave a short address. Tonight we will have our dinner with the ladies Martin and Boyd. Our goose is still strutting about self conscious that his number is not up yet. Quintie is happy and had a healthy romp this morning with Punch. Miss Boyd and Dr. Eva Hala have charge of our Mission hospital.

Margaret Harcourt (now Mrs. Ginn) and her husband Wesley spent their honeymoon at Mandu and we had breakfast with them at the ladies bungalow on their return from Mandu. They are now spending their Christmas holidays in Mhow, and will then go north but they are not sure yet just when the Bishop will station them. D.J.F. has been laid up since Margaret's wedding and Bill has also been ill with gastric ulcers for a couple of weeks. He is now reported to be on the mend. Cadet Bacon is still training and Capt. Dobson is on duty in Delhi.

Yesterday I had a letter from Mary Anderson of Vancouver, she reports the marriage of Lorna. My brother Will and Lillie were at the wedding in May. I don't know what Lorna's husband is doing but they live in Vancouver.

The Maharaja of Ratlam acknowledged my Christmas card by telegram yesterday. We were having dinner at the Mission hospital when the wire came. There has been no recent word from Marion. Oh yes, there was too a couple of weeks ago. She is engaged at St. Josephs.

We have some thought of spending a few weeks next summer with the J.T. Taylor's at Mt. Abu. Bhabriya is helping us here and sends greetings. A nice card from Miss McLeod and Miss Gruchy says "Nothing lies beyond the reach of prayer except that which lies outside the will of God"

We are ever mindful of you.
Lovingly
Father

1943

Mid JANUARY

Bulk of 11th Division moved to Changi Village and then became "C" Group S.A. under Lieutenant Colonel Fitzpatrick. Jack stays behind.

11th Division becomes G. & W. area being nearer – I go as 11th Division Group Medical Officer to some 700 plus men. Live in Headquarters mess, nice garage room overlooking Channel. Pretty spot and quiet. Room with Petherbridge. Hot water shower! P.B's chickens!

Major "Squire" living with us. Village in ruins. Not a front to any room as former shop!

Medical Inspection Rooms of the Manchesters taken over with Warrant Officer Davies. Indian Army Ordinance Corps and a Bombard living in it, and Asst. Surgeon Devine and Kashan assisting at early A.M. sick parades. Also, Captain Dr. Lunds. Captain Waring Indian Army Ordinance Corp got a wash basin installed! Lieutenant Colonel Cornelius, South area, Asst. Director Medical Service. He put one Royal Army Medical Corps, Medical Officer who was court martialed to assist me for two days!

Found the Prisoner of Court Martialing in Medical Inspection Room as a patient! All trouble nothing new. P.M. roll calls in village street – turn out in battle dress and marching. Commanding Officer slapped one day for dismissing us without permission by mistake!

JANUARY 12, 1943
Telegraph
Simla, India
To- Rev. F.J. Anderson U.C.C. Mission, Dhar

Your son Lt. W.G. Anderson has been reported prisoner of war in Malaya from 15th Feby 1942. Any further information received will be communicated at once.

14:30 Hrs 12th Jany.
Casualty **[Dept.]**

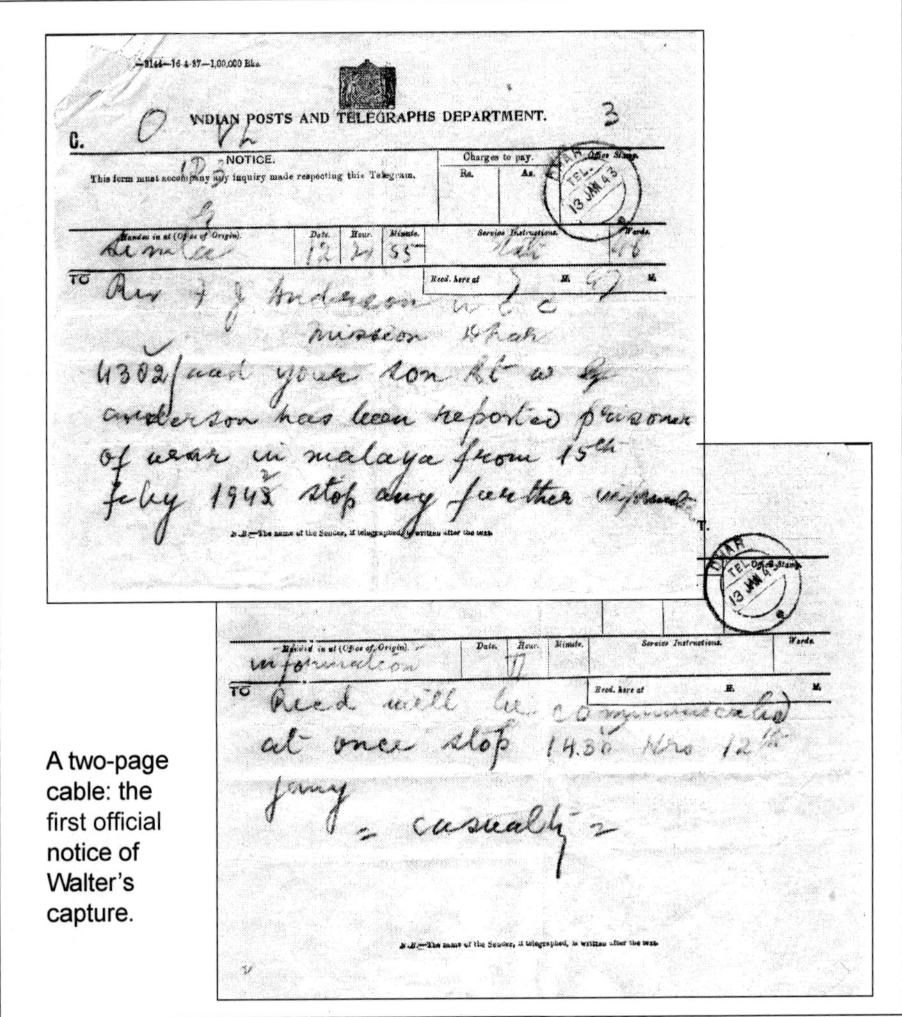

INDIAN POSTS AND TELEGRAPHS DEPARTMENT.

NOTICE.
This form must accompany any inquiry made respecting this Telegram.

Charges to pay. Rs. As.

Office Stamp. DHAR TEL. 13 JAN 43

Handed in at (Office of Origin). Simla | Date. 12 | Hour. 21 | Minute. 55 | Service Instructions. | Words. 46

Recd. here at

TO Rev F J Anderson U C C Mission Dhar

4302/cas your son Lt W G Anderson has been reported prisoner of war in malaya from 15th feby 1942 stop any further inform

N.B.—The name of the Sender, if telegraphed, is written after the text.

Office Stamp. DHAR TEL. 13 JAN 43

Handed in at (Office of Origin). information | Date. | Hour. | Minute. | Service Instructions. | Words.

Recd. here at

TO recd will be communicated at once stop 14.30 Hrs 12th jany = casualty =

N.B.—The name of the Sender, if telegraphed, is written after the text.

A two-page cable: the first official notice of Walter's capture.

JANUARY 19th, 1943
[From Mother]
Dhar, C. I.

My Dear Walter

The last letter written to you was at Christmas. It told you about Dr. Campbell's passing etc. the end of Oct. and beginning Nov. This will tell you we are well, except Father's cold in head. Dr. J.T. Taylor has been very ill with Paratyphoid, but is now considered to be fairly safe on the way to recovery. He still has Vera and assistants for night, and Louise with male nurse for days. Andy was called and came by air for ten days. He has now gone again. Bill Taylor seems to have Gall Bladder trouble like I had. He is taking course of treatment for four months. He has not worked since Oct. He will take classes from Feb. 1st. Marion is well and Ann is growing fast. A good picture being sent me. Mrs. Waters still much of an invalid. Jimmie Baba is developing nicely and nice looking.

The Audit is finished. Bill was not able to come so Baxter and Gardner did it. Now we want to help McLeod down in the valley. Hilda goes home.

On Wed. 13th we had a wire to say you were reported a Prisoner of War in Singapore, so the long silence is broken, and relieved. Thanks for this much – is our feeling.

Many friends send love to you with all good wishes possible. Yesterday brought Air message that Uncle Bryce had passed away in the South on Nov. 21st from "coronary heart trouble". Nellie and Florence very sad and lonely. He had not been well for some little time. Still he did the driving, to the South. They had been settled about three weeks, when he finally felt that they should call a doctor. This was done and he was left more comfortable. Then in a day or two he was worse, and again rather desperately, he said "call the doctor", Auntie Flo went to telephone and before she or the doctors got there Bryce was gone. Nellie was alone and it was a most harrowing experience for her. His body was put in the vault, to be buried in the Spring in the North **[Nellie and Flo were Mabel's sisters]**.

Nellie writes herself, a long letter – as though she was trying her best to be brave and courageous. I have cabled them since the 13th via Canada.

We don't yet know where we shall tour, as Father is still busy in the office. One thing is certain you don't have to worry about us, quite the reverse. I wish Bessie could get some word of Jack. Bessie is very well and not so thin as she used to be. The children are lovely. She likes living in your bungalow. She helps in the hospital, about four hours a day and is paid for it.

Now I shall let this go for now. Loads of love, and best of wishes from many friends. Father looks after your affairs, so don't worry.

Best love from
Mother

JANUARY 31st, 1943
[From L.A. Davenport]

REV. & MRS. F.J. ANDERSON
DHAR, CENTRAL INDIA
College Street United Church
Toronto

Dear Dr. and Mrs. Anderson
The session and members of College Street United Church rejoice with you in word having come from Walter. During these trying days our prayers have been with you. They still are and always will be. You are very dear to us all. It helps us always as we think of you – our workers for Christ – in that part of His vineyard. May His richest blessing be upon you and your dear one. 'In His Keeping we are safe and they **[sic]**. *Our love and good wishes always.*

L.A. Davenport — *C.A. Gowans*
Clerk of Session — *Minister*

FEBRUARY 6th, 1943
[From Mother]
Dhar, C. I.

My Dear Walter
I posted my last letter to you on the 20th of January '43. I wrote of Uncle Bryce's passing away from Coronary heart trouble and also told you that you had

been reported as Prisoner of War, Malaya. That is the only word we have had. It did greatly relieve the strain, by just breaking the silence. How we hope you are well. Take good care and be as cheerful as possible.

Dr. J. T. Taylor is now making a slow but steady improvement. Vera is home again. She is starting a little nurse training class and has two from her old institution here. Eva goes for her post-graduate course. A Christmas card came from Aunt Laura **[married to Mabel's brother Jack]**. *A regular letter from Aunt Nellie also. Uncle Bryce was ill before they went south and should never have driven so far. Bill Service passed through – he remembers you well, and very complimentary.*

Lorna Colwell has been married. Dr. Wallace writes. Beryl has taken a church at home. Heavy work for her. Marion now lives on Windermere, nearer work. Baby Ann is reported very attractive. Marion says that little Ann calls all water, whether in a lake or in a glass "tup of tea", so when Marion was talking to her about "Uncle Walter" Ann nodded her head and said "tup of tea". Miss Martin is on tour. Father has not been well enough to go yet. Another heavy cold. He coughs now so it will pass off soon. He has had the Auditors and he too has audited other accounts.

I had a letter from Margaret and they have been appointed to the charge of a Vocational School. She wrote when she heard of our telegram, about you. Bhabriya is still with me, though temporarily. He will not go on tour. Miss Cates had some of her precious school supplies stolen – hardlines. Dr. Alice Jane now has Dr. Smith working with her, and Dr. Jean has taken the place of Smith. Eva Hala now will supply two months for Mrs. Peters who has leave. Eva has six months study-leave from March. Ida and Bob have a baby son. When they return we shall see him. Moir and Margaret are on tour. Moir will officiate again this summer in hills, and live in Ellengowan.

Mrs. T. B. had Typhus – not so bad a case as mine. Dr. Alice has her parents now living with her. Vera has some stamps for your collection – Father also is putting away all he gets. My little box holds what I get!

Quintie is the same little friend as ever. She misses motor rides now. Father had an accident with his glasses three days ago, and when his cold is lighter he will have to go for one new lens. He had just got new bows on – so a screw was left loose, and they fell apart to the cement floor! He is using an old pair.

I wonder if you ever got the letter of "sympathy and good will" from Dr. Scott. Now I shall have to close. There is one thing I am sure of, that you don't need to worry about things here (we are all quite well **[this space was censored]**

Bessie has no word yet, but she is in good flesh, and the children lovely. Bessie works four hours daily in Hospital, and enjoys it. Habil, Eva, Vera etc. all wish to send you their best regards. So many others too, including Hugh and wife. Take care of yourself and others, wherever you are.

With our constant love and concern, always.
Mother

[The following letter to Walter surfaced among other correspondence as we were finishing compiling this book. Written in 1943, it was apparently not received until well after the war. It is the only hint we found of a romance in Walter's life, and there is no indication that, private person that he was, he confided it in anyone. It is included to give a broader and deeper picture of the man.]

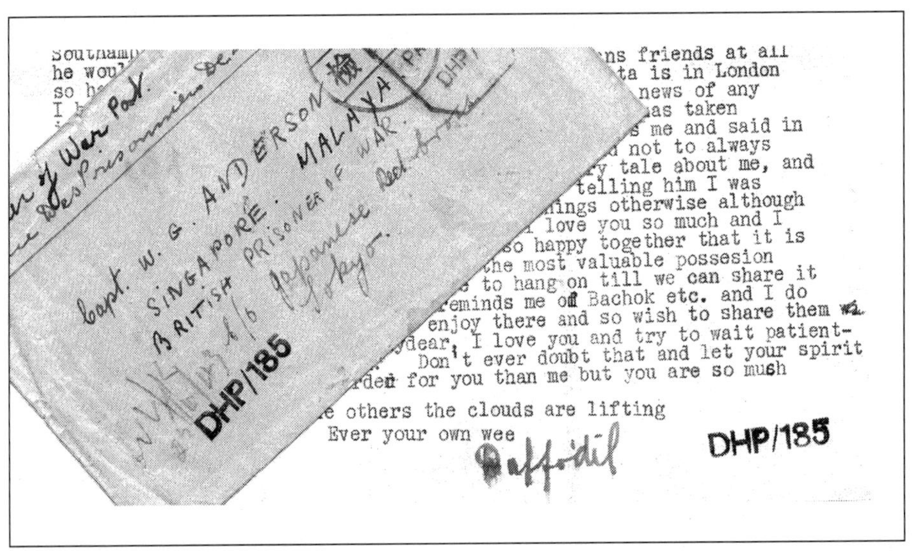

FEBRUARY 25, 1943
[small section of the address cut out, apparently censored]
c/o Kenya Branch, British Red X
P.O. Box 712, Nairobi, Kenya

Dearest, dearest Andy, **[assume a nickname]**

I wonder if you have received any of my letters yet. I do so hope at least one has arrived by now. I have not received anything from you yet but am hoping I may do so soon. It is sure to be slower to reach me as you do not know my address. I have written before to tell you that I had a cable from Norah to say she had heard from the War Office that a Captain W.G. Anderson had appeared on the lists from Tokyo therefore the news was regarded as official that he was safe in a Malayan camp. I was terribly thrilled and excited at first, but now have the feeling that it does not refer to you, but that they have got the initials wrong, and it is someone else. Anderson is unfortunately such a usual name. I shall write to you as a civilian and to the Malayan Camp also so that one day one of them will reach you. It is hard to know what to think as one gets no news of you at all, but rest assured that we are all alright here and tell everyone not to worry unduly about their wives, we are all looked after very well by the Government and Life is not hard for us really.

I am very well indeed, and am settled down to Army life quite cheerfully again. The girls are very nice indeed, and I like my work, although the hours are quite long for the heat. Still it is better to be in an office in the tropics than out of doors. Have plenty to do in my off time and lots of nice friends, and the living conditions are very good considering there is a War on. Don't worry, Dearest Heart, over me for one moment. I live very comfortable on my pay and am saving for my leave in S.A. next August when I go to stay with a friend. I want to see as much of Africa as possible while I am here, so far I have seen very little as the five months I was in Durban as I was working in the Naval office I did not get time to get around much. I went one week-end to see Alva but that was last March. I hope you will get news from your sister and Aunt Clara, how worried they must be, poor dears. All is well with my Father, had a letter from him today saying how glad I must be to hear from Norah that you are safe. I wonder so much if that Captain is you or is it a mistake.

Darling Heart, it is over a year now but never mind, it will all come right one day and we shall forget all this when we are together again. I haven't changed at all, sometimes I feel I shall never grow up inside me however I may look outside, and you will always be just Andy to me therefore all I could wish for. There is none to compare to you as far as I am concerned, and I am still as proud of you as ever. Oh Andy, you have made me so happy and I am so glad we had those months together, it was all so perfect.

Tell Robert I had a letter from Phyllis who is with her aunt in London, and she and Mrs. 00i and Mimi are all well. R. has a job in Southampton, Father tells me. I do not communicate at all although he would like me too **[sic]**. *I do not write to my Malayans friends at all so have no news of those who went to Australia, Rosita is in London I hear. Ted is in Ceylon and Arthur is Mid-East, no news of any importance otherwise to relate. Father is a pet and has taken everything very well in the circumstances. He misses me and said in one of his letters I am to go* *home after the War and not to always wander. Imagine R. has told him some tragic fairy tale about me, and quite worried him but I wrote him a long letter telling him I was content, happy and secure and would not have things otherwise although we had struck a bad patch at the moment. I love you so much and I know you love even more and we have been so happy together that it is the only thing that matters, we've got the most valuable possession there is in the world and we only have to hang on till we can share it all together again. So much here reminds me of Bachok etc. and I do the same sort of things I used to enjoy there and so wish to share them with you. Always remember, Andy dear, I love you and try to wait patiently till we are together again. Don't ever doubt that and let your spirit fail you, it is so much harder for you than me but you are so much stronger and tell all the others the clouds are lifting.*

Ever your own wee
Daffodil

THE TIMES OF INDIA

400 Women Marched Singing To Prison

1942 INCIDENT

TOKIO, September 4: Four hundred British women marched 10 miles to a Japanese prison singing: "There'll always be an England" after the surrender of Singapore in February 1942, Major David James, Liaison Officer between Lt.-Gen. Arthur E. Percival, the Singapore Commander, and the Japanese, who has now been released from a prison camp in Tokio, told me today, cables Astley Hawkins, *Reuter's* special correspondent.

"They were lead by a British officer's young wife, wearing shorts, who got them into ranks and started singing", he said. "They were uneven at the end of the march, but reformed into ranks to enter the prison, still singing".

The prison was the Changi prison outside Singapore, in which were herded all British civilian women, while captured troops were concentrated in prison camps under canvas. Children went to prison with their mothers, carried on lorries provided by the Japanese.

Major James, who speaks fluent Japanese, managed to arrange for a half-hour meeting between the women and their husbands and fiancees on Christmas Day.

Soldiers in the camps made toys for the children.—*Reuter.*

A report from the *Times of India,* relating an incident in 1942, where British women, many of them wives and fiancees of British men imprisoned by the Japanese, marched ten miles to the Changi prison outside occupied Singapore. As they marched, they sang "There will always be an England".

FEBRUARY, 1943

We **[all POWs]** send second post card on February 22nd, 1943.

This is the second postcard Japanese authorities allowed their captives to send.

MZ 23691. CAPT. W. G. ANDERSON
FEB. 22 ND. 1943.

DEAR FATHER AND MOTHER :-
PRISONER OF WAR. QUITE WELL. DONT WORRY. TRYING NOT TO RUST. HOPE PREVIOUS CARD RECEIVED. TRUST ALL WELL. LOVE. WALTER.

俘虜郵便

馬來俘虜收容所 檢閲濟

PASSED DHP/6

REV. AND MRS. F. J. ANDERSON
U. C. C. MISSION, DHAR
C. INDIA

DHAR DELY. 14 NOV. 43

The Rev. and Mrs. F. J. Anderson of the United Church of Canada Mission, Dhar, C. I., received a post card from their son, Dr. Walter G. Anderson, on Sunday, November 14th, and presumably from Singapore. The message dated February, 22, 1943, was addressed to his father and mother and reads, "Prisoner of war. Quite well. Don't worry. Trying not to rust. Hope previous card received. Trust all well." The place of origin is not given. The 'previous card' referred to was received on August 11th. It was dated June 20, 1942. Dr. Walter Anderson was the Mission doctor at the hospital in Ratlam, C. I., before entering the I. M. S. for service in India and overseas.

A Toronto newspaper reports the receipt of this rare word from a Japanese POW camp.

Headquarters mess better organized and food more attractively prepared. By now the Local Purchase system functioning well and helped my area – orders 2 weeks in advance – got peanuts and bananas mainly – but once a good pair of canvas shoes – couldn't get a sarong **[kilt]**. Good walks and several good concerts in Southern area.

MARCH 6th, 1943
[From Mother]
Dhar, C. I.

My Dear Walter,

I posted last to you on Feb. 7th. It's a rather long time ago. I wish I felt more confident that these letters were reaching you. Of course, I know it will take a long time for them to go through, at least.

To have had the report that you were Prisoner of War, did greatly relieve, but it was so long coming – almost a year. In this last month the Nurses Graduation was attended by Vera, had visit from Habil's wife, we celebrated Hospital Sunday and an Honour Roll included your name among Prisoners (I.M.S.). Only a few at a time seem to be published. On 20th Feb. Benji killed and brought to me a cobra 5'5" long, it was ready to lose its 'kanchla' **[skin]** *and it looked more venomous than ever I saw one. About four days ago a smaller one, thought to be a viper was killed. We did not get out to do any touring. Father was not well enough until the season was so far past that it was no use. Miss Martin is home and at present on a shopping trip to town by bus. She is returning today. Vera has had a few days in bed – throat etc. I had a pleasant trip to Burra Bungalow, and its garden with Princess P. – Vera also went. It's very modern and beautiful now. Her Highness was away for adenoid operation. Mrs. H. and Helen came out for the Nadkar daughter's wedding, and turned up here late at night. We took them in for over Sunday. Strangely, none of us, not even Miss Martin was invited to wedding. Some mishap, somewhere. Dr. J.T. Taylor does well. Bill and Mary Taylor in Miraj where Bills Op. is over. Mrs. Harcourt and Helen went to Dak Bungalow first and didn't like it – so came here! Beckwith came through on Monday but he could not wait for Mrs. Harcourt to make calls and get ready so went on home after breakfast.*

After Red Cross Miss Martin and I were invited to see a film with Pushpamala and Mrs. Kher. It was quite enjoyable. I have been making nightsuits **[pyjamas]** – *I don't doubt you need some.*

Gruchy is visiting Vera this weekend. I am having them all for dinner. Your Medical Journal comes. Wish I could send you some to read. Now it's time to post, so I shall close. Don't worry about anything here, all is "OK". We can do all of that! Take care of yourself.

Our constant remembrance and love
Mother

MARCH 19th, 1943
[From Rev. A.A. Scott, another missionary]
United Church of Canada Mission
Indore, Central India

Dear Walter,

At last Council meeting I was asked to write to you on behalf of Council, and assure you that we have not forgotten you. I have been very slow in carrying out my instructions. For a time I did not know exactly how to address a letter to you, and then, later on, so many things came in the way that I did not get it done. However, at last I have got started. Doubtless you have been hearing from your father and mother, for I know they have been writing regularly, so you will be kept in touch with news of our Mission. Things are going on much as usual. The men's side of the work is very much handicapped owing to shortage of workers. As you will know, Grant and Clark have not been able to return to India. Dobson and Bacon have taken commissions in the army, and Baur has gone back to his own Mission. In the Hospital at Ratlam Dr. Hodge is still carrying on, but I think she plans to go to England this year, and we, as yet, have no plans for the place after her departure. However, everything is going surprisingly well in spite of all the difficulties which are bound to occur in war time.

I suppose you have come across Jack Leech quite frequently. His wife and family were in Ratlam for a time. I'm not exactly sure where they are now.

If you get a chance to write, please do so, and let us know how things are going with you. Meanwhile, you may be sure that you are often thought about by your old friends in Central India.

With all good wishes,
Yours sincerely,
A.A. Scott

MARCH 24th, 1943
[From Mother]
Dhar, C.I.

My Dear Walter

My last letter to you was sent on the 6th and it's considerably warmer today than then. In my last, I did not tell you of our call to Mandleshwar. We had two days there and Father was investigating some trouble, and busy all the time. Hilda Johnson has just gone and now Miss McLeod is carrying on. She has been laid up for over a week with 'flu'. We think Bryce's and Quinn's will be with Hilda. Brave people! Ruth got her Music Exams off last year, and was teaching at the school. As our bus came back along the valley I could see Rupmatti etc. The atmosphere was clear. I thought of you! (When am I not thinking of you?) I must have said that Bill and Mary went to Miraj – now they are home. Bill made a good recovery, and is supposed to have brought his stones home with him! Dr. J.T.Taylor. is getting along well, and they have just left for Mt. Abu, taking Bhabriya with them! They rented 'The Briars' **[an Irish Mission House]** *there. We expect to join them about a month from now – if we can get away. Miss Coltart goes for Apr. Mrs. Toombs was due back from M – with Bill and Mary. She had been detained for Xrays after her 2nd operation for goiter. We hope this will be sufficient! Mrs. Waters recent Airgraph sounds as though Marion had moved again and has Ann boarding out somewhere near her, owing to broken nights and too much work with her, for the good of the Hospital job. That must be done I suppose.*

Father still sends help. Mrs. W. still rests 18 out of 24 hours, so is not well yet. Dr. Armstrong sends best wishes. They get letters and cards from Donnie – since October. "Don is fighting boredom by teaching Mathematics, Saxophone, etc". He bailed out. I had to go to town and see Ear Specialist last week. I inflated the tube and injured left ear and the Dr. says it ruptured the drum, so I am only hearing (the things I'd like to hear) on one side just now. Lots of noises, day and night, in injured side. Stayed overnight with ladies at Hospital. Louise Scott wants to write to you. If I have to go in again I only go as far as Doctors residence in Cantonment. When this subsides I want tubes blown out.

Father has gone to a meeting of Dr. Campbell's Executives and is due back this evening. He will see Bessie and the children. She and Una, with their three children will be where Moir and Margaret stop, 'Ellengown'. Moir takes services for six weeks. Hugh and Becky go to Kodai to Cliff's house. Cliff in Port of Spain. Bob C. still studies for PhD this time! They have baby son.

I am all alone – and feel very much alone. We have killed five snakes in the last five weeks! The first was Feb. 20th and was a cobra 5'5". That was on a Sat. On Feb. 18th as I was working about I was near a back window and saw Quintie just outside in the shade. She rose up to come to back door and she wailed so stiffly that I spoke "Quintie dear, what is the trouble" she seemed to be anxious to get in, and hearing my voice she tried to trot toward the steps. Her little forefoot, she could not raise high enough to make the step and immediately sprawled over the steps in a convulsion! In half a minute it subsided and she wailed away a few steps and another started. We rushed about, put her blanket on the ground, etc and again, she got up and sat on it. Daniel gave her sour milk, water etc. but other convulsions followed (terribly severe ones). I ran to Hospital and when I came back with a dose Father had her wrapped, quietly in her nice red blanket Mrs. Taylor gave her. I had notified the Vet, so I sent her body to his Hospital. His verdict was "snake bite" though there were no marks on her body. Her nose or mouth may have got stung. I hated to tell you about this and felt that I couldn't in my last letter. She was in the very best condition, and what a grand little comforter she had been to me this past year. The house seems so empty. She was so nice and so gentle to the last moment. Her eyes turned green and very clear. The next snake was also a cobra, only a few inches shorter than the first. The last two killed were not likely so deadly, another variety. This is most unusual for this time of year.

Mr. Beckwith sends a man tomorrow to start investigations of our leaking roof – so for some days at least it will be noisy, dirty and unpleasant. (Sudden sounds hurt my ears, so will be glad to finish). Hope you got mail at Christmas time, and later. Love, in heaps and our continued remembrance and that of friends.
God bless you my dear.

Ever yours
Mother

MARCH 26TH, 1943
[From Father]
United Church of Canada Mission
Dhar, Central India

Dear Walter

This morning a contractor was to begin turning tiles on the roof of our bungalow in an effort to stop some of the leaks but it is the day for throwing coloured powder and water **[celebrations for blessing people]** *and the Hindus will be too busy at that for work. So the din on the roof has been postponed for at least another day.*

Last evening Miss Boyd, Miss Martin and Dr. A. T. Matthew (a South Indian lady in Margaret Harcourt's place here) were in for a game of Rook. Miss Boyd only looked on. She is leaving on the 30th for a three months vacation in Srinagar. Miss Martin and Dr. Hilda Smith go later to Simla. Bill Taylor is back from his gall bladder operation at Miraj and has gone with his wife to Landour. Mrs. Buchanan, Mrs. Smillie, Mrs. McMillan, Mrs. Scott are already there. Their husbands and Bessie Leech will go later. Also, the Waters, Moir is to do some practicing at Kellogg Church this summer. The J. T. Taylors have gone to Mount Abu taking Bhabriya with them. We expect to join them about April 20th and hope our roof repairs will be finished before that.

The Bryces and Hilda Johnson have gone on furlough; quite a bunch will be due to go next summer.

Mother and I paid a visit this month to Mandleshwar, Indore, Rasalpura and Mhow. I was in Ratlam last Tuesday and Wednesday on business in connection with Dr. Campbell's Will. I spent the night in our old bungalow (now Buchanans) and saw Bessie Leech and her two children at the Campbell bungalow. They all looked well and expect to go to Landour about the end of April. She is longing for news of Jack. Her family allotment, like ours, comes regularly. Bessie gets a little too for part time work in our Ratlam Hospital. I hope you see Jack sometimes. Is David Angers there?
Keep well and smiling. With every good wish.

Lovingly
Father

End of MARCH –
I got first mail – 5 letters! Jack got 61 in one batch from Bessie! Incident of food poisoning in Gunkha mess!

APRIL 4TH, 1943
[From Louise Scott, another Missionary]
U.C.C. Mission,
Indore, Central India

Dear Dr. Walter,

One day last week we had the pleasure of a visit from Mr. & Mrs. **[refers to Walter's parents]**, *and in the course of conversation I asked for your address in the hope that I might write to you. I wonder if you will receive it? I shall go on the assumption that you will and give you a little bit of the C. I.* **[Central India]** *news.*

Miss Clearihue is in Indore this weekend; there is an Executive Medical Commission meeting on Tuesday, so she came down ahead of time for a visit with Dr. Anderson. As usual the Medical Commission have problems that seem so difficult to solve, and the latest one is a supply for Ratlam. Dr. Alice Hodge who has been there for over a year, only came temporarily and is considering going this month, so now for someone to replace her. That I think is the purpose of the Executive meeting, and just what will be the solution one hardly knows. What about coming back to help us out!! How I do wish you could **[the rest of the sentence blacked out by censors]** *Dr. Jean Whittier, Miss Hilda Johnson and Mrs. McLeod returned to India last year, just about this time. They had quite an experience in getting here, and a long tiring trip. A new nurse came with them. Miss Bucholtz from Western Canada. She has been in Neemuch with Dr. Jean Whittier studying language, and then will come to Indore this July, when I depart for Banswara. She is quite a buxom lassie, not unlike Miss Cates, and should be able for lots when she gets into things, she seem to be an awfully good sort. Miss Florence Taylor was supposed to return to India with Miss Gruchy, last July, but she was unable to get away, she will relieve me if and when she comes. And then I might have a chance to get into rural medical work.*

Shivghar is still going; I would hardly say strong, but Mr. Buchanan is quite keen and that helps to keep anything going. Miss Boyd moved to Dhar after Margaret Harcourt left to be married, and with her is an Indian doctor, Dr. Mathew, quite smart and very nice. Margaret married a teacher from the M.E. Mission, Mr. Ginn. I do not know him. The wedding was in Mhow, in the Kirk, and most of us from Dhar and Indore were there.

Mr. & Mrs. Bryce left for Canada recently. A bit unexpectedly, though they had been hoping to go this year. Hilda Johnson went also with the same party. Others who were due to go, Miss Martin, Miss Boyd, the Grahams, are planning on a longer holiday in India instead of going home at this time.

Nurses' examinations have been on for the last two weeks, and now we are able to breathe once more. However, holidays start tomorrow and that means short-handed for some time. I expect to go off in about a week or so. I am going early so that I shall be back for a little while before going to Banswara.

Dr. Taylor had quite an illness just before Christmas. All were quite anxious about him, but are glad to say he has almost entirely recovered. He and Mrs. Taylor left recently for the hills, where we hope he will complete his recovery. Miss Hilliard and I were on duty with him for the greater part of his illness, and Dr. Andy Taylor was called down from his duties. Bill Taylor returned from Miraj the other day after having an operation. Gall bladder I think it was. He seems pretty fit though quite weak. He and Mary have gone up to Landour. Shamis preceded them with Mrs. Scott and Isobel. So Indore is a bit depleted in the meantime. We can still scrape up a set for tennis, but it is terribly hot to play.

We are quite busy at the hospital. Dr. Smith came here after Council last year. It is great having her, she is so keen on medicine, on everything actually, and having things done properly. It keeps us busy trying to make the nurses understand. Just now we are having some building done, and that makes the place look such a mess. The Lab is being enlarged, you will remember that Dr. Smith is so keen on that department, then we are having a house for an assistant made from some of the Dispensary rooms, and also a new septic tank; the last is where my interest is focused, since it will mean less work for the nurses, and keep things so much cleaner... at least I hope so... who knows!

I do not know much about the news of Ratlam. Miss Boyd is anxious to get back there, she is not very enthusiastic about Dhar. Bessie Leech is helping out in the Ratlam hospital with some of the teaching, she is living in Dr. Campbell's bungalow. The children are very sweet, and seem to keep well.

[One line blacked out by censors]

I went to a picture in Mhow about a week ago, not bad, but not as good as Jeannette MacDonald can be. Last year's Council meeting being held in Indore was quite an experience. I think most people liked it very much, it was much more friendly, not so much 'en masse' idea, though we did have tea all together, and the regular social evening.

This is a very sketchy letter, but I do wish you to know that we have you very much in our thoughts. I wonder if you have met Jack Leech. Our prayers are with you both. Here is a good prescription I heard the other day, when a member of your profession was advising a patient to go away: 'The internal climate of your body needs a change', something like that. One does hear some odd remarks.

With every good wish to you and to Jack if you see him.

Most sincerely,
Louise Scott

APRIL 20th, 1943
[From Mother]
Dhar, C. I.

My Dear Walter

I don't believe I have written to you before in this month. We certainly keep our minds busy thinking about you, and longing for a word from you, hoping you are well, and many other wishes connected with you. All of them good!

Bessie only had word of Jack on April 1st through Canadian Red Cross! She will continue to live in your bungalow and work at the hospital. Dr. Hodge and parents leave soon and Dr. Jean Whittier comes to take her place.

Your bank reports all balances paid up to April 1st. The Quinns, and Bryces and Hilda are not here now.

We had an Airgraph from Marion a few days ago. Imagine our feelings when we read that she had taken Larry back again last fall. She keeps us in constant worry. She said Dr. and Mrs. Waters had been coaxing her to write it.

Yesterday afternoon the old gentleman across the way passed away very unexpectedly. Most relations were away, some on business and some on holidays. They are still waiting for some to return, ere they cremate.

I read a letter from Donnie Armstrong to his Mother. He had to bail out.

It has not been very hot yet. I have tried to get ready to leave tomorrow morning. We join the Taylors for a little while.

It is not easy to think of going – much easier to just stay right at home. I shall make this short and write before so long again. You will get more than one at a time anyway, I suppose.

Hoping you're as well as we are – yes more than hoping.

With deepest love from
Mother

MAY 1st, 1943

Order to clear out South area – Most men gone in "F & H" Forces – remainder go into general barracks in Selerang and all officers continue as "C" Group South Area and we got allotted bungalows in Australian Imperial Force area! For us a still better change – Headquarters mess bungalow and lovely front upper window looking up Channel.

Report casualty cases brought here so Japs allowed us only electric light after some time!

A great labour moving all our furniture – bag and baggage, chickens **[chickens for Japanese consumption]**.

MAY 15th, 1943

"J" Force of 1000 plus, left for Japan, with Jack on it as official padre by the A.C.G. ? "G" and "W" area closed down and officers join us.

MAY 17th (?)

300 – all officers left us as final group (officers party) of "H" Force – "Lambs to the slaughter". Told going for camp administrator duties in nice climate among the hills! Lieutenant Colonel Whittenberg. Officer Commanding and Major Tilling adjutant. I have always had a guilty feeling for categorizing certain officers within the limits! Packed lorry loads! Changi now reduced to about 5000. Hard work for the few fit men left with wood and ration fatigues. Weekly checking of cards and categories of all men and Assistant Director Medical Service re: their fitness to work and this rechecked by Major Portal.

Australian Imperial Force area perhaps the best area organized – electric lighted convalescent Depot and amputation case block **[area]** – eye center. Y.M.C.A. gramophone, outside concerts, (Japanese Roman Catholic sentry passes us into chapel). Australian Imperial Force concert party professionals remain – professional comic and lady impersonators – one clown said he was going to return to Malaya with a circus show. Animals he would train. This clown's slogan "You'll never get off the Island".

Got our daily news read out in Headquarters mess from a typed sheet brought by appointed person who took it around to groups from their hidden source. Might be interpreted by Nips coming to buy Parker Pens!

Heartening to know of fall of Tunis etc. Subject just drops from Syonan Times Shimbun **[Newspaper]**.

MAY 19th, 1943
[From Father]

United Church of Canada Mission
"The Briars" Mount Abu
Rajputana, C.I.

Dear Walter

I am much ashamed that this is my first letter to you from Mount Abu. We are here with the J.T. Taylors and in spite of the low altitude and warmth, enjoy it quite well.

It is not a very extensive hill station and the many short circular or curved roads, together with a deep blue lake about one mile in circumference provide for daily walking exercise. There is boating on the lake and hills to climb for those who want that kind of exercise. Landour and Kashmir are much favoured by our Mission folk this summer. Dr. Jean Whittier is to take up your work after the holidays when Alice Hodge hopes to depart. Marion apparently keeps well though she does not write often. She will probably be seeing Hilda Johnson and the Bryces in Toronto soon. Also Dr. McMaster and Bertha Manarey.

Dr. J. T. Taylor is steadily improving after his very severe illness. He takes much longer walks than when we first came up here. The fingers of his left hand are numb and one foot gives him trouble sometimes. Last week we walked every afternoon to the Club grounds to watch a cricket tournament. The Lawrence School boys won the finals. We have been to the movies twice.

I shall look after your Insurance in July when it is due. The Aetna is all paid up. We are keeping pretty well and expect to return to Dhar about the middle of next month.

[One line cut out by censors]

We hope you will be permitted to write us soon.

With love and best wishes
Father

JUNE 1943
"Smokey Joe's" opened in June and was a great success. Dutch certainly did run Snack cars. This was a combined affair.

JUNE 4th, 1943
[From Mother]

Dhar, C.I.

My Dear Walter

The last letter I sent off to you was from Dhar just as we were leaving. Father has written from here, and I sincerely hope you get the few letters we do send you. We don't write very frequently. There seems little use sending letters very often, yet I think I shall write more often from now on. The mail delivery system there should be more organized now.

We came up here (the Taylors were already here) in late April and have about twenty days here now. Dr. Taylor's activities have been very limited, but as his strength returns he gets about a little faster.

The roads are so numerous and so well paved that walking is clean. We have had some interesting walks to see views, temples, gardens, golf, football games, etc. We are right at the P.O. so Father is glad. No letters from Marion up here, but had some from others about her. She and Lawrence made up last Fall. All other news is either good or very good. Mrs. Waters can get out a little more now. Randall Stringer is married. Mrs. Waters went to the wedding.

Moir is again officiating at Kellogg Memorial for six weeks. Wee Jimmie is not very well at present. Irwins in Kodai, Martin in Simla and Boyd, McLeod, Hilliard, Clerihue, Whittier etc. in Kashmir.

So many complain of wet weather here, it was dry and warm – we have no use for blankets yet! Keep as cheerful as you possibly can, no reason for worry outside your own circumstances. Remember we are with you in mind all the time. Dr. and Mrs. MacKay say if and when you write Walter please give him very earnest good wishes from us both and tell him he has been much on our hearts during these painfully long days of suspense.

Best love from
Mother

JUNE 14th, 1943
[From Mother]

"The Briars"
Dhar, C.I.

My Dear Walter

As you did me, so I'll do for you, and send you a few lines on this date. I miss you very much and on this day especially, I feel that you will have been thinking of me and would write if you could. It has been a quiet day in a way.

Dr. and Mrs. Taylor went out to lunch, and we two had curry and mango fule **[similar to a milkshake]**. *Mrs. Taylor asked two ladies, Yankee, in to tea from next door to take "pot luck". She had also ordered a cake, though I am the housekeeper this week. The two ladies enjoyed tea and we played MahJong with them afterwards. Next day they found it was a birthday!*

Dr. and Mrs. Taylor were out to lunch that day. The Taylors gave me an "ivory elephant necklace", and Father gave me some Eau-de-Cologne and hankies. The latter very much needed, and I know you will be needing many things like this. How I wish we could send you things! How I wish a lot of things! We do try to be patient, and wait.

We heard yesterday that Mrs. Davidson had had an operation which was successful, but there was fear of malignancy in the 'pancreas'. Since Mrs. Beckwith is going, Mr. Davidson will now get off with him if possible. Mr. Davidson is at present in the Nursing Home with Malaria, and he is growing cataracts in both eyes, so he ought to get away. He would not listen till he heard of Mrs. Davidson's condition.

We find that we may have a Dr. and his wife as guests for the rain. Passing through they want to spend some months in India, and we have lots of room.

There has been some excitement over more wild animals here. Another person has been killed and partly eaten. This is the third and two or three animals have already been killed, two panthers and a tiger. This one is reported to be a "Black Panther". Women and children will, and I suppose they have to, persist in going out into the rocky jungle for wood etc. There were several persons about when the last woman was attacked last Sunday.

We have been, especially Father and Dr. Taylor, enjoying some good books and various kinds. Mrs. Taylor is sending some to Andy by one returning to duty. Present plans are to leave here next week. Shall be home the evening of 25th, Aunt

Nellie's and Ann Louise's Birthdays. Colds better, cough less, and quite well. Dr. Taylor's heart was tired yesterday, so he lay for some time.

Heaps of Love
From Mother

JUNE 20th, 1943
[From another missionary, Florence Gruchy]
As from U. C. C. Mission
Ratlam, Central India

Dear Walter,

You are constantly remembered in Ratlam hospital – herewith a few lines to greet you, from the hill tops where Tena Baxter, Emily Maxwell and I have enjoyed a grand holiday.

You will already know of the changes in Ratlam. I found a very different place when I returned last year. Alice Hodge was fine and it was a privilege to have her parents there too. They left on June 8th. We were all away but Rev. F.J. Anderson and Miss Patterson came to represent us. The congregation and Staff gave them a grand farewell expressing of genuine gratitude and affection. Jean Whittier will occupy the Russell bungalow with her Auntie. I miss Vera – You will know of her new venture but it is a great help having Bessie Leech. One of our third year boys got the only sup. in exams this year – Pharmacy again! Our graduates get registration now with the C.P. **[Central Province]**

This all sounds very stilted but the 200 word limit bothers me!

How we wish some word would come from you!

We remember you with pride and gratitude and sympathy and await your return in ardent faith and hope.

Yours affectionately
Florence Gruchy **[Missionary teacher]**

JUNE 25, 1943

"K" Force. All medical left Singapore in evening, I'm on it! About 200 orderlies and 25 Medical Officers not told why we are going. Glass rodded etc. again. Most men about ready to be sent away – feel need of change after 1 year now and hope of better food etc. Crowded lorries in

Selerang Square arrive Singapore Station in dark and put into Box Cars with Nip guards – in dark, 25 men and kit to 1 box car, on floor.

JUNE 26th, 1943

Some time about 1 am. Train moves off – cross causeway in moonlight to Johore Bahru. Very cramped sleeping. Nights cold if rain and wind blows in, and in day, metal car almost too hot to touch. Three places in day for rice and fish or stew. Each car to carry black 6 gal. containers. Also difficulty getting enough drinking water and sharing out of bottle also. Have to shit all over track or near it as opportunity offers, with permit or not of guards. Company of Koreans with us. Interesting tall trees in Johore. Also see neglected rubber plantations of all ages, P.N.D. trees – Changi trees. Germans in Johore boundary. All station names in English obliterated and painted over in Kata Kana. Sometimes can read through.
"K" Force - Officer Commanding Major A. Crawford of V. E.
Adj. Major B. Anderson A. I. F.
Our box car had water on the floor and next one coal dust.

[area here left blank]

26, 6, 43 – Reach K. Lumpur about 6 pm.
Shave on track platform!

27, 6, 43-
Reach Ipoh - noon – Indian (I. A.) in mufti put on siding – coffee queues. Sleep out on ground – guards walking about us all night.

28, 6, 43 - All day on siding – chance to bathe at a tap. Bomb damage of oil and gas tanks. Nips and coolies removing iron goods and rails. See train of coolies going north.

29, 6, 43 – Leave Ipoh after noon

30, 6, 43 - Reach Taiping at 9 pm. Pretty mountain jungle between Ipoh and Taiping. Captain Brown, train Medical Officer – one patient ill and given platform airing at Taiping.

JULY 1st, 1943
[From Father]
United Church of Canada Mission
Dhar, Central India

Dear Walter

A letter to you is as good a way as any to celebrate Dominion Day and Canadian history, for the past year will not be without interest to Canadian students.

We returned from our Mount Abu vacation on June 25th and found the Dhar landscape looking delightfully fresh and inviting. Miss Boyd followed us a day or two later but Miss Martin will not be back for another month. The summer has been hotter than usual from all accounts and even the hill stations. We were well pleased with our Abu visit except for the excessive warmth there. I would be glad to go again if the weather prophet would insure cooler weather.

The Bryces, Dr. McMaster, Miss Mannarey and Miss Johnson are now in Canada. We expected Bob Clark back but hear that he has taken on a pastoral charge temporarily. Dr. Jean Whittier takes over your work this month. Miss Scott is in Neemuch. **[The next sentence cut out by censors]** *Simla sends your allotment regularly and I will pay your Insurance this month as I have already done re your rates. Marion and Larry are together again and she is preparing for her second child in August. Just how far Larry provides we do not know.*

I have been busy catching up correspondence and accounts since coming home and am beginning to see daylight again. The ladies – Dr. Matthew and Miss Boyd are to dine with us tonight. Sorry we cannot offer them ice cream. Dr. J.T. Taylor is much improved and will undertake his seminary duties this year but for the last time. Mrs. Davidson has been ill in Canada but is convalescing.

We two are carrying on as usual. Quintie we miss but Punch comes in sometimes to see us and get a bone.

With love and very best wishes and hoping to hear from you.

Yours lovingly,
Father

JULY 1st, 1943

Alor Star early morning – flat rice country Padang Bisai about noon – Thai border. See first Thai "band box" or "poster" uninspiring. Warned to carefully salute Nip officers and non-commissioned officers at next big station inside South Thailand. Inside Thailand again is jungle – not tall. Railway Stations filthy – never cleaned – job to get water.

Thai girls sell hard boiled duck eggs and seed bananas – experience from so many Prisoner of War trains going up the Kra Isthmus **[land bridge connecting Malay Peninsula to Asian mainland]**. This a blessing. Kra Isthmus– disappointed at no special scenery – not even able to see sea but once briefly near a station.

1st chant 2 – 3 A.M. reach Prai (opposite Penang Is.) and here have to get rice and tea and be counted.

JULY 3rd, 1943 (?)

Early A.M. cross large river, Port Buri? Arrive BangPong about 11 am. – leave train. Roll call – walk to coolie huts – customs search. All march around. Told we'll be here some time. Realize kit must be dumped (sorry brought it).

JULY 4th, 1943

Sudden word to be up and fall in at 3 A.M.! March in dark along track a mile? and climb into open train loaded with sleepers. Bitterly cold early. Wind up on top. Arrive Kamburi (Kanchanburi) 5 A.M. March to Prisoner of War camp – eventually find it! Put into certain huts. Tired. Find a coffee canteen! First sight of open trench latrines with bamboo bars for feet – full of huge maggots. Water shortage in camp. **[A few words of text illegible and corner of page damaged].**

Few Indians in this camp. Coolies and Thai elephants seen at one point working on some junction line, probably going into tip of Burma?

[empty space]

PRISONERS OF WAR IN JAP HANDS

Arrangements For Letters

NEW DELHI, July 3.

Arrangements have now been made for the despatch of postal communications to prisoners of war and civilian internees in Japanese hands, says a "communique". Only unregistered letters and postcards can be sent at present. They must be clearly written or typed and posted in the ordinary way and not sent to the Red Cross Commissioner to be forwarded.

Such communications may be written in English, Urdu or Hindi, but the address, including the address of the sender, must be in English. They should deal with purely personal matters, care being taken to see that no information of any kind, which might be of any use to the enemy, is given. No references to naval, military, aerial, economic or political matters are allowed, and movements of any members of His Majesty's forces or any warship or merchant ship must not be mentioned.

In view of the difficulty the Japanese may have in censoring letters, it is recommended that both letters and postcards should be brief and clear. No postage stamps need be affixed on the letters, but they must bear the inscription. "Prisoners of War Post." These arrangements are provisional and liable to alteration.—"Associated Press.

Clipping from New Delhi newspaper, describing how letters and cards to POWs were to be written and dispatched.

Meet Ransom, Baswell and Thompson at Kamburi of International Red Cross. Dispose of more kit!

JULY 5th, 1943 ?

Examined at Nip Medical Headquarters! – lecture on "American beasts" from Nip Colonel! – map of new railway. Threat if not pass!

JULY 6th, 1943

Lecture by Nip Major on Cholera and Malaria precautions in coolie camps and afternoon demonstration of water pump and filters. "K" Force divided into small groups.

JULY 7th, 1943

Most of "K" Force leave morning train on top of sleepers. Scenic Railway! Wampo bridge after Aruhem. Plenty of fat Thai cattle in jungle. Kambury bridge iron – ack ack guns seen. Arrive Wangai at dusk. Get off. Awful lorry ride in dark to filthy spot in the trees. Smooth out spot to lie down. Rain in the night!

JULY 8th, 1943

Find we are in the shitting perimeter area of Tamil coolie camp! Tried to dry bedding. Get 2 tents from Nips. Divided into Wangai Party and Nike party (younger). Tim Hog's fingers incised by Nip – no anaesthetic!

JULY 9th, 1943

Wangai party groups (Indian Medical Officer and 4 others) report at Nip office for posting away. Long wait. Find a British Other Rank friend working cholera spray at Nip office – gives me a boiled egg! Some of us waiting got a meal from near Dutch camp – food seemed good! Nasty rumours of bad treatment of "H" Force officer's party – not far off. Nip Group 9 merged with No. 8 of Bill Cowen and 2 of my men sent with Major Royal Army Medical Corps. Anderson & White.

Cowen and I to go to Takanun. Jap Medical Major commissioned to look at us! We are taken to same Nip unit to move.

Railway from Kamburi followed course of the Kay Noi (?) River to beyond Nike. Rail at this time only extended to one station beyond Wangai. Big P.O.W. camp at Tarso near Wangai. These Nips later in charge of No. 4 group P.O.W. Padre Alcock laid out the growing cemetery at Tarso. Major General Aide De Camp kept in Kamburi – too weak. Japs annoyed. Captain Todd and Marshall to remain in Wangai - Begin bamboo hut building!

Groups – Captain W.H. Cowen – Royal Army Medical Corps
Captain W.G. Anderson – India Medical Service
Quarter M.. – G.R. MacTighe – R. A. M. C.
Sergeant G. Chandler – Cambridge Regiment
Lieutenant/Corporal G. Walls – R. A. O. C.
Sergeant Bob Dunning – R.A.O.C.

JULY 10th, 1943

Part of Nip unit leave before day light – we are fairly free at this time, though have to gather bit of fuel for Nip kitchen. Some Dutch work in Nip kitchen – first taste of Nip food – served out of basket. Bathe against order in the river. In evening walk to station Thai canteen and met Major Henderson bringing in a sick coolie to Hospital in trolley! First real contact with Nips, pidgeon English, etc. Chandler's marriage book appeals to them!

JULY 11th, 1943

Off before daylight in luggage lorry – terrible mud roads. Get into barges in river – two – pulled by motor. Rugged and wild rainy scenery all day – up strong current was slow – zigzag around bends and rocks. – See Thai boats and yellow robed priests – Pagoda on a peak. Saw P.O.W. gangs en route slaving high above on hill side – rain, dull, mud. Arrive Kinzaiyok P.M. Nips all ride, we tramp in the mud to Nip camp hut. Now we sample real Nip treatment – no food till Nips eaten – Boot, nuisance in hut – mud.

JULY 12th, 1943

Where to wash? My basin useful! Try to give group talk on Cholera to lads who really begin to get frightened of it! Cowen and I meet Dr. Kanzaki – lesson in Nippon - go!

Nearby P.O.W. camp frightful – mud, flies, nearly all have diarrhea or dysentery in tents. We are warned not to go into it! See few men during day. Our lads put to work by Nip Medical Sergeant – dig trench. Cowen and I manage to walk off to a P.O.W. Hospital – terrible – units, almost skeletons lying there close together. Captain Pitt had Renal Colic and later dysentery and yet had to work (Allen later was drowned at sea) – 4 tents and little space – Dysentery and Malaria and some Cholera cases sent away.

Meet Dutch interpreter from Kamburi and a Nip looking for two "escaped" doctors! The Nip confusion – these men posted to Nip Kamburi headquarters had been put on our train by mistake for Wangai!

Many Thai motor boats chugging away on river – first see Thai flag – broad center red with narrower white and outer blue.

Special Cholera camp in Kinzaiyok for coolies, P.O.W. and all – a very few British personnel – segregate and useless Jap spray – many, many deaths daily – some coolies buried before dead – One of our lads taken there to spray, comes back with long face.

Conditions of P.O.W., we saw on all sides truly frightened us. Had to stand in rain and wind from before dark till after dark. Kinzaiyok noted for its sickness.

JULY 13th, 1943
[From Mother]
Dhar, C.I.

My Dear Walter,

Since returning from Abu this is my first letter. Came home June 25th. I wrote you just before leaving there. Coming via Baby's home I brought a small boy to Hostel. (Coming home, we met a man who says our mutual acquaintance Shivaji has been removed and things greatly improved). In good time the rains have come, and schools reopened. Less children about and quieter now. Your favorite view toward the gate is very fresh and green, I wish you could see it. In last news Mrs. Davidson's operation was over, but it revealed trouble in the pancreas, malignant, and Messrs Beckwith and Davidson go home.

Marion's Airgraph, now says "John Mullin got married last week to Margaret Campbell, and went to the Falls for weekend". Very busy officers can't have much honeymoon. A word about his mother – she has been ill with Asthma and in bed, and has lost forty pounds. David is the only one at home. Even last Saturday I saw J. Leech's name, for the first time. Do you meet?

Never so glad that you studied medicine. Oh, they say a foolish optimist is better than a wise pessimist. When Vera was over she told of an old woman who declined an invitation to a picnic, thinking they would walk and next day she said – if I had known I could have rode, I would have went! Aunt Nellie asks me to say they are well, and Florence driving her car now. Letter also says Uncle Jack may stay south for the summer – but she doesn't expect him to. Letters from Donnie Armstrong coming and will come from John Colwell. We are getting good shower today. Evenings are clear and sunny, usually.

Letters should go to you more frequently than we send them, I fear. Later – I am expecting guests for a month or two, soon a doctor and his wife retiring and stopping off for a few months.

Very best love and prayers of many people, go from Aunt Nellie and Auntie Florence, Vera, Taylors, and many others who always remember you and enquire for you.

My heart is ever with you – keep cheery.

Love
Mother

JULY 13th, 1943

Had to work roofing Nip kitchen and new Nip latrine built beside P.O.W. kitchen – so learn to handle the "chaku" or atap. Nip food awful – rice and pumpkin stew. They do boil water for drinking. See a P.O.W. mental (?) case rage when in little stream getting water – Officer gives K.O.? to quiet him! Cowen refuses to work ! (Bashed into it later!)

JULY 14th, 1943

McTighe, Chandler and I leave in the morning with a Nip Warrant Officer for Takanum in Nip landing craft boat with motor and supplies.

We are left out in open bow in pouring rain, though room under cover. Chandler was shaking. Some slow trip up river all day. Arrive Takanum evening in rain – left to find our own way! Tired, dark, carrying kit – ask for Dr. Ida – no one knows! Eventually find horrid little Dutch shed to sleep in.

JULY 15th to 23rd, 1943

Begin work in the new Nip camp. Carry load of peanuts to docks and Chandler hit on the head! Load lorry to come back with supplies – I nearly fall off! Dutchman backed (my partner carrying)! I clean out refuse pit by hand! Help build Nip bamboo hut and bali bali – flattening and splitting bamboo. Clearing jungle – Dutch get to go for latrine – fetching bamboo from the jungle, making steps – bamboo and stone. Carry both water for Nips from river below. A.M. and P.M. "tenko" **[roll call]** – I learn parade orders in Japanese! (We clean up Nip hut floor each A.M.)! Nip prayers to Tokyo. Annoying being called as servants just after collecting food etc.! Tea for Nips. Hot water for us. No time to dry out wet Kit.

[There is a gap in the diary here, with narrative missing.]

Meet P.O.W. and ask direction – a Hospital is the wrong place (for Japs only) – get an English speaking Nip out of bed – goes to an office to phone – many "asokas" – finally directed to lorry driver's camp for night, but McTighe was sent by Nips from place we're to go, so they then direct us. Called by Nip cook to get food "speedo" and Chandler goes naked in the haste. – Nip angry!

Nips worship and bow towards Tokyo each A.M. and do physical Training. We have to line up too and "Benjo"!

Nip Sergeant Major, changes subject when Chandler tells him during rest period he was paid $4.00 a day in Singapore to hold up hands while Nips made cinema of "Capture of Singapore"! Bathe and clean tools in river below – get news of Sicily! Nips move into new hut when finished and we move into their old ones afterward – on a day set as a holiday! Funny looking. Dr. Ida – tells us to go to Dutch coolies.

JULY 24th, 1943

I at morning – escorted by one Nip to second Lieutenant Aoto's camp, four kilos (?) away – carry my kit all the way in the mud and hills – hardest job I ever did – fell once! Join up as Medical Officer to Captain Jonker's Dutch camp. Captain Hock (Vet.) acting Medical Officer.

JULY 25th to AUGUST 2nd, 1943

Frightful conditions of Dutch mud camp. 150 – 175 men in old torn tents – most on ground. Latrine impossibly situated – night shittings on ground. Sickness plenty – dysentery acute, malaria, Painful Heels, Beriberi, tropical ulcers. Camp only ten days old and so dirty! Camp location from Nip camp with stream between! Order for fencing in ! Dense jungle along. Working horrors – up before daylight and dark when return. Men always treat leaks – rain – bedding etc. wet. Filth about tents. No sanitary squad, only Kurtz as orderly. A.M. muster roll – some pretend to faint! Sometime fetch out the sick and drive some to work. Everyone frightened of Lieutenant Aoto – bully boy. I get permit to evacuate a bunch of sick – some looked not too bad, but died later. Some Quinine tablets and a little Rivanol, the only medication. No bandages or dressing. Try to save dead men's mosquito nets! One ulcer case treating himself with urine! I ask for sanitary squad – get two men for two days – Dutch officers missed them for hair cutting etc. work not done. Food is better – irregular times – some meat – fried eggs and coffee. Thai boatmen in by river!

Captain H. Jonker O.C. N.E.I.F. (Netherland East Indian Force)
Captain J. Hick Camp near site of future Takanum state
Captain Weiffenbach Group 25 ? of No. 2 base
Captain Menlokr ? P.O.W. Camp Takanum
Lieutenant DeJonge (naval)
Cdt. Sergeant M. Knipers
S.M. Bugter

Speeds work on Railway embankment and small log culverts and bridges. Aoto threatened his men – Harakari – must be done by certain time when steel laying party would come. Slave driving – I'm often called up through the mud and uphill to some Eurasian Dutch – ill or collapsed. Permission to take him home from Nips.

Night work sometimes to finish a job – called up in dark to see a man – no torch or light to see way up hill – hell getting there – lads with no clothes covering them in wet – heat up my chaoti **[a loin cloth approx. 2'x4']** at bamboo fire and wrap it on chaps alternately with some other, while he lies on a mud-carrying frame!

Dutch are mostly Eurasians, some very black, e.g. Klink, who looked exactly like he was descended from Ethiopians – we called him "Haile Selassi"!!

JULY 30th, 1943
[From L. Scott]
U.C.C.M.
Neemuch, C. I.

Prisoner of War
Military No. M.Z. 23691
Lt. (now Capt.) W. G. Anderson
Indian Medical Service
Last Serving at Singapore

Copied from the Circular letter from Dr. Armstrong, dated Toronto May 28th, 1943

"Item 12" Perhaps you will let me have the rank of both Bacon and Anderson. In addition to the cable from India, reporting word received concerning Walter Anderson, being prisoner of war, we had from the Under Secretary of State for External affairs, Ottawa, letter dated Feb. 11th (supposedly 1943) as follows– "according to official information from the Japanese authorities at Tokyo, Capt. W. G. Anderson is a prisoner of war in Malaya".

You have probably heard that Welford Russell has received a promotion and is now Major. He will be Sr. surgeon in one of the Base hospitals in England.

Louise Scott

AUGUST 3rd,1943

One Dutch in coma with cerebral Malaria (died later). I have to leave camp and walk 4 kilometers down to P.O.W. camp at Bangan. (Night work there removing rice stores from rapidly rising river, man nearly lost!)

AUGUST 4th, 1943

Japs. find where I'm to go! – walk back 1½ km to Nip camp of 2nd Lieutenant Shemidzen, Royal Engineers. Dr. Ida here. I play 2nd nurse to Nip cholera patient and have to give him my mosquito net. – have to sleep in tent with proven cholera carrier! I do general camp chores for all contact group of Nips and washing clothes.

AUGUST 5th, 1943

Some fever – pre-malaria attacks. Enjoy hot water, no tea – rice and pumpkins. Cholera patient improving. Elephant walks around tents one night, crunches old ringer solution flasks and eats bamboo shoots. Funny Jap system of spraying.

AUGUST 6th, 1943
[From Mother]
Dhar, C.I.

My Dear Walter,

I have not been able to get much use of this machine **[typewriter]** *lately, so many persons using it just now. I should have written several days ago.*

Dr. and Mrs. Sheridan came but had a muddy time getting in from Ratlam by bus. Finally, after hours, the doctor walked in the last three miles and found me waiting in the car at the statue. I took him in and we went out to rescue Mrs. Sheridan. They will find it very quiet here, and dark from heavy rain, but they assure me they won't be lonely etc. Younger persons would. We are told that His Highness shot a record tiger down on the borders, not long ago. Also there were two alligators found to be in Nat Nagra Talao, and they were caught and finally shot (in the eye!) by His Highness. They had travelled overland during the hot season in search of water.

About two weeks ago Miss McLeod got word of her sister Isla's death. You and I met her on the lake trip at Muskoka. Miss McLeod is not very well at present and is in bed. She has low fever. Vera had to leave when she had not been home very long, to get the nurses training classes started in Banswara. Miss Cameron has retired and the new Superintendent has not arrived yet. She is due now.

Vera will no more than get back again when she will go to chaperone the girl nurses in a Gov't Hospital so we are having to do without her. Miss Martin is back from holidays, but she doesn't look very well. Hilda Johnson is happy to be with her parents again. She is talking of studying Theology. I wonder what Mrs. Bryce will study this furlough. Bob Clark has taken a church. They have a baby son. Cliff is living in his Father's own town. Last week we got a shock when word came that Alice Anderson had died, and the time of the funeral was given. We drove in with Miss Martin's car and she came back with us. Dr. Alice had been complaining of her back since April. She had been in bed a fortnight and wrote Father that she was "going away next week". She had no holiday. Dr. Smith went in to see her very early in the morning (when she was up with a case) and found her unconscious. Then there were two convulsions, but she never regained consciousness and she died a week ago today June 30th. It was a stroke and most unexpected! The church was crammed, and every doctor in the big hospitals were there. Mr. Beckwith managed everything, with aid of Seminary Students, and St. Johns Ambulance Corp. etc. Flowers everywhere. Capt. and Mrs. Toombs were there. I sat with Dr. Hilda Smith. Dr. Alice didn't even have high blood pressure, and altogether this was most unexpected. An xray had revealed some abnormality in her back the week before. They did expect serious trouble there. We shall all miss her very much.

How I long to know how you are, Walterji. Dr. Alice once said how she "grudged your skill". Louise has gone to Neemuch Hospital, Bessie helps Miss Gruchy. Daniel Lakha is now doing housework for us and he is doing very well with it. Harrison looks after the car and he knows how to drive, so I must try him out some day.

Keep up your courage, it helps to keep one healthy. Outside your immediate circumstances everything is all right. Marion is housekeeping again, and will have another child by this time. I do hope things are going better with her family.
Constantly remembering you with best of love.

Mother
Dr. Wallace sends best wishes for you.

AUGUST 8th, 1943

I return to Dutch nicer camp with great relief. Find Vogel in coma with head wound – He was hit in head with shovel by Jap on Aug. 6th – typical intra-cranial hemorrhage – Quinine I. M. **[inter muscular]** times 2, no effect he died 9th August.

AUGUST 9th – Sept. 1st, 1943

Conditions in camp worsen – sick increase – Tropical ulcers, dysentery, beriberi, malaria, painful heels – 9 deaths, one suicide in river. I report to Lieutenant Colonel Williamson Royal Army Ordinance Corps of No. 2 base camp Takanum. When I went to draw camp pay instead of Knipers, Major Max Pembuton gave me a little M & B sulfa. Kraen refuses to work, acts wildish, Japs tie him to tree all day, even burn with cigarettes, Sortick ob. **[died]** Beriberi. Young Van Ginkle ob. Malaria. I rescued Johan from work! Later becomes my Medical Orderly in Takanum, owner of Noemplak Hotel.

In Shemidzu Thai camp one bearded Nip puts a straight razor into my hands and lifts up chin for me to shave (not cut) his throat! What a chance! Presents me with soap for washing out clothes.

[empty space here]

Dutch spiritless and apathetic. Tree fell on Statt? Hanchow Horai sometimes shows feeling for P.O.W. – always bows at grave. Young Nip interpreter from California. Railway embankment finally built in time for steel-laying party to lay the tracks.

AUGUST 15TH, 1943

[From Father]

United Church of Canada Mission
Dhar, Central India

Capt. W.G. Anderson I.M.S. No. M.Z. 23691)

Dear Walter

The eleventh of August was a red letter day for us when about two o'clock in the afternoon your post card of date June 20th 1942 was delivered to us.

There is nothing we have longed for more than a direct message from yourself. We have waited long and now we do rejoice and thank God and His human instruments in Government and Postal Services for the realization of our great desire. Bessie also received a post card dated the same day from her husband Jack.

We have been busy passing the glad word on to others and all who hear rejoice with us in the glad tidings from afar. We told the inmates this morning at the Leper Home and their faces lightened up as they listened. They send their best wishes.

Now that the trail has been blazed from you to us we look expectantly for more to follow soon if you have written again since June of last year as you must have done. Your message has rejuvenated us.

We are well and wish you all the best.

Lovingly
Father

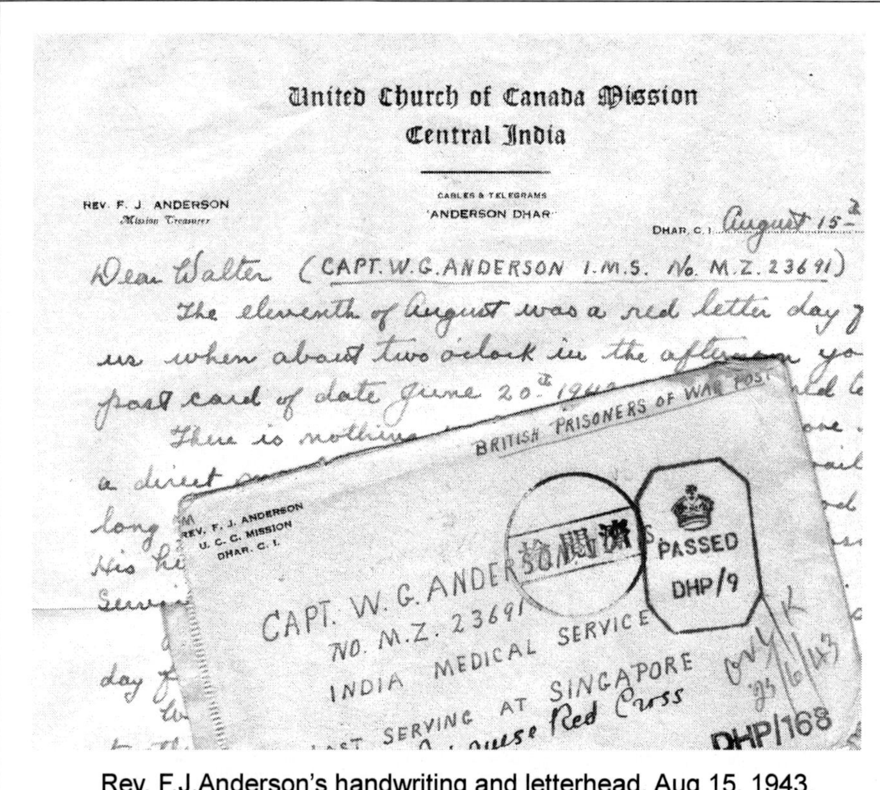

United Church of Canada Mission
Central India

REV. F. J. ANDERSON
Mission Treasurer

CABLES & TELEGRAMS
'ANDERSON DHAR'

DHAR, C. I. August 15

Dear Walter (CAPT. W.G. ANDERSON I.M.S. No. M.Z. 23691)
The eleventh of August was a red letter day
us when about two o'clock in the afternoon yo
post card of date June 20th 194

Rev. F.J.Anderson's handwriting and letterhead, Aug 15, 1943.

Late AUGUST

About end of August we evacuate by boat. Another party of sick (many later died, including Kraen of jaundice). "The Baron"! Knipers ill with mild Blackwater fever!

SEPTEMBER 1st, 1943

Sudden search of camp by Lieutenant Aoto, ordered - any proof of contact with Thais? Corporal Tanioka who speaks English, answered in search of my notes re: "length, depth, height" etc !! Advance party with Dr. Heck, left two days before for new camp site near Brankasi. Search due mainly to finding a Dutch officer in a camp near Brankasi, openly cleaning a revolver! Nips tied him up to a tree! Lucky!

SEPTEMBER 2nd, 1943

Camp moved by train to new site near Brankasi – what a chore carrying all camp and Nip baggage and supplies and tents and mats, and the sick Olivier, up to the tracks. Also sick Vanolu Graff with ulcers, Weisthoff, hit on head by "Schevine" with bamboo stick to load train quicker. Train only small, open trucks drawn by 6 wheel convertible, Diesel motor! New site beside track about 1 Km. from Lieutenant Colonel Flower's big steel-laying camp.

Very fortunate weather, most days. Work in breaking stone to fill in along the tracks. Get some extra food and medical supplies from nearby P.O.W. camp. Lieutenant Stahli, a missy Doctor from Java helps. I get caught by Aoto going to see dentist in P.O.W. camp without his permission! We get Jap atebrin for Knipers. My first real dose of Malaria! Went to P.O.W. camp with Tanioka to look for matches or lighters. Had some supper there with Captain McGovern Indian Medical Service of New Zealand. Remarkable hospitality of officers in tent I visited! Lieutenant Hughes there gives me some peanuts! Aoto's reputation spreads to this camp! Holes in tents worse! Johan makes a good medical orderly and can speak English so well. Captain Jonker shakes terribly with Malaria.

SEPTEMBER 5, 1943

[Telegram from Father]

United Church of Canada Mission
Rev. F. J. Anderson
Mission Treasurer

Capt. W. G. Anderson I.M.S., Singapore

DEAR WALTER
MARION'S JOHN RANDALL BORN JULY 18
VISITED RATLAM RECENTLY
BECKWITH DAVIDSON TRAVELLING HOMEWARD
ANDERSONS SHERIDANS SAW "GOODBYE MR. CHIPS"
YESTERDAY MHOW
LOVINGLY
FATHER

SEPTEMBER 5TH, 1943

[Postcard from Mother]

Dhar, C.I.

MY DEAR WALTER,
MILLIONS THANKS FOR
YOUR "BRIEF" CARD
RECEIVED AUGUST '43.
REGULATIONS ALLOW
25 WORDS NOW.
HOPE YOU RECEIVED
SOME LETTERS+
LOVING GREETINGS
MOTHER

LETTERS TO WAR PRISONERS

Japanese Restriction '43

NEW DELHI, September 2.—The Government of India learn that the Japanese authorities require that letters and postcards to prisoners of war and civil internees in Japan and Japanese-occupied territories must in future be limited to 25 words only, and must either be typewritten or written clearly in block lettering, says a *communique*.

This restriction comes into force immediately, and correspondence posted after this announcement which does not comply with the above restriction may not be delivered by the Japanese Government, who claim that the restriction is necessary to simplify censorship so that correspondence can be speeded up.—*Associated Press*.

Newspaper report of Japanese restrictions on correspondence addressed to POWs to 25 block printed or typewritten words.

SEPTEMBER 15th, 1943

My diary taken and burned by order of Aoto.

[Walter told his family later that he had used a little 2" pencil to write in his first diary, it was easy to hide. After his diary was confiscated and burned by his captors, Walter had to recoup what he could remember, which explains time gaps in previous entries. He did manage to make notes that he could refer to when re-writing his diary. Also, throughout the remaining diary he still fills in events he remembers which we have put into chronological order.]

SEPTEMBER 23rd, 1943

Move camp again by train, Oliver worse!

SEPTEMBER 24th, 1943

All day in a train on siding at Takanum Station. Sleep there under train at night. Rain and sun, out in open, only boiled rice. "Stone Camp". Young Klinklogman ill on train with head in my lap – urinates over side of truck. The "bull" Nip cook, threatens him with, cut bag out!

SEPTEMBER 25th, 1943

We arrive at Sambae Camp site near Takanum, across a side river. Hurry to unload train. The "Schevine" kicks dying Olivier as we lift him off the train. Olivier died eight hours later! This called the "Sambae" camp – out in the open clearing – site of an old Australian Imperial Force camp where many had died of cholera in the spring. What relief to be out from under tall trees. Here we have built bamboo and atap huts to live in – what comfort!

Better food here, as Knipers allowed to go with party down to Takanum boat landing and buy supplies from Thais – he sells his wrist watch for 75 ticals **[Thai currency]**! We officers can fry eggs (duck) and make up various hot "sambals" and often cook served "nassi goring" and snacks. Occasionally I cook hot omelettes with brown sugar in "Pop" in early morning and I put a lime in it or brown sugar. Can get "Kachang ijjon" and sprout "teagay". Men's work not so hard – they elevate a section of the railway and cut away embankment. General health of camp better, but have three deaths! Olivier who had been in

Canada, (dysentery, malaria and jaundice), Cardinal, Beriberi case and DeBus with Flu or pneumonia meningitis.

Another Dutch group camp, with Captain Kaisbert Commanding Officer, camp beside us and set up a coffee shop! Medical Officer here was good and professional surgeon – Captain Dr. Valmar vander Mohler of regular army. He had a small microscope and looked at stool smears for E. H. ? Got Aoto's permit to evacuate a party of sick to Takanum Base P.O.W. camp, two or three kilometers away and old torn tents were taken there. Engelbert there (legs big with Beriberi) gets huge carbuncle on his back – no dressings available – terrible!

Johan does good work in separate little hut as medical orderly. Blijenbey, his friend lives with him there. We also have a small hospital tent. Ulcer of man working in Nip kitchen cleared by using maggots. Artz with malaria with delirium, out wandering at night! "Wild Strawberry Tree". Hear jungle hens cackling! Small coloured snakes – heard once a frog squealing as snake tried to swallow it! Kitchen boys mistakenly begin to saw up a log in Aussie cemetery close by to be used by them as the memorial!

Doctor Mohler's treatment for tropical ulcers – syringe with alcohol soap solution or wash with soap and water. If not healing – maggots.

Engelbert, Dr. Mohler suggests and we use maggots, half size, put in a bottle with water and emptied on to a bit of gauze and quickly applied to wound. In two days and nights, they had eaten slough away. But terrible stench for poor Engelbert. We get him into cook house job for tidbits, etc. Tragedy of his wife believed dead and both children. (Tragedy of him later in December 1944 – early 1945, killed by our bombing of bridge near Takanum camp.) **[This is one of the notes apparently inserted later in the diary by Dr. Anderson himself.]**

Aoto invites us officers to a Jap movie and we hear the Nip band that was to play for the Railway completion celebrations.

I get paid 102.50 Ticals each for two months here! Aoto unreasonable – example – first ordering three copies of death certificates, then later injuring one, was a fool for making so many out!

Word of another camp move – so I ask Aoto for permit to evacuate another six sick men – answer "no" and hits me on the head with sheathed sword. (Even his head Sergeant afraid of him and asked me once to report him ill with dengue!) Aoto stands two Aussies up to a tree for not standing to attention with fingers straight!

SEPTEMBER 29th, 1943
[Postcard from Mother]
Dhar, C.I.

My Dear Walter
Again many thanks for your "brief" card.
Mullins cable love for you, hoping you're keeping well
not suffering from cold.
Busy and well, LOVE
MOTHER

OCTOBER 3RD, 1943
[Telegram from Father]
United Church of Canada Mission
Dhar, Central India
Rev. F.J. Anderson
Mission Treasurer

Capt. W/G. Anderson
Indian Medical Service
Singapore

DEAR WALTER
TORONTO AIRGRAPH REPORTS MARION
AND CHILDREN WELL. SO ARE WE
HOPE REMAIN HERE IN SERVICE TILL JULY 1945
COUNCIL PROBABLY AGREEABLE
CHEERIO
FATHER

This map shows the stops on the railway being built along the River Kwai. The dates show when Walter attended his patients in various camps there in 1943. He also travelled there in 1944 and 1945.

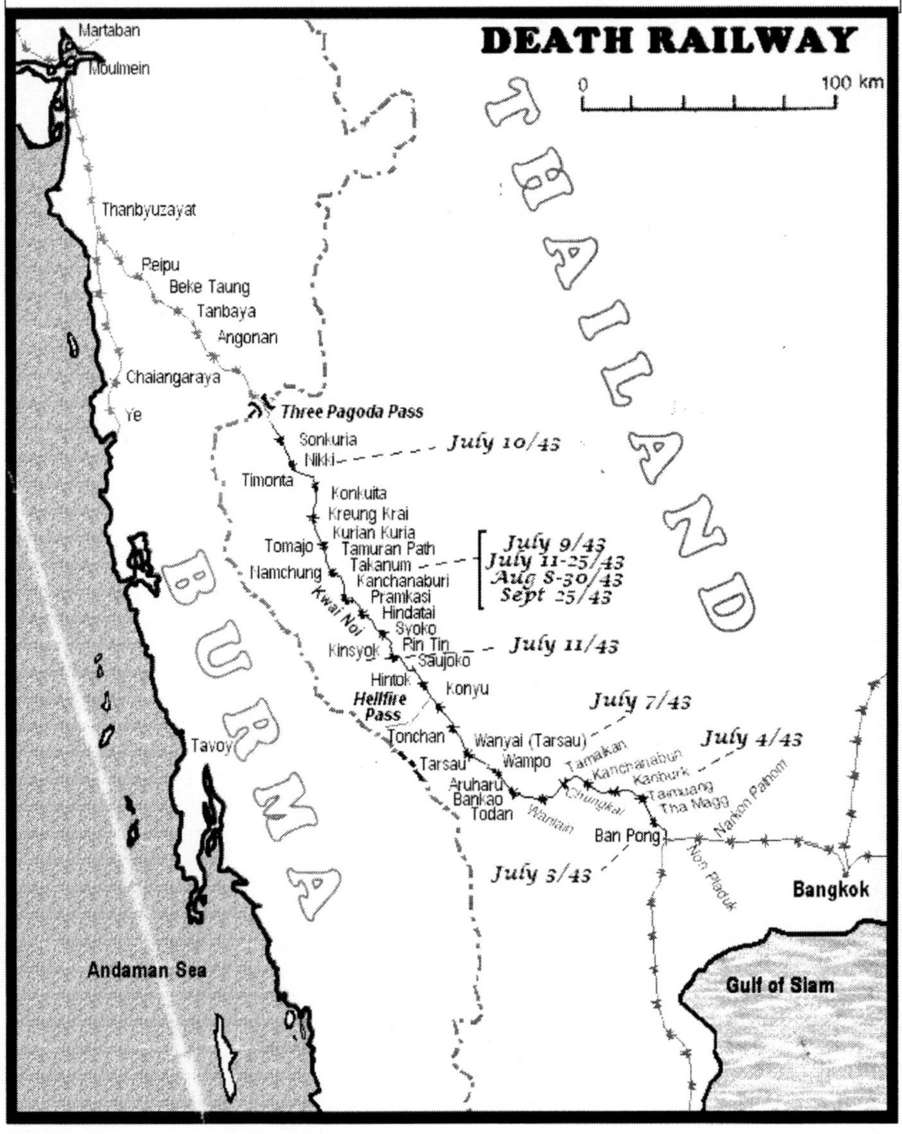

OCTOBER 3rd, 1943

On October 3rd, 1943 we were able to send one printed post card home. Via No. 2 P.O.W. camp Thailand, but could not date it. This was my third and last time of writing as P.O.W. and luckily all three cards got to India. **[This entry was apparently inserted later in the diary by Dr. Anderson himself.]**.

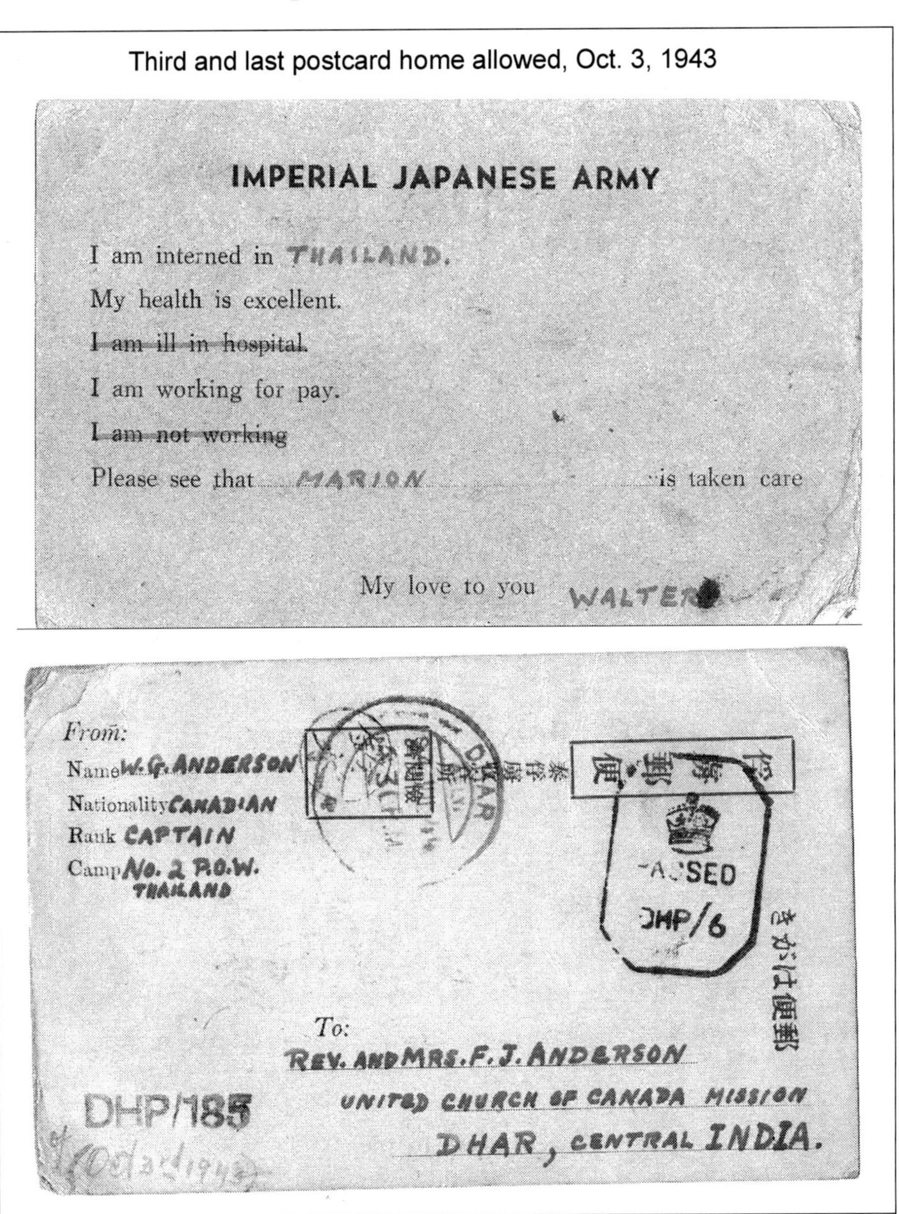

IMPERIAL JAPANESE ARMY

I am interned in THAILAND.

My health is excellent.

~~I am ill in hospital.~~

I am working for pay.

~~I am not working~~

Please see that MARION is taken care

My love to you WALTER

From:
Name W. G. ANDERSON
Nationality CANADIAN
Rank CAPTAIN
Camp No. 2 P.O.W. THAILAND

DHAR

PASSED
DHP/6

To:
REV. AND MRS. F. J. ANDERSON
UNITED CHURCH OF CANADA MISSION
DHAR, CENTRAL INDIA.

DHP/185

Third and last postcard home allowed, Oct. 3, 1943

OCTOBER 17th, 1943
[Telegram from Father]
United Church of Canada Mission
Dhar, Central India

Capt. W.G. Anderson
Indian Medical Service
Singapore

DEAR WALTER
PASTOR ZAKHI RESIGNING MOTHER MARION SELF WELL ALBION PROGRESSING ALL GOING MISSION COUNCIL TWENTIETH LOVELY WEATHER THINKING OF YOU KEEP UP COURAGE
CHEERIO
FATHER

OCTOBER 1943

Railway being built from both Burma and Thailand ends meet and was completed at Kon Quita, October 17th, 1943. and formal opening ceremonies held there October 25th. I well remember seeing the first real steam locomotive going slowly over the line in October 1943.

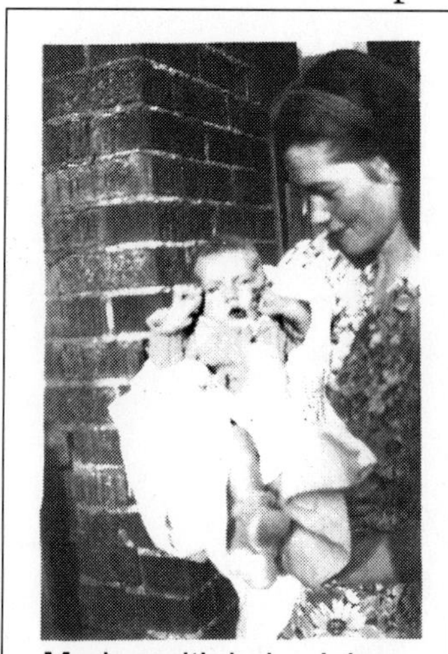
Marion with baby John Randall, 3 months, Oct. 1943.

OCTOBER 23rd, 1943
Toronto, Ontario, Canada
[Christmas Card from Marion, not received until Dec. 27, 1944]

Dear Walter;

Glad to hear of your post card although short and over a year old. Mother was glad! Have a son John Randall – born July 18th, 1943. He's fine. Ann had her tonsils and adenoids out. Well, John, Bob, Alex etc. well. John married. Everyone asks for you continually. Best wishes for your welfare.

Lovingly
Marion

OCTOBER 25th, 1943
[Postcard from Mother]
Council, Indore,

My Dear Walter
My third card. Second Eastern mail
mostly lost in accident enroute. None from you –
longing to hear. All going well here.
Love from all
Mother

NOVEMBER 6th 1943
[From Mother]

British Prisoner of War Post
Personal Number M Z 23691
[Written in pencil:]
Medical Officers Harbour Camp Prachai
Capt. W. G. Anderson
Indian Medical Service
Last serving at SINGAPORE
Dhar, C.I.

MY DEAR WALTER
HOME FROM COUNCIL.
MANY LOVING GREETINGS FOR YOU. FATHER NOW SECRETARY TREASURER DURING SCOTTS FURLOUGH. OUR HEARTS LONG AND WAIT FOR YOU.
LOVE
MOTHER

NOVEMBER 8th - 23rd, 1943

Move by train to Tamajan. (I have malaria on the train!) We unload the train at noon – were up long before daylight – had to cut down and take along all our own atap roofing! We sleep at Tamajan in a few dirty little shacks.

Colonel Flower's camp and Hugh Henderson with Nips, not over 2 kilometers away. We get a herd of cattle for camp. They stampede one night and the other camp catches one and kills it! Some of our lads work at a nearby Nip ferry across the big Kay Noi. Our men work building a road running up over other side of the river and also a bridge over a side river – all thick jungle. Have to cross ferry to work each day and means long way to walk back and forth. About 97 men now in our camp.

Joined at Tamajan by about 200 – 300 coolies. (Tamils, Malays and Chinese). Visited one day by Captain Cowan who brought my pay. Dr. Heck and I alternate in helping Captain Wiffenbach clear jungle and build huts for our new camp across the river. Location good for water and bathing by a river. Able to build fairly decent huts with platforms – "bali bali"– for all. Little hospital hut. Aoto insists on a fence!

I dig the camp "benjo" **[latrine for bowel evacuation]**! Officers had a decent small benjo covered with logs. DeVere killed by falling tree. Others injured. Nip humor to put Johan ("Christo") to work on road – Knipers and I get him off! We are joined by 300 – 400 native coolies for road work. They have no doctor.

NOVEMBER 14th, 1943

[Telegram from Father]

United Church of Canada Mission
Dhar, Central India
Rev. F.J. Anderson
Mission Treasurer

British Prisoners of War Post
Capt. W.G. Anderson
Indian Medical Service
Singapore

DEAR WALTER
JACK WRITING BESSIE REPORTS TALKING WITH YOU – PROBABLY DECEMBER – ABOUT FRASER CAMPBELLS DEATH. WE EXPECT REMAIN INDIA ON DUTY THROUGH 1945
REMEMBERING ALWAYS
CHEERIO
FATHER

NOVEMBER 14th, 1943
[Postcard from Mother]
Dhar, C. I.

Dearest Walterji
Second card came today. So glad! Jack's mentions you. He got letters, hope you do. All well here. Don't permit discouragement.

Many greetings, LOVE
Mother

NOVEMBER 23rd, 1943

"Wiffenbach" camp. Best Dutch camp so far – huts and bali bali for all – number of men about 76? (Our small party under Horai at Tamajao ferry and another at Bangan ferry). We are more to ourselves in our little jungle clearing, and beside a rushing small river. Nips were away across the river. Cattle from herd killed twice a week. Weather good – clear cold moon! Light nights. Bundles of atap en route to Nip camp, often hidden near ours to be sure of enough roofing for our huts.

Coolies from Tamajao come over to new jungle camp site along small river below us. Nips always upstream of course. Nip called by Dutch "Adamson" appointed to be "doctor" to coolies. Sickness in their camp rapidly increases – Tamils and others are most unsanitary. Tamils all wait around and won't use camp open trench latrine.

Hanchow Tanioka put up P.O.W. and coolie camps. Some Dutch working parties, but mostly Dutch put as small "mandurs" **[foremen]** over parties of coolies on the road – they all speak Malay. One elephant in camp to heave logs, he squeals when these are too heavy!

Derrick Helder (East Surreys) brought to be the motor truck driver for Aoto. Men more spirited as road built and work lighter – sing sometimes and play bamboo flutes. Some letters for them from Takanum camp. Aoto beats Knipers when asked to give the mail out! Knipers tied to tree by Aoto for buying from a Thai boatman without his permission! A Thai canteen is established near coolie camp. Their prices high – later ordered closed by Japs. Quite a lot of Nip cavalry (Dutch recognize units from Java) going up by road each day to Nike and into Burma.

Once crossed Kay Noi on bamboo raft to give an intravenous injection of Bagnan to a sick Nip. Japanese medical orderly took a fancy to my syringe!

DECEMBER 15TH, 1943
[Postcard from Mother]
Dhar, C.I.

Dear Walterji
Shall broadcast you Friday,
Greetings from Council, MacKays,
others.
Second card received thankfully. New
medical lady will study DHAR.

LOVE Mother

[Because it was stated in the press that mail to POWs should only contain 25 words, correspondence was abbreviated. In the previous postcard, "broadcast" indicated that she would let family and friends know that she had received word from him via radio.]

Early DECEMBER 1943

Went to Tamblon Paton twice; once walking close behind two elephants (with two Nips on one)! to see about death of a Dutch lad in Cowens camp. Again went on December 23rd and got one month's pay for November.

In December 1943 Nips admitted Italy was finished. We live in rumours of Germany weakening.

I am astonished one evening to hear Tamioka whistling "Swing low sweet chariot"! His mother said to be Christian. He learned it in Kobe.

We see quite a bit of Thais from Kampong. A Kampong across river from us. Naked Thai men bathing were tattooed heavily from knees to waist like shorts! They travel by boat and elephant, wear a short sword in their girdle. Women chew betel nut!

A few nights before Xmas, we hear first plane (allied) going over to raid Bangkok! What a thrill! Lieutenant Aoto (now full Lieutenant) excited, has his Dutch night watchmen (awake fire guard). Keep water to pour on fire!

Hoft died of strange malignant malaria? And bright lad brought from Banyan with massive pneumonia and suddenly collapsed and died.

"Adamson" can't treat coolies – so Johan and I are called to go over from 5 – 7 pm. (Tokyo time) every day and do treatments. Dysentery, malaria and ulcers rapidly increasing. A Chinese overseer, Mr. Lee, helps me check coolies and get their number. I know no Malay at this time. Nips give us a small tent for treating. All these coolies live in tents without bali bali. One or two coolie deaths occur daily. We find them sometimes lying out on ground where they died and are left till working coolies come home and bury them. Two tents are put up as a "hospital", but no one to care for those in them. Dr. Ida sent some medical supplies for us all, but hopelessly inadequate. Frightful maggotry tropical ulcers – make Johan nearly sick dressing! Nip Corporal fell on bridge and fractured a rib with his bayonet – I have to attend him for 2 weeks B.I.D. **[twice daily]**! Sergeant Major Bugter has toe fractured by elephant tossing a log. Captain Wiffenbach gets dysentery relapse, then complications of thrombosis of left leg.

Difficulties of growing maggots when you want them: – got meat twice a week – fresh bits of meat tended to dry up too fast and not rot. Eventually, when maggots in it, large red jungle tree ants carried them away. Tried again – next time, after maggots developed – dog swallowed rotten meat and all! So finally grew maggots quickly from saving the stinking slough itself and adding rice and water. This brought the blue bottle flies!!

Christmas Day DECEMBER 25th, 1943

Busiest Christmas of my life! Everyone seemed to be sick. Finally Johan ill and I treat Nip Corporal Dutch camp and all coolie treatments alone. Derik Helder brings me sweet biscuits and condensed milk from Takanum village, so then I celebrate Christmas with him at night. Captain Jonker conducts a Dutch service.

Bangnan ferry Dutch group joins up with us again before Christmas. I report every two weeks on illnesses for Dr. Ida. Aoto sees 30 cases of malaria reported – angrily tells me these are only colds and no mosquitoes here, so how can there be Malaria!

As work finishes the men got excited about possibly being withdrawn to Singapore and Java! Aoto and party are to move on into Burma, allegedly to Akyab.

Hanchow Tanioka's treatment of P.O.W's better than when others in charge. I have to send in list of temperatures of those ill and not on parade. Few mosquitoes now but Malaria relapses and Flu fevers plentiful. Tropical ulcers in the men still bothersome – have to grow and use maggots again on Van DerGroot, Klink, Orie, etc. Orie's skin ulcer particularly bad with black bone of tibia showing. Some maggots entered the bone spaces!! But have probably saved his leg and life? One of two brothers with Beriberi got bad ulcer – whole foot ulcerated and fly laid maggots stripped up tendons sheaths – frightful – he died December 31st. **[Another example of his going back later to fill in some information in his diary.]**

1944

JANUARY 1st, 1944
[Telegram from Father]
United Church of Canada Mission
Dhar, Central India

Capt. W. G. Anderson
Indian Medical Service

DEAR WALTER
HAPPY NEW YEAR. IT WILL BE. PASTOR SINGH (RATLAM) DIED. PNEUMONIA. PASTOR ZAKJI RETIRED. SAM ABRAHAM CONDUCTED MORNING SERVICE.
ALL WELL PROSPECTS BRIGHTER
FATHER

JANUARY 1st, 1944

I'm suddenly homesick! Tanioka gave Johan and me present of some sugar! The Corporal with rib (now Sergeant) gave me a tin of Campbell soup!! This is Nip holiday. We officers call on Aoto to wish him a (un) happy New Year!

JANUARY 2nd, 1944
[From Mother]

SERVICE OF PRISONER OF WAR
No. M.Z. 23691, Capt. W. G. Anderson,
Indian Medical Service,
Last serving at Singapore, Malaya.
C/o Japanese Red Cross,
TOKYO. JAPAN
Dhar,

Dear Walter,
Hope you got my broadcast.
Regret to record the death of Pastor Singh last week – Typhoid-Pneumonia.
All else going well.

Lovingly,
Mother.

JANUARY 2nd, 1944

Nips celebrate with wrestling bouts for all Nips, Dutch and coolies. Prizes!

JANUARY 6th, 1944

Our Dutch sick taken away in a lorry. 7 pm I am transferred to the coolie camp. New Japs taken over, become my "new master"!!

JANUARY 8th early morning

Aoto says goodbye and Captain Jonker and his full Dutch party march off to Kurian Kurai to await withdrawal to Chungkai. I am left – depressed – no feeding arrangement. I live in with an Eurasian, DeCruz, dresser **[helper]** from Singapore. Dutch left me some split peas etc. which I share with him. New Nip thinks camp condition is dreadful! Holds handkerchief to his nose when walking around sick coolie tents!

JANUARY 10th, 1944

Aoto's Nips march away – to Burma. Former Dutch camp now desolate and stripped by coolies.

JANUARY 11th or 13th, 1944

All but 100 sick coolies (left in care of DeCruz) and I, in afternoon, strike camp and set out on a four day hike, carrying all kit to new camp site up the line. We follow the new road. Camp 1st night near Kinchung, where McTighe brought me some orange pekoe tea! First met Lim Djin Pin here. Strange feeling tramping along trails with these coolies, just like one of them. My heavier kit carried by different party's coolies each day (under protest)! Tiresome, up and down hill. Mr. Lee, overseer, and I are fed by Alor Star Mandur **[head coolie or foreman]** en route. 2nd night stayed in old hut near Kurian Kwai bridge. Saw Chandler next morning at bridge where road crossed Kay Noi. 3rd night in camp at old Timonta, Captain Frans here but unable to visit him.

JANUARY 13th, 1944
Office of the Deputy Field C.M.A.
Officers (I.A.) Casualty Accts. Sec.,
Simla,

To: Rev. F.J. Anderson
U.C.C. Mission, Dhar (C.I.)

Dear Sir,

It is observed from the records maintained in this Office that your son Captain (then Lieutenant) W.G.Anderson, embarked from India for service Overseas on 23rd January 1942. He disembarked in Singapore, but the date of his dis-embarkation is not available.

It appears that on arrival in Singapore, he was requisitioned by the R.A.F. and again – embarked ex-Singapore for another station in Malaya, in the beginning of February 1942.

In the correspondence on record in this Office, his name is shown as Captain W.G.S. Anderson.

As there appears to be no other I.M.S. Officer bearing this name, it is presumed that the complete name of your son is Captain W.G. Anderson. Please confirm if this is correct.

The favour of an early reply is requested.

Yours faithfully,
[signature not legible]
Deputy Asst. Field C.M.A.

JANUARY 14th or 16th, 1944

Afternoon, we all arrive at new camp Timonta, back in a forest clearing, 1 km. from the Railway Station. Joined here by Djin Pin and his coolies. I sleep this night in Nip hut.

[These undated entries apparently comprise a record Walter made during his trips to treat the ill, up and down what would later be called "The Death Railway", along the River Kwai between Thailand and Burma – see map on page 126]

Bangkok – Moulein Railway
(Nonpradok to Thanbyugayat – 415 Km.)
Nonpradok
Bangpong
Tammang
Kanburi
Tamarkan
Wanran
(Chungkai)

Aruhiru
Wampo
Wanyai (Tarso)
Rintin
Kinsyok
Syok
Hindatai

Bramkasi
Takanum
Namchung
Tamajao
Tamoran Path
Kurian Kurai
KonKoita
Timonta
Nike
Sonkurai – Thailand

Chaiangaraya – Burma?
(3 Pagoda Pass-305.8 Kilos? – Piatonju – 3065)
Anganan – 310.5
Miseli
Kiando
Apalon

Anakuin
Thanbyozayat 415

JANUARY 15th, 1944 to JUNE 7th, 1944 **[The following section of the journal apparently covers the time when Walter was being moved from station to station and later, June 7th, he filled in what he could recall, from scribbled notes.]**

At Timonta **[Railway Station]**. About 600 **[labourers]**. I select a high bit of ground and Nips get coolies to build a bamboo and atap hut for Djin Pin and me. Mr. Lee and Hong Lee just come in to live with us! So 3 Chinese and I! Have a Tamil man "boy" to do cooking and get our raw rations from the store daily. (Ramaswami – quite devoted to Djin Pin). Had a 2nd boy for awhile, gathering firewood and carrying water from the only muddy little stream that ran by the camp down near the Japanese Hut. My good pen knife stolen, which I lent for peeling vegetables. Frightful lot of mosquitoes here, feel them biting through net at night! Tall trees left in camp clearing – with old thick 8" vines hanging from one to another and twisted on themselves, up 40 feet! Wild banana trees plentiful about us but the fruit only finger size and only black seeds held together by pulp. For a time camp had three large and one baby elephant belonging to some Burmese. Baby liked to chase the coolies and sometime bit and injured them. Later, our Burmese had an elephant stolen! Japs could do nothing since elephants caught in the forest legally belong to the Thais!

We are always on Tokyo time! Work was from muster roll (just after daylight) about 8 am. till a little before sunset – making the road, parallel to railway and carrying small stones to it from the big river bed about a mile away. After coolies went to work accompanied by Nips in charge, now armed with rifles and bayonets because of occasional allied air raid along the Railway and also protection from Thai bandits. We had breakfast (pap, or dry rice with curry stew or dry salt fish fried), then Djin Pin and I did dressings, sitting outside hut in boxes and coolies would bring banana leaves to spread on the ground. After ulcers and wounds dressed, we made our rounds of the hut to record and treat those sick with a fever, and not at work. Mr. Lee accompanied me and was interpreter in Malay language. Had to record names and party member, disease etc. This took till noon. Coolies' rice carried out to the ward by kitchen staff on poles between two men. Had our lunch of rice and occasional cabbage, white radish, yams, sweet potatoes, whatever vegetable available, about 1 pm or 2 pm, then had much of afternoon to ourselves except for any special sick to be treated. Then in the evening or late afternoon, after bathing (out in the open with always some Tamil women nearby) when first coolies returned from work, we began dressings again – this clinic larger than morning, since mostly coolies back usually about dusk and then ate evening meal of same kind of food. To bed at 8:30 or 9 pm. after battling mosquitoes and sitting in moonlight.

Rations were coolie rice (Nips had clean white variety), and as available dried spinach, pumpkin, long white radish, yams, salt fish dried, occasional sweet potato and a little tea and curry powder and salt and chillies and tamarind and sometimes Kochang ijiu we bought from Tamils. Tried to always have hot curried stew with the rice, though Mr Lee and Hong Lee didn't like it. Djin Pin managed the meals.

JANUARY 17TH, 1944

[From Rev. Frederick J. Anderson]

The United Church of Canada Mission
Dhar, C.I.

To- Office of the Deputy Field C.M.A.
Officers (I.A.) Casualty Accts. Sec.,
Simla

Sir,

Communication No. 6620 of date January 13th, 1944 received.

The complete name of my son is Walter Gilray Anderson. There is no "S" in it. I do not know definitely the date of his disembarkation in Singapore but received from him a letter dated No 4. I.R.C. Singapore February 8th, 1942. Also a cable dated February 9th, 1942 announcing his arrival though not specifying that it was on the 8th. I judge that it was the 8th for he would lose no time in writing and the cable followed next day which was a Monday.

Your communication was news "that on arrival in Singapore he was requisitioned by the R.A.F. and again embarked at Singapore for another Station in Malaya, in the beginning of February 1942".

Two brief post cards have come from him.

1. *Dated June 20th, 1942 and received August 11th, 1943*
2. *Dated February 22nd, 1943 and received November 14th, 1943*

Neither card stated place of origin. Both stated that he was Prisoner of War. The second card said "Prisoner of War. quite well. Don't worry. Trying not to rust. Hope previous card received".

We were glad to receive these two cards.

Yours faithfully,
F.J. Anderson

JANUARY 22nd, 1944

A week before my Birthday Djin Pin experimented on a "cake" – mashed yams and sweet potatoes, a few mashed bananas with little maize flour and brown sugar begged from Nips and layer of thick sweetening – strained Kochang ijiu – The whole put in a round tin and steamed 6 hours in pail with water, covered by banana leaves and served cold in slices with sweetened condensed milk (4.50 Ticals a tin) poured over it! Very good. He repeated this on Jan. 29th for my Birthday! The first time celebrated the Chinese New Year and his own Birthday Jan. 24th (?). One day, I bought a duck for 9 Ticals from a nearby Chinese Thai Camp where Djin Pin and I had twice been called by the Nips to see sick Chinese who after gave us free coffee and sweet egg noodles. Dr. Pin spoke Nippon – so did all our talking with Japs in charge – handy for us. Later we lost our "boys" to the work and these replaced by children and later by a young Chinese lad.

JANUARY 26th, 1944
[Telegram from Father]
United Church of Canada Mission
Dhar, Central India
Rev. F. J. Anderson
Mission Treasurer & Gen. Secretary

DEAR WALTER
SCOTTS, GRAHAMS, GIBSON, HUGH, GOING ON LEAVE SOON.
GOING TODAY NAGPUR NCC MEETINGS.
MARION LARRY CHILDREN REPORTED WELL
ALL WELL HERE.
LOVINGLY
FATHER

JANUARY 28th, 1944
[Postcard from Mother]
DHAR, C.I.

Dear Walter
I am thinking very specially of you today and tomorrow. Father is away at NCC meetings. Be of good courage. I may visit Waters two days.

Lovingly yours
Mother

FEBRUARY 1944

Our Coolie Parties – Alor Star (Telugus)

Johore (Malays with some Chinese – Hindustani & family)

Segamat Lama (Tamils)

& Segamat 'B' – a few Tamils

Djin Pin Parties – Perak (Telugus)

Kuala Lumpur (Tamils & Chinese)

Malacca 'B' (Malays & Tamils)

Each party led by a Mandur Besai, with small section Mandurs under him. Only some of Telugus and Tamils have their wives and families with them.

In all six overseers: Mr. Lee and Krishna work with us; and Hong Lee, Mr. Adman, Mr. Awong and a Cingalese, with Djin Pin.

When Captain Cowen passed through in February, he left me a copy of "Greater Asia", published in Rangoon, brought down by Australians. Told of Nips advancing in Imphal and quoted "Manchester Guardian", that Japs were 40 miles inside India and time the British Government did something about it! Made one a bit depressed!

One day about end of February '44, the Hindustani barber, while cutting my hair, told of going into the forest from work at noon hour and meeting a party of bearded sahibs having coffee. He offered to come again and shave them, but they said they kept moving, not to be found by the Nips! Could this be a party of allied paratroops spying out the Railway? Looking over at the mountains beyond the tracks and thinking of these men somewhere there possibly, gave me a thrill. Barber said I could not meet them by moonlight. Later, I dismissed this all as merely soothing balm from a well wishing Indian.

One day Indian National Army troops were marching past to Nike and into Burma – their medical orderly came into camp to fetch me to see one with abdominal pain and constipation – fallen by the road wearing K.L. made bayonets! and carried a Tommy Gun. Indian National Army troops were taunted by Khuda Bruxjagah – replied they had their own reasons for going into Burma and we're not telling.

As time went on, we had nine and more sick – sometimes 50%. 200/250 remaining in camp. Japs got annoyed. Often Djin Pin and I called out to check over remaining coolies kept squatting at muster roll. I hated this and it is difficult to judge a coolie who says he can't work early in the cool morning. The less ill-looking sometimes made to go to work and reduced to half day pay. When a lot sick, no mid-day food was served in camp, but this didn't reduce the many sick.

Work became hard and Nips got rough with the coolies and so many stayed home also from fear and laziness. Some Telugus arrange with head Mandur and go off secretly all day to buy food in Kampunga? Or Nike, 6 km away. I can never locate all the total daily Alor Star sick for this reason! Some K.I. Chinese stayed in gambling all day making money there! Many Malays shiftless and lazy – like children. Only Tamils seemed to help each other when sick. Small coolie groups run away from time to time.

Deaths in camp in five months totalled 83. Mostly Malaria, Dysentery, Beriberi, Tropical ulcers and occasional Pneumonia, Emphysema, Meningitis, Gangrene scrotum etc. Our medical supplies (very inadequate for 500/600 labourers) of Quinine pills, Creosote pills, several solutions and gauze bandages, came from Nip Butan headquarters at Konhosta! Nips did come one day and we vaccinated camp. Also vaccines were sent for Cholera, Tuberculosis, Dysentery and Plague and we had to try injecting the whole camp with their first dose a half c.c. and second dose 1 c.c. after ten days. Coolies didn't like all these needles and less and less take the injections! Nip Medical Officer was a one star "Mineraijekon?" or Cadet who visited occasionally.

FEBRUARY 20TH, 1944

[Telegram from Father]

United Church of Canada Mission
Dhar, Central India
Rev. F. J. Anderson
Secretary/Treasurer

Capt. W. G. Anderson I.M.S.
Indian Medical Service
Singapore

DEAR WALTER
ALL WELL. DOBSONS HERE TEMPORARILY. HAD GOOD LETTER FROM MARION NOW LIVING WITH LARRY AT

MALTON ONTARIO
DAVID GRAHAM, MISS CAMERON ARRIVED CANADA
LOVINGLY
FATHER

Early MARCH

About beginning of March, Captain Cowen and Walls passed through with coolies from Kuichung going to Suma. Nike 4 km. above us. Dunning had already gone there in February. (Captain Deverall died in coolie camp there toward mid/end of January, soon after I arrived at Timonta, but I did not know it then. Captain Brown had buses called from Nike for him but too late!).

MARCH 7th, 1944
[Postcard from Mother]
Dhar, C. I.

My Dear Walter
Longing for further word from you.
Aunt Nellie and Mrs. Mullin send much love. David now six feet and heavy. Leper patients salaams.
All well.

Loads of love
Mother

MARCH 1944

In March, Djin Pin got leave of ten days to go to Bangkok to buy medicines. In camp we raised a sum of money and I made a list of a few simple things. Thus we got cotton wool, a scalpel, potassium iodide, tincture of camphor co., eucalyptus oil, magnesium sulphate, also a pair of shoes (19.50 Ticals) menthol, etc.

Had first real allied air raid the day that Djin Pin left for Bangkok – three planes before sunset suddenly came over a hill and went up and down the Railway line, bombed in Nike and machine gunned in old Timonta, killing a few coolies in the segregated camp hospital where Owen's was in charge. (Owen in Dec. '44 got a piece of shrapnel in one arm from bombing.) Camp air raid routine: The doctor goes to the centrally located "jagoh's" huts, all coolies in camp squat in rat trenches around each hut (long huts over 100 ft.) not allowed to run into the forest and stopped if they do. In March Japs told coolies of allied paratroops landing near Kanburi, and to guard against this, young men were picked out and trained in bayonet drill with sharp bamboo spears – spearing a dummy gunny-bag and making the unpleasant Jap noises! The coolies seemed to be amused by this. We had two other raids before June, but nothing happened in our camp.

Pathan Jagoh one day, seeing Djin Pin and me doing dressings quoted the lines ("wise mullah Khatra man, wise Latrin Khatin jan!".) His name – Khuda Baklal and was very friendly and with his brother would walk into our hut anytime – we had no privacy! Nice to talk Hindustani, but difficult to follow his Pushtu. His was a Malay jagah, who had said he fought against Japs with the Johore State Forces! He was friendly enough.

Malacca A. Mandur Besai, and one of his Kitchil mandurs had been in the Malay Regiment.

Djin Pin suddenly taken away to Bangkok again (end of March or early April) by Nips from headquarters at Konoitai going on holiday – to show them around (and help them finance themselves by selling Quinine!) – I protest, so much work alone and Djin Pin asked Nips for assistance – Lieutenant Colonel George Walls is sent to me from Suma Nike – takes over case of Djin Pin's coolies – with me till we left in June. He gave me a long large needle that fit my syringe – a great help. Now could do and did do 2 chest aspirations for thick phlegm (one case yielded 6-9 cigarette tins of pus), abdominal paracentesis, (2 cases) and several lumbar punctures for meningitis (about 4 cases – one was good looking Tamil girl – following mid ear abcess)! A young Tamil Christian dresser, Pierce Andrew, English speaking, appointed to be Medical Orderly for the Nips (who frequently got fever with severe headache) but was not much good – poor chap got meningitis, was evacuated to Nike coolie hospital where he died.

APRIL 1944

About April 1944 an isolated "hospital" hut was built, but this became really a segregated death house – dysenteries, gangrenous scrotums and penis, gangrenous legs and beriberi, emphysema etc. Big red jungle ants crawl over the sick and into their eyes – frightful. All the food they can take is rice "Kanji" which only makes them weaker.

Our Nips left to go to Mandalay in Burma, after a period of hard training, but the Butai was badly affected with Malaria – how many would survive? Replaced by a new Butai of Nips – always dislike Nip changes: devil you know is better than devil you don't know! Departing Nips are generous and sell off remaining food stores, sugar etc, at low price to the coolies. New Nips in charge very suave and sly. Sent a Chinese coolie lad to borrow a "Bangkok Chronicle" newspaper in English that Djin Pin had brought back. Built long addition to the camp hospital or "death house", all camp sick had to move over there. Then built a hut for "doctors" beside it.

Nip camp adjutant who got the gaunt fever and had headaches and wouldn't take Quinine, later reported died of Malaria in Mandalay. The Nip Corporal camp Commanding Officer friendly enough to me – said Japs had Calcutta, soon take Delhi, then I could go back home! Called me to give him Quinine injection one night for Malaria – my needle broke in his buttock! But got it out okay. He took Djin Pin and me to see Jap movies in Nikes. Coolies all report he was rough on them. He was survivor from Nips routed in Solomon's, drew bayonet one morning on a Chinese Mandur and kicked him into the rat trench around hut. Another Nip Corporal, fight one night came to our hut and hit Djin Pin with bamboo, then beat up sleeping coolies who fled screaming!

Main coolies' huts were fine, each about 60 yards long. Bamboo poles, atap ("chaku", in Nip) roofing, and split bamboo platforms from old huts in other camps, full of bed bugs. Some Alor Star coolies did weird fortune telling some nights.

Soon after arriving in Timonta the first dysentery patient attempted suicide by cutting his trachea with a brother's straight razor! Got bleeding stopped by pressure – he died of dysentery days later! Nip Officer Commanding said to call it "Malaria" if he died! Everything was Malaria! Became very hot in the jungle in April! One day in April the Nip Lieutenants assembled all in camp and held a 1 –2 minute silence to honour all coolies and P.O.W. who had died working on the Railway.

MAY 1944

In May, a little boy, Nephew of this man, and Son of Alor Star No. 2 Mandur, was accidentally killed by a Nip soldier who pushed him accidently into a ditch he was supposed to be digging. Boy was dead when brought to us back at camp. Same Nip beat with bamboo a Tamil man whose foot ulcers I was cleaning at the time. This man had come into camp and left the Nip truck he rode loaded!

Malay coolie boy (only one left with Alor Star party) had large non-pointing abdominal wall abscess – lay out in all night rain, wakened us at dawn crying "Allah" – had no scalpel yet, so obliged to incise him through normal skin with safety razor blade (no anaesthetic!) – got 2½ quinine bottles (about 20 oz.) of thick pus, and he recovered. Another time I removed two bone sequestra (one 2 inches long) from his tibia, and treated him for Malaria etc. (And, last I know he was still working in December 1944.)

Tamil man who had been driver for Royal Army Service Corps in Malaya died of pneumonia (Djin Pin's patient). Coolies were buried in very shallow graves and too close to camp (men didn't want to walk far after work at night!). Nips decided a new road was to come into camp through the cemetery and made coolies dig up the bodies and move them – then abandoned the idea! Terrible smell and I saw the poor driver's toes sticking out of the ground two weeks later! I frequently wore a pair of this man's Khaki shorts which he had given Djin Pin, who passed them onto me being too wide for his liking!

Walls and I named different men who came for repeated ulcer treatments – e.g. "My Task", Nelson (because he stretched out) Wellington, etc! cleaning ulcers a terrible chore and painful – made most Tamils say "Ai-yo yo yo..!"

MAY 11th, 1944
[Postcard from Mother]
'Bellevue', Landour

My Dear Walter,
We have been here a few days.
Several send greetings, among them Abdul.
All well. Longing for you.

Lovingly
Mother

MAY 31st, 1944

We move into the new hut. It is a nice and large hut, but across a mud stream and on very low land – very muddy. Walked back through jungle a mile to the big river – one day to bathe, another day with the Nips who dynamited the river for fish. A few days after moving to new hut, word comes that camp is to be broken up and small parties of coolies distributed to several camps further up the Railway line. Walls and I and overseers to move too. Moves are such unpleasant things. Walls and I had been getting malaria about two or three weeks – he more than I!! Meantime Djin Pin (never able to settle after Bangkok trips and selling Black Cat cigarettes. Prater Chai cigarettes, etc. he brought back) had got ten day leave and gone off to Bangkok a third time, borrowing my water bottle! He had borrowed 30 Ticals before from me. Walls wouldn't lend him his bottle.

Two truckloads of "sick" once evacuated to Nike Hospital by Nips in consultation with chief Mandurs and without any reference to us in medical charge.

In May came sudden storms – strong winds blew down tree branches and damaged the atap – then following rain came through roof! when ground soaked, trees could blow or fall over – and one such crashed into Malacca B. hut next to us one night just missing some coolies. Others were killed at old Timonta. A storm in the forest can be very frightening.

(Outside this same Malacca B. hut one night in June after we left, and when Sergeant Chandler was there, a coolie went out and was so badly mauled by a tiger; he died). We heard reports of tigers from near other camps, (but never saw one myself). Frequently could hear barking deer in the forest and frequently the hooting of monkeys.

I get monthly pay of 50 Ticals. Djin Pin got 60 ticals. Overseers much more. Tamil overseer Krishnamurti a queer one – congress dress, etc, always complaining and "sick" with many tin trunks of luggage – was carried on a stretcher one day to Nip hut to sign for his pay! – to impress the Nips, but it made every one laugh!

Hong Lee's acute attack of asthma for one week – couldn't lie down in sleep. I cured him to his surprise by taking 6 c.c. blood from his arm and injecting it into his buttock – he slept quietly that night! Treated me thereafter to coffee!

JUNE 7th, 1944

Walls and I with overseers leave camp with last party of coolies. The sick left behind. Caught in downpour of rain in morning on way to Timonta Station. Wait there from noon till 9 pm. for train! At last, coolies and us loaded into open train trucks and arrive in Nike where we change over to empty box cars on another track and spend the night. Medicine box and Djin Pin's one chest and alarm clock carried by coolies arranged for with Mandur. I keep these to be sure he will come seeking them and bring back my water bottle from Bangkok.

JUNE 8th, 1944

We wait till about 4 pm. on the siding at Nike station. I get another morning attack of Malaria. On same track heading down was trainload of P.O.W. mostly Dutch, being withdrawn from points on the Railway in Burma – many bad with dysentery and in pitiable states but given no medicine by Japs and train kept standing.

Coolies bring us some "opam" (rice pancakes) to eat from some Tamil place in Nike. About 4 pm we get orders to move into another open truck train – a terrible scramble with coolies and their luggage – we don't know where we are going! Coolie parties allotted to different trucks. As the train stops at points along the way, certain parties of coolies are ordered off and reinforce the local labourers. We suddenly pass the Three Pagodas and realize we are then over boundary into Burma.

At Anganan the overseers are all ordered down – no one knows anything about Walls and me, so we remain on with one party of coolies left, Segamat Lama! We get out with them at next camp Kiando. Nips are puzzled but give us a small hut to sleep in and a "boy" to cook our food. The Dutch "panicher" belonging to DeVere I had was most useful – nothing else to wash and cook in!

A Tamil Christian dresser from Vellore, speaking English, was at this camp, and could speak to Nips for us – very fortunate.

JUNE 8th, 1944
Nike to Kiando

JUNE 9th, 1944

Luckily Nip Butai "doctor" (a funny elderly man) was in Kendo camp to give cholera injections. He had Walls and I give a few to prove we were medicals! He left later in the day for his headquarters at Anganan and to arrange where we should go. Most coolies here Tamils of Seramban party. Nip hut over by rock cliffs used to quarry stone for road and Railway. Had underground shelters since it had been sprayed by allied plane machine guns.

Our Sergeant Laura very sick coolie, we had brought with us semi-comatose, died, - clinical Malaria?

JUNE 10th, 1944

We wait about camp – mostly sleep. Did not get to visit a large P.O.W. cemetery across the tracks – this had been a P.O.W. camp and was about 2 Km. away from Kendo Station. Met a coolie ill with tuberculosis clinical, formerly of the Madras Sappers and Nurses.

JUNE 11th, 1944

Kiando to 3 Pagoda Pass

With the Indian extra train dresser and coolies to carry our stuff, Walls and I walk back about five kilos along track to Anganan (310.5 kilos). Here Nip "doctor" hands us over to Hanchow Hiono (Five Star civil – military, not soldiers), and we walk back another four kilos with him to camp Piatonju only 1/4 mile from 3 Pagodas Pass. We are fed here in Nip hut and I remain posted here (306.5 kilos point on Railway). While Walls walks on back into Thailand and is posted to coolie camp at 299 kilo. Malay overseer Mr. Adamson also came with us and spoke English. I found our Timonta and Tamajan Johore party coolies here. Their Mandur spoke English.

Spent 6 months and 6 days at Piatonju (3 Pagodas camp) – in some ways, the pleasantest period of the whole 3 1/2 yrs. as P.O.W.! Hanchow Hiono, Tanico and five other Nips run the camp – small – about 150 coolies. Railway here curved almost like an "S" – or less? Nips live in their hut on one side of tracks and coolies live on the other side in old P.O.W. huts (huge long things, two tiers, that must have housed hundreds of P.O.W.) now falling down and only held up by many support poles. I live in Nip hut with them and share their food at same table. We can't speak other than a few words of Malay, but I'm treated respectfully and no interference in my work. Am quite free to go all over camp area clearing and encircling jungle. Perak party coolies (Tamils) here had been joined by our old Johore gang (Malays and few Chinese and Hindustani men). Johore sick neglected since leaving Timonta have bad tropical ulcers, particularly one Hindustani man with multiple ulcers on legs and small Malay Mandur with whole foot maggoty and ulcerated. Took me till two and three o'clock doing dressings and cleaning ulcers. Patients smell so foul, others near them can't eat! I go twice a month on certain days to headquarters at Anganan for a few medical supplies and report names and illness of all sick.

Meet up here with Walls and other dressers who have longer to walk in along track. I seem to get a bit more medicines than some others! (– little white or rivinol gauze, quinine powder, creosote pills now finished, juso soda tabs, shoso bismuth tabs? Kaienja cough sed. tablets, aspirin, charcoal, magnesium sulphate cinnamon tablet combination packet for dysentery, bandage, potassium permanganate, plasmoquin, rivinol solution – all in very small quantities except the Quinine powder). Also walk to Anganan to get paid (50 Rupees in Jap Burma scrip) last day of each month with Mr. Adamson. Meet Hong Lee and Mrs. Lee each time in office. Hong Lee treats me to coffee! Look forward to meeting Walls fortnightly and get any news.

In June the Johore Chinese Mandur and another Chinese both died of pneumonia. When very ill and unable to smoke their opium they just died. Nearly all the Chinese coolies smoked opium (including Mrs. Lee, but not Hong Lee!) which was supplied in little tubes cheaply by the Nip headquarters!

JUNE 28th, 1944

Nips evacuate party of sick to Nike coolie Hospital, include Malay Mandur with bad ulcer, who died on reaching Nike station.

JULY 3rd, 1944

[From Indian Red Cross, to Rev. Anderson]

INDIAN RED CROSS & ST. JOHN WAR ORGANIZATION
TEL: ADDRESS "INDCROSS"
"KEVIN GROVE"
Simla, India

Rev. F.J. Anderson,
United Church of Canada Mission,
Central India,
Dhar, C.I.

Dear Sir,

Reference your letter dated the 24th June, 1944.

Owing to the Japanese Government's refusal to allow a Red Cross representative to function in Malaya we are mainly dependent on the Japanese themselves for giving the location of Prisoners of War camps and they have not yet given the exact locations of the camps in Malaya but simply report people as being in 'Malaya Camps'.

In Thailand the camps are numbered but had your son been there his postcards would have said so.

You are advised to continue to address him at Singapore. Letters are just as likely to reach him this way as any other. Unfortunately, as far as we know, only a very small percentage of letters reach Prisoners of War in Japanese hands even when the exact camp in which they are interned is known.

Yours faithfully,
[signature not legible]
Major-General,
DEPUTY CHIEF COMMISSIONER

AUGUST 4th, 1944
[From Indian Red Cross, to Rev. Anderson]
INDIAN RED CROSS & ST. JOHN WAR ORGANIZATION
TEL: ADDRESS "INDCROSS"
"KELVIN GROVE"
Simla, India
No. GS/PWE

Mr. F. J. Anderson,
United Church of Canada Mission
DHAR, Central India

Dear Sir,

Thank you for your letter dated the 27th July 1944 informing us that your son Capt. W.G. Anderson, I.M.S. is now interned in camp No. 2 Thailand which has been noted.

Yours faithfully,
[signature not legible]
Major-General,
Deputy Chief Commissioner

AUGUST 1944

About August 11th, an allied small "reccy" **[reconnaissance]** plane suddenly came low over trees and gave us an unexpected fright and thrill!

Also after big coolie hut built, a two room "sick" hut was built, and a tiny dysentery hut.

Both coolies and Nips planted out gardens and actually got a few onions, chillies and brinjals **[eggplant]**, from them after the rainy season. In August a new coolie hut built and new cook hut and all old P.O.W. huts torn down – said Nips, they looked from the air like a big camp!

Many rats in Nip hut – at night big holes showed in my wool socks, pieces out of my rubber stethoscope tubing, a hole in my new 39 Ticals light green shirt just bought from Bangkok by Djin Pin; and the string holding up my little mosquito net cut so it fell on my face! and rats would walk over my head and feet! Nips borrowed a cat from Chaiangaraya.

One Nip in charge of cook house (Roman Catholic wife in Japan who used to correspond with a Scottish Roman Catholic girl) gave me a Khaki cloth patch for my shirt coat. The older Nip gave me a pair of old wooden clogs. My Malayan running shoes about worn out. Wood clogs sometimes eaten at night by white ants from the floor. Nips had the usual big room – like green and blue mosquito nets.

Coolies work here all maintenance of Railway line, laying fresh crushed stone, mending embankments washed by rains, changing sleepers, levelling tracks, repairing culverts and bridges by cutting and adding new logs, placing railway marker, etc. Nips always careful that all tools washed and counted in evening and put away in tool hut – in charge of a bearded Tamil from Salem!

Presents from Nip headquarters were given out from time to time to Mandurs and coolies who worked best – eg. leather belts, canvas shoes, a sarong, cotton vest and trunks etc.

Two cases of theft in camp!

(1) Aris and another Malay, stole and sold – caught when goods of young Malay "boy" identified – tied up to trees all day and night without food and drink; bitten by mosquitoes, got swollen neck and ankles and wrists, shouted out often in distress. Aris got badly infected leg. He was taken with sick coolies to Nike but just left at the station, and reported as "runaway" to Nip headquarters at Anganum!

(2) Theft by Javanese cookhouse Mandur – tied up to tree and threatened by Nip lighting a dynamite fuse but wouldn't confess – he got loose in the night and ran off to some camp!

In August & September, 3 Malay boys died suddenly of heart failure – one on Sept. 5th had been to work that morning. He and the mentally deficient lad with cardiac Beriberi (ob. **[died]** 2nd Sept..), both shouted loudly before death from great distress – angina/anemia? Terrible to hear and not be able to do anything!

SEPTEMBER 6th, 1944

A second party of sick taken to Nike and Mr. Adaman and I go along with one older Nip. Waiting on 5th morning at Chaiangaraya Station for train, a Nip General passes – yellow flag – in special atap hut structure on open train car – funny to see these – he salutes Nip wood column there to Nip dead. We wait, but can't get a train to Nike, so return to camp – walking back Mr. Adaman and I stop at 3 Pagodas and eat our lunch – fried curried chicken and rice! Hanchow Hiono had loaned me his Nip billy can and the chicken was cooked by Adaman – grand! Next day got to Nike with coolies – got Malaria attack – rode back in the engine.

In September Walls brought me a "Bangkok Chronicle" telling of Allied landing in South France and surrounding Marseilles. Old Nip had just told me at Nike Station that English had surrendered to Germans! Where? Also Walls had word of an Allied air raid, night, on Nompradok when ninety six P.O.W. in all died from the bombing of one part of the P.O.W. camp.

OCTOBER 1944

Repeated Nip cholera inoculations was one very good thing. About October, Nip lab people from Nike came and did "glass rodding" of coolie cook house staff – our one and only coolie woman hid in the jungle. Small grayish bamboo scorpions sometimes sting coolies. One fell from roof on to my bed one night. Lucky to see it!

Djin Pin came up from Nike to visit in June – got back to Timonta from Bangkok to find us all gone. He then enquired at Butai – medical headquarters at Nike. Brought back my water bottle and gave me a present of Shakespeare, "Moment in Peking" by LinYu Tang, and four "Bangkok Chronicles", giving news of first week of Normandy Allied invasion!! I hand over his alarm clock and medicine box!

Djin Pin called again 2 or 3 weeks later, now posted to Tadin camp, near Major Nardell, between Kiandos Apalon in Burma. I read

Shakespeare through twice and memorize passages – what a boon in this Burma jungle in the monsoon rains!!

I am lucky to get Nip food – rather tasteless but so much better than coolie food – white rice, miso soup, miso fried with onions was very good and most tasty of all (one spoonful enough for a plate or bowl of rice), sweet potatoes, ducks eggs, onions, pumpkin, small brinjals, dry sweet ginger meat (ding dang), occasionally beef and chicken boiled in little pieces along with green onion tops in a curved dish as we ate it; sweet Kochang ijiu balls in tenth day holidays. Prophylactic 0.3 gm blue sugar coated quinine pill A.M. and P.M.; also some Vitamin B or yeast tablets for the table while they lasted.

Two Chinese lads were cooks, one quite comic "Chankuls". We often had wild greens to eat, sweet Sorin shaped like a tall dandelion, only eaten by Nips and Chinese. Interesting that different coolies ate different wild greens. Water supply from a boarded well beside jungle stream at foot of coolie camp.

Nips had a little bath house always with water in big metal drums heated and a board platform to bathe on – I was allowed to bathe at night after Nips all finished – but the advantage of hot water!

Major Andrews and some Aussies work at Nike Hospital, but we had no opportunity to see them when handing over coolies at the Jap office.

Only 8 coolie deaths in Piatonju camp, and none after Sept. 11th while I was there. After parties of sick evacuated to Nike, I had very little to do. Wandered around the huts, sick attended to early, observed all the native life of the jungle around when not raining and visited with Mr. Adrian who lived in separate little hut with Jahore Malay Mandur. He had belonged to Malay Royal Navy Volunteer Reserve in Singapore and before that to Singapore Volunteer Corps.

I took Malay lessons from him, writing words in a book **[see p. 158 - this tiny notebook was found among his papers]** and soon could speak simply to understand coolies' complaints. The Hindustani men to talk to were a comfort. I learned counting in Tamil since many Tamils couldn't speak Malay and I had to always get the sick man's number and name!

Work slackened off in Monsoon Aug. – October and coolies get leave to send men up to Anakuin in Burma and of course often to Nike in Thailand, to buy extras like coffee, brown sugar, chickens and coffee etc.! I twice bought smallish chickens for 10 rupees each, and they were shared by Mr. Adman, who fried them in curry sambal after being duly and properly cut by a Moslem Malay! Adrian and I also had coffee with sugar sometimes during morning or at night, and then shared my orange pekoe tea given by McTighe and now lost its savour! General health of coolies improved with these extra purchases.

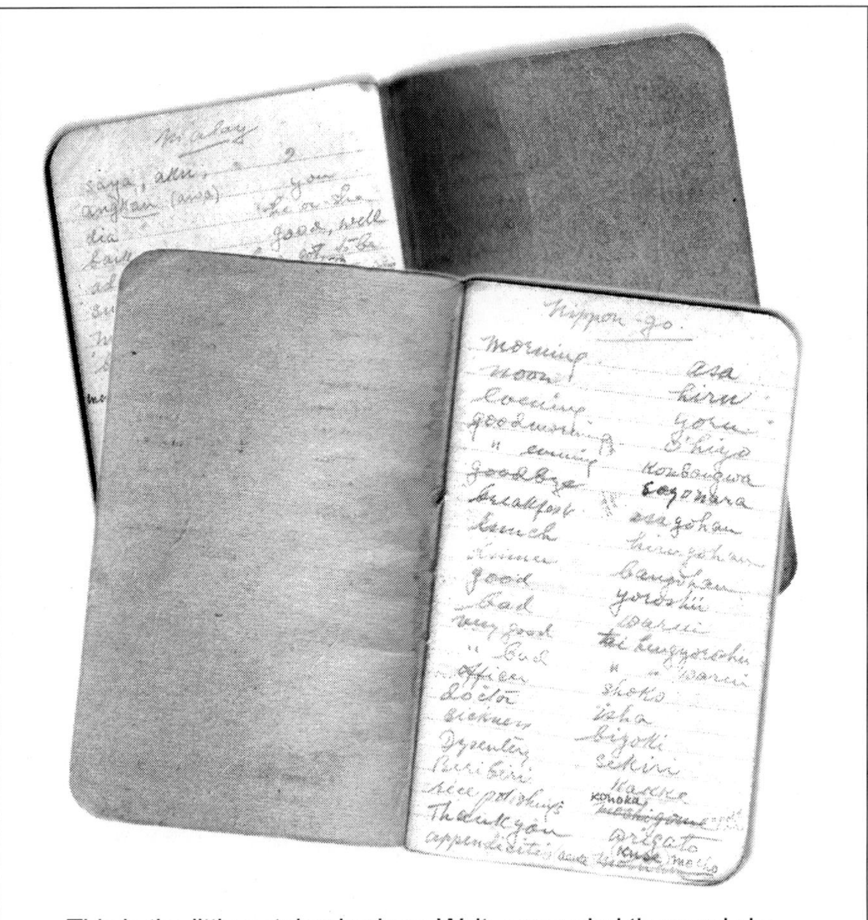

This is the little notebook where Walter recorded the words he was learning, Nippon (Japanese) in the front of the book, Malay in the back.

OCTOBER 15th, 1944
[Telegram from Father]
United Church of Canada Mission
Dhar, C.I.
Rev. F.J. Anderson
Secretary – Treasurer

CAPT. W.G. ANDERSON
INDIA MEDICAL SERVICE
P.O.W. CAMP NO. 2
THAILAND

DEAR WALTER
INQUIRE ABOUT NEW PRIVILEGE
AND SEND SHORT CABLE FREE
ATTENDED PRESBYTERY INDORE
LAST WEEK
RECEIVING LETTERS FROM MARION
ALL WELL BEST WISHES
LOVE
FATHER

[OCTOBER 1944 Continued]

In October '44, Hanchow Hiono's Nips were withdrawn and this section of railway taken over by another 5 star Butai with Headquarters at SonKuroi. (Medical supplies still from a new Nip Medical soldiers in Anganan). Coolies Tamils put on a farewell program one night, went in a body with some gifts to Nips one afternoon and offered a cock which was out! Sorry to see this group of Nips go, since we had been treated well by them on the whole. Hiono stayed to the last alone, and introduced us to new Nips – Head Hanchow Goto or Gotosan, with just three others. Their treatment of me just as courteous as the others. Goto was a regular fussy old woman with funny cackling voice – and rather hard on the coolies.

All this section of Railway and small Butai's were under the big or main Konasawa Butai of Nike. Officer Commanding was Lieutenant Colonel Konasawa, said to be a black bearded Manchurian.

New Nips at once brought in a group of about 35 Superior Javanese Railway workers (from Java and Wango). These looked healthy and stocky, but soon many had Malaria and bad headaches like the Nips!

Goto gave our hut to the Javanese and built a new and nicer hut for Nips with board platforms and table with benches – and called me in to live there too. We had sweet Kochang ijiu soup with rice flour dumpling. Some nights before going to sleep, the Nips are very fond of having the Chinese "boys" massage them! Goto asked "Swami" with the beard in charge of tools why Nips were called "master", but I called "Tuan"?! He seemed to think Tuan superior! Java lads made to do morning physical training and say prayers to Tokyo and Java, like regular Nips. Head Mandur said he worked on Railway line in Java when train wreck occurred that killed several of British troops landed there from our convoy in February 1942. I had met up later with some of these brought to Changi as P.O.W. en route elsewhere.

Coolies had to work hard now, cutting and carrying heavy tree logs for bridge repairs and also dig air raid shelter trenches for us.

Piatonju camp only about a quarter mile inside Burma from the 3 Pagodas. The Three Pagodas were small, (8 or 9 feet high) square base and fancy hanging tinkling ornaments around the "gold" top – all three in a direct North-South line, and pointing North to a narrow dip between two camel-back mountains about one mile away. To the South West was visible, a deep ravine edge which became a valley to the West and opened out into the distant plain. Pagodas looked quite old. A memorial pillar to some Japanese soldier was stood in line to the South, and a small Hindu (Tamil) shrine was at the base of the north pagoda where the Tamil coolies sometimes put offerings of paper money! The road and rail tracks ran right beside the pagodas. Between them and Chaiangaraya station was probably the highest point on the railway, with exception of one spot near Kinzaiyok or Bramkasi. Always a strong feeling standing in boundary between two countries – more so here in the mountainous jungle, over 305 kilos from Nompradak.

During and after monsoon, jungle undergrowth increased greatly, specially the common weed growing up to five feet with little fuzzy mauve fall flowers in clusters. Our camp area okay, so not affected with mud as in some places! About September – October very many kinds of brilliant butterflies seen, but still very few new kinds than I had seen before in the Nilgirisiu? in South India. Trees too tall to see much bird life – saw one hooper. Saw wild chicken (look just like small Indian Village fowl), often in tracks, when walking to Anganan. Frequently hear them cackling in the jungle, Javanese lad caught one that came close and ate it!

Many kinds of jungle ferns seen growing in the moss high up in trees – also certain orchids (Major Bruce Anderson Australian Imperial Force told me later, he collected forty different kinds of orchids; while an English Officer had an excellent collection of butterflies). Bird like Indian King Crow but with two long paradise tail feathers in black, was quite common.

Interesting huge flying squirrels seen after the monsoon, at dusk, silhouetted in tree against the sky – looked size of small monkey; climb to top of tree, then glide away to base of another tree, perhaps 60 – 80 yards away, and gliding around some trees in the way! Many small coloured snakes, one green viper!

New Nip food rations seemed better than before – fair amount of meat from Nike. Chinese cook made "croquettes" with chopped meat and onions!

A new dresser, H.B. Luis, Indian or dark Eurasian from Malaya, posted to camp, knew very little! Couldn't speak English well anyway.

A Tamil, very ill with pneumonia – Luis and I kept a temperature chart for him and I kept him alive with rationed small amounts of my own M & B tablets I had brought from Changi for personal use. I kept feeling I had to spare him a few more tablets, as he worsened whenever tablets stopped. Terrible to feel you hold power of life and choose who to let live and who let die when drugs limited! This man recovered enough to be evacuated to Kinzaiyok coolie Hospital early December.

NOVEMBER 1944

Mr. Adaman was withdrawn to Nike in November. The Nips made a box trap (a chicken head bait) and caught a big grey striped wild cat one night. This was drowned and stewed and eaten! Too strong! Tamils caught iguana and made curry of it, white meat – tasted like young chicken.

Great disturbance one night when Tamil jagoh down the track saw two eyes shining – thought it tiger or thieves! Whole camp took up cry – Nips rushed out with rifles – to find a young black and white steer from Anganan Nip Camp – tied up and killed for camp meat next morning and nothing said to Anganan!

Great camp clean up because of expected inspection by Nip big Number 1! – He stopped a few minutes and did not even get out of his trolley car!

All during monsoon Nip troops (young two star privates etc.) and war supplies, cases, lorries, occasional light tank etc. moved on into Burma. Many open carloads of old sewer pipes or oil pipe lines (?) came down into Thailand. Often train loads of Nip sick and wounded (?) came down from Burma to Nike, and these were a very sorry looking lot.

After the monsoon I spend many afternoons alone, clearing new Jungle growth from the P.O.W. cemetery close to our huts and hidden by growth. It contained 68 graves – 5 Aussie and rest all Dutch. Special big dedication cross in all Burma cemeteries. When entrance lastly cleared, Nip laughed and inferred I was preparing a place for myself in case of being hit in an air raid!

I get permit to go to Walls 299 kilos camp for Christmas Day; where Walls was to lay on a chicken curry feed etc. Great plans go astray! As monsoon stopped, allied air activity increased – almost daily, planes passed high over head – could tell the difference in engine sound. Camp alert gong would be rung! How I wished one would let down a rope! And I dreamed of signalling my name in Semaphore **[apparatus for signalling]**!

Because of cold weather in November – December at night, we kept a constant log fire going in a pit inside hut. Did same in monsoon to dry out damp clothing and blankets. One night a plane passed low overhead and Nip adjutant soaked himself in a hurry to dump a full four gallon tin of water on the fire!

In November, through the Nips and coolies, I had word of Americans landing somewhere in Philippines.

DECEMBER 8th, 1944

About 5 P.M. had regular allied air attack – could see many distant planes, but one circled around our area – dropped a bomb at Sonkurai headquarters and one in jungle near Chaiangraya Station. Could hear repeated bombings back near Nike. Occasional little bursts of machine gunning. All very exciting – hiding in slit trench in jungle out of the clearing. Nips seemed to have known of this "Anniversary" raid, and were on the lookout for planes. Coolies all excited and told to run into the jungle. No actual damage to lives near us done.

DECEMBER 10th, 1944

Another raid about six pm. – this time I counted twenty great four engine "Liberators" in formation turn right over us, fairly low and few minutes later, could hear roar and feel earth tremble as they dropped bombs on Apalon in Burma. An iron bridge at Apalon or Anakuin had previously been hit. Very thrilling! Scared too! Coolies get letters from Malaya, telling of Nips badly bombed there too – they know the war going against the Japs. Nips had told coolies English are trying to converge on Mandalay.

Few days later, word came of a fairly heavy air attack in a Butai headquarters in Kamburi. (The Medical Butai Headquarters was burnt out in it)

Train with some of our coolies going on leave to Malaya said to be machine gunned.

DECEMBER 17th, 1944

Sudden order for me to be withdrawn to Nike! Trolley car waiting on the track! What a scramble to "pack" things dumped into a big basket and dumped into trolley. (Nips to be moved soon too – Piatonju to be taken over by Artillery group!) Meet Walls at Sonkurai and we are taken on by trolley to Nike – there to Nip Headquarters! and then carry our stuff on over the bridge to coolie camp where we join Major Bruce Anderson and an Australian Imperial Force orderly and McTighe spend night talking over "news" e.g. fall of Saipan and Tojo.

DECEMBER 18th, 1944

Making our coolie rounds with Major Anderson and get sudden orders to leave in the afternoon. New coolie women and children from Malaya, swollen with beriberi and anemia. We met up with Dunning and Chandler and kit at Nip Medical Headquarters. My kit far too heavy

– carry it on a pole! Chandler is in a straw hat! We help to lower a big petrol drum into ground hole and a Nip is crushed in thigh, when it slips out of ropes.

Waiting for train in p.m. at Nike station I meet the former Timonta Hanchow (now two star Corporal) returning "to Japan" from Mandalay. He says former Timonta adjutant died "of malaria", (speaks Malay). We get into train evening on top of red lead bars! – leave when dark.

DECEMBER 19th, 1944

Arrive at Kinzaiyok O.K. in the A.M. – spend the day off on a distant siding in case of Allied air raids. Given two fried eggs by British Other Rank cook in a Nip kitchen where we walk to get food. Three Nips are with us. Train comes again at dusk.

DECEMBER 20th, 1944

Arrive in the morning in Kanburi – Leave train (abandon my split boots) and hide in trees during reccy plane raid. Fear of bombs or machine guns in train! Escorted by Nip Medical Sergeant to Dai Ni Coolie Hospital Camp. All kits opened and searched at Gate! Meet Major Crawford again. We then join "K" and "L" Force in the camp. Only a few of "K" Force still missing. Find I was the last out of Burma, though Major Davies, Australian Imperial Force, later went in again to Apalon for short time.

Only Captains Wallace, Young, Dawson and Lennox are employed in Dai Ni on coolie wards. The rest do only camp chores – eg. Water parties to river.

I get a sleeping place between Major Hugh Henderson Royal Army Medical Corps and Major Crankshaw, Australian Imperial Force. Nice to be amongst your own kind again! About 300!

DECEMBER 20th – 31st, 1944

Dai Ni, large coolie hospital camp, many long bamboo atap huts out in open, near railway track, about one and a half miles from big P.O.W.

Officers camp and Kanburi town. Nip regiment Medical Headquarters since early December bombings and five Nips in charge. "Poppy" is an old Major who lived in coolie canteen and liked to sell bananas and play with Tamil women! "Puss-in-boats" is Sergeant Major. Lieutenant Colonel Benson Royal Army Medical Corps is our Officer Commanding ("L" Force) but is "ill" in bed. Major Crawford actually in charge.

Many of British Other Ranks and Anglo Indian lads seem to behave a bit out of control! We march to office for "tenko" **[review during which beatings took place]** roll call in Japanese, in the dark A.M. and P.M. Also native dressers parade! Very poor.

I see some of my former coolie patients here. We are not allowed to talk to coolies or dressers. Found Djin Pin living with other Nip group at far end of camp.

Daily water parties about a mile to Kay Noi River 4 or 5 in A.M. and 3 in afternoon to bring water in pails and buckets – back on bamboo poles for kitchen and Nip baths. Two of us to a pole. We occasionally get a dip in the river on last trip. Really no other way to bathe. Officers take turns in daily charge of water parties. Trouble when some of men drop out and parade, number is reduced. I had this trouble December 31st and had to chase out a chap again whom the Nips stopped. Chaps do secret trade with Thai vendors on way to river when Nip guard not near.

"Poppy" allows us Christmas day holiday and lets us buy an old ox for dinner – frightfully tough – old meat – can't eat it! We are allowed to have 11 A.M. Xmas service. Major Crawford read the lesson, I read prayers and Captain Todd spoke – service held in sick hut.

I speak to the men one night on Canada in only ten or fifteen minutes, notice after parade.

Major Mardell and I go with Captain Clarkson to big P.O.W. officer's camp before New Years for dental treatment. Major DeSolganoff of Indian Medical Service is Senior Medical Officer there, we find all officers there have books and watches and pens and all valuables removed by Nips and we find a search going on. We don't like that atmosphere!

We were yelled at by Korean guard at the gate. See a big seventeen foot deep and wide trench around the camp.

[This was the end of Walter's diaries and the very last page in his small journal. However, we did find little pieces of papers with various information and have tried to fit them into these pages where we felt it would continue the remaining story. Walter did write some wonderful letters to his parents once he was free and they are also included.]

The author's workspace, piled high with just a fraction of the materials she culled from boxes and shelves of letters, notebooks, photos, reports, clippings and little scraps of paper. In order to compile and research this book, all that and more had to be sorted and organized for this volume.

1945

FEBRUARY 20th, 1945
GENERAL HEADQUARTERS, INDIA,
Adjutant General's Branch,
Simla

Rev. F.J. Anderson
U.C.C. Mission,
Dhar, (C.I.)

Dear Sir,

I am directed to inform you that information has been received from the India Office, that your son No. MZ-23691 Lieut. W. G. Anderson, I.M.S., is interned in No. 2 Prisoner of War Camp Thailand.

Any further information received will be communicated to you without delay.

Yours faithfully,
Jnr. Comdr.,
For Adjutant General in India

[Added in pencil:]
asking source & date of information 26.2.45

MARCH 6th, 1945
GENERAL HEADQUARTERS, INDIA,
Adjutant General's Branch,
Simla

Rev. F.J. Anderson,
Secretary – Treasurer,
United Church of Canada Mission,
DHAR, CENTRAL INDIA
Dear Sir,

I am directed to acknowledge receipt of your letter dated 26.2.45 and to say that the information regarding your son Lieut. W.G. Anderson, I.M.S., was forwarded to us by the India Office on information given to them by his next of kin resident in the United Kingdom.

We regret we have no definite news regarding the British Prisoners of War who were reported to have been sunk last July, but, you may rest assured that any information received here will be communicated to you without delay.

Snr. Comdr.,
For ADJUTANT GENERAL IN INDIA

[Note how confusing these letters are, the one dated Feb. 20/45 knew where Walter was. Lack of communication I suppose.]

MARCH 23rd, 1945
Dai Ni to Dai Ichi

MARCH 25, 1945
[From Father]
United Church of Canada Mission
Dhar, Central India
Rev. F. J. Anderson
Secretary – Treasurer

Capt. W. G. Anderson
No. MZ 23691
Indian Medical Service
POW CAMP NO. 2
Thailand

DEAR WALTER
CAPT. ROLAND BACON (MISSIONARY)
KILLED THIRTEENTH
CAPT. FISHER, YOUR CAMP, INFORMED
HIS FATHER IN ENGLAND OF RED
CROSS GIFTS RECEIVED. GOOD NEWS
LOVE
FATHER

APRIL 1st, 1945
[From Mother]
Dhar, C. I.

Dearest Walter
Tis Easter Sunday and we are away to church, as usual, except that we seem to carry out a routine, with heavy hearts.

Prayer and Love
Mother

APRIL 6th, 1945
Dai Ichi to Tamaran

APRIL 15th, 1945
[Telegram from Father]
United Church of Canada Mission
Dhar, Central India
Rev. F.J. Anderson

CAPT. W. G. ANDERSON
INDIAN MEDICAL SEVICE
POW CAMP NO. 2
THAILAND

DEAR WALTER
PRESIDENT ROOSEVELT DIED
LAST THURSDAY. TRUMAN NEW
PRESIDENT
ARTHUR DOBSON RETURNING
TO MISSION SERVICE JUNE
WE GO "OAKVILLE" LANDOUR
TWENTYSIXTH
ALL WELL LOVE
FATHER

APRIL 25TH, 1945
[Telegram from Father]
CAPT. W.G. ANDERSON I.M.S.
INDIAN MEDICAL SERVICE
POW CAMP NO. 2
THAILAND

DEAR WALTER
BECKWITH ARRIVED
ENTERTAINED REV. GERALD BELL
OF WEST CHINA LAST WEEK END
WE GO TO 'OAKVILLE' LANDOUR
TOMORROW. MOIR LEFT TODAY
LOVE
FATHER

MAY 5TH, 1945
[Telegram from Father]
United Church of Canada Mission
'Oakville' Landour, C.I.
Rev. F. J. Anderson
Secretary – Treasurer

CAPT. W.G. ANDERSON
INDIAN MEDICAL SERVICE
POW CAMP NO 2
THAILAND

DEAR WALTER
HAVE ENJOYED OUR FIRST
WEEK HERE.
LONGING FOR YOUR RETURN
AND WORD FROM YOU.
ALL GOES WELL WITH US.
MOIR GRANTED EARLY
FURLOUGH
LOVE
FATHER

MAY 25th, 1945
Tamaran to Nakoni chari??

MAY 26th – 27th, 1945
Nakoni chari ?? to Bangkok

MAY 28th – 29th, 1945
Bangkok to Sraburi & Pratchi

JUNE 2nd, 1945
[Telegram from Father]
United Church of Canada Mission
"Oakville' Landour
Rev. F.J. Anderson
Secretary – Treasurer

CAPT. W.G. ANDERSON
INDIAN MEDICAL SERVICE
POW CAMP NO. 2
THAILAND

DEAR WALTER
HALF HOLIDAY OVER
CELEBRATING IN MUSSOORIE TODAY
LETTERS FROM MARION RECEIVED
ALL WELL WITH US
HOPING FOR REUNION THIS YEAR
BEST WISHES, LOVE
FATHER

JUNE ??, 1945
[Telegram from Father]
United Church of Canada Mission
"Oakville", Mussoorie, U.P.
Rev. F. J. Anderson
Secretary - Treasurer

CAPT. W. G. ANDERSON
INDIAN MEDICAL SERVICE
P.O.W. CAMP NO.2
THAILAND

DEAR WALTER
REVS. HILDA JOHNSON AND BRYCE
BACK IN INDIA.
WOODSTOCK SCHOOL SALE SUCCESS

SLIGHT EARTHQUAKE JUNE FOURTH
PLAN LEAVE HERE FOR DHAR
TWENTY SEVENTH ALL WELL
LOVE FATHER

JUNE 24th, 1945
[From Mother]
Landour, Mussoorie, U.P.

My Dear Walter

We are getting ready to return to Dhar, on Wednesday, after holiday. Moir and Margaret going home with children. God Bless you.

Love,
Mother

AUGUST 6th, 1945
[Telegram from Father]
United Church of Canada Mission
Dhar, Central India
Rev. F. J. Anderson
Secretary – Treasurer
CAPT. W. G. ANDERSON
INDIAN MEDICAL SERVICE
P.O.W. CAMP NO 2
THAILAND

DEAR WALTER
SENT FREE CABLE THROUGH RED
CROSS TODAY. ALL WELL.
GOOD WEATHER. HOPES BRIGHTER.
SUNSHINE PEEPING THROUGH ALL
CLOUDS EVERYWHERE
GOOD CHEER LOVE
FATHER

AUGUST 16th, 1945

FREE !!!

These are two (enlarged) pages of the miniscule (1.5"x3") calendar that Walter created and maintained, to count off the days and months of his internment. The ones shown here cover the periods of January to May, and June to November 3, 1945.

AFTER THE WAR

AUGUST 31st, 1945
[To Parents]
Camp at Prachai, Thailand
[subsequently noted:] *rec'd Dhar Sept. 11th, 1945*

From Capt W.G. Anderson I.M.S.
Letter No. 1.

Dear Father and Mother

This is a sudden unexpected opportunity of writing a letter which may or may not get through but is worth trying. One hardly knows how to begin, or what to say all at once! I've only been able to send you three postcards in the three and a half years – 1st of June 20 '42, which you received, then Feb. 22nd '43, and by mere chance the last was Oct 3 '43!

Your letters up to Nov. 1st '42 were rec'd on April 4th '43; and letters from Nov. '42 to 7th Mar. '44 I rec'd 27th Dec. '44. None since. A Christmas card of Marion's posted 24th Oct. '43 came Dec. 27th '44.

No need to worry about me – well and probably heavier than when in India by a few pounds. I had Malaria at least 19 times to date, and Beriberi **[deficiency of Vit. B]** *off and on, from poor food at times, but now things are better.*

In brief, I was in the Indian Reinforcement Camp outside Singapore on landing, and later had to move into the city where, for the last few days of the battle, we had a "sticky" time from the general bombing and shelling.

When the Japs took over, we as P.O.W.s went to Changi Cantonment **[February 16, 1942]** *on Eastern tip of the Island. Jack Leech and I were together until he went off in a party to Japan, on May 15th '43, as Chaplain. He was well.*

I remained in Changi till June 25th '43 having been Med. Officer all the time to various groups of the 11th Division. Only European troops, of course, were in Changi.

Indians were taken elsewhere. When settled in we had a fairly good time, though food was poor and we wondered when we would be free again!! June 25th I left for Thailand with a group of M.O's going up the Kra Isthmus by rail. We were distributed among the camps working on the Burma Thai Railroad, but not with our own troops.

From July '43 to Jan. '44 I was doctor in a coolie camp of about 500 Tamils, Malays, Chinese and a few Hindustanis – people to whom, at least, I could talk. I lived with Chinese overseers and a good Chinese Dresser who alone spoke English. He was a great help and brought me a few things from Bangkok when he was allowed to make the trip; also interpreted to the Japs in charge. A Scottish Med. Orderly was with me in this camp for two and half months, otherwise I've been the only European.

June to Dec. '44, I was in a smaller Coolie Camp just inside Burma and lived all the six months in the same hut with the Japs. The Hindustani coolies also came to the camp. A friendly Malay Overseer alone spoke English, and I learned some Malay to talk to the patients. I read through Shakespeare in this camp.

We're now just waiting for arrangements to take us away. Some go by plane but the sick first.

It is certainly thrilling to be able to write again. Your letter last year said you would still be in C.I. **[Central India]** *in July '45 and I trust this finds you there. Hoping to see you again in the near future.*

With love
Walter

SEPTEMBER 1st, 1945
Pratchai to Bangkok

SEPTEMBER 2nd, 1945
[To parents]
In the Godown Sheds on the Docks, Bangkok

Dear Father and Mother

This is the first official air mail we have been allowed to send. I wrote one from our last P.O.W. Camp at Pratchai (near Sraburi) Thailand August 31st but we were told it was not official and was hoped to be able to be put aboard a plane by an officer coming to Bangkok. It was the first chance worth taking after such a long period! A medical party was suddenly called on the evening of August 31st to come to Bangkok harbour at once for any medical jobs there might be in connection with sick ex-prisoners of war brought here. So far we have been waiting. Light sick and gradually parties of others were to be evacuated a few days after we left straight from an airodrome near Pratchai camp. I had half the medical ward in the camp hospital while there.

We got everything soaked that night in the open lorry in a heavy rain but it was worth it on the first stage of the journey home! The Thai driver brought us to an empty wing of some big building at 1:30 a.m. where the Thais provided us with real wooden beds, and served us a good breakfast on real plates and a tablecloth! – The first tablecloth and real bread and butter and milk that I have had in the last three and a half years! We then made our way to the sheds here amid many cheers of Thai children and others in the city streets as we drove through. Their sympathies have certainly not been with the Japs.

Well, I won't give any events that happened during this long time – I gave a brief outline in my other letter which may have got through. I will only repeat in case not, that I am absolutely o.k. and looking forward to being taken back to India. Many are going by plane from here daily but of course medicals should be among the last to go and perhaps with heavy sick, in hospital ships. Present arrangements, however, are that a large new hospital unit is being flown here soon and there is a chance of some surplus medicals then getting away. By air to Calcutta would be a great thrill. We hear something that ex P.O.W.s are all going on to Bangalore for a while first. Very glad to get a third bunch of mail from you this a.m. some short letters and cards of varying dates from October '43 to October '44. The last addressed to Thailand shows me that my third P.C. to you (undated) of Oct. 3, '43 got through. Also glad to know you will be in C.I. through 1945. I must have Christmas at home. Being up in the Thai Burma jungle I did not get your broadcast message of December '43 or your cable of October '44. But I don't think they would have reached me in any case. But many thanks all the same. Closing now as I have no envelope (one just to hand!!). We can send an airmail once a week. I hear ex P.O.W.s have been evacuated from Japan so I hope Jack Leech is in India by now. We hear by radio the Japs officially have signed the end of the war this morning. Plenty of armed Japs still around here but they only look at us! Nice to have the big wide river in front of us, Bangkok is some miles upriver from the sea though the tide rises and falls. The city itself has many modern buildings, road circuses etc. but is very picturesque with typical Siamese architectural temples and palace.

I might say that April '43 I received a letter from Moir and one from Dr. Campbell written in July '42. I heard from Jack Leech in a later letter from Bessie that he **[Campbell]** *had died November 1st. News in the same mail batch. In December '44 I received letters from Miss Louise Scott and Miss Gruchy. Very sorry to hear of Dr. Alice Anderson's death. Glad a new doctor has come. News received of the death of Mrs. D.F. Smith, Pastor Singh and poor Quintie. I won't write more now but must possess my soul in patience till the great day of getting away comes. Love to you all and Marion and regards to friends till I see them. Sorry this has to be pencil. Have no ink.*

Walter

SEPTEMBER 4TH, 1945
[To parents]
Bangkok Airport

Dear Father and Mother

Another chance to get off a few lines (3rd). My last was written in the Docks Godown on the 2nd. The same afternoon I was posted out to the Airport Hospital here in connection with Indian evacuees etc. It certainly gives one a thrill to see so many planes coming in every day, loading up men and taking off again so soon. Only three weeks ago if we heard the familiar sound that planes make we would have had our eye on a good shelter or hiding place so as not to get mixed up in anything, unless, of course one was in an open and recognized P.O.W. Camp. Even then it was a bit uncomfortable if the planes came very close. However, the last camp we were in at Pratchai we seldom saw a plane.

I expect we may be leaving here very shortly as the new people take over. Hope to get another good look around Bangkok. It is such a picturesque place. In front of our Pratchai Camp was a huge rocky hill with a Buddhist Pagoda and temple on it. It has always been the ambition of many of us to climb to the top and get the view of the country around. This wish came true so unexpectedly! Buddha himself is supposed to have rested on a ledge of the rock up there.

Today I am wearing a fairly new and decent shirt, shorts and stockings which I have managed to keep by the whole time for just such an occasion at the end! Lady Mountbatten may be inspecting the hospital today. There is a pretty Canal in front which makes good swimming. The Siamese climate is really on the whole better than mid-India – always green.

(When war ended in Singapore February '42 I had lost everything except what I had in pack and haversack on me! Have managed to pick up or buy things here and there. Should have left that trunk etc. at home). Hoping to see you soon.

Love Walter

SEPTEMBER 5th, 1945
[To parents]
Airport Hospital
Bangkok

Dear Father and Mother

Herewith the 4th letter since freedom dawned! Without going into details of the many things that happened during the last years, for which there is quite time enough later, it is a bit awkward now to be able to send mail fairly frequently. Even pencils and any blank paper were taken away from us latterly and writing became almost a lost art. A few pencil stubs were allowed in the Camp Hospital wards, but limited. I've always managed to keep a small indelible pencil in the bottom of my purse! Since last Dec. the Nips began putting the screws on and searches were put on at any odd moment to try and catch us with prohibited articles. It is astonishing sometime how the Nips were fooled. I must say that certain valuables handed in were given a receipt and these things recovered (such as my ring) after the end.

Hoping to get another trip into the city today to have a good look around and see what there is going in, I think with a Thai doctor.

Again love to all and hoping to see you soon.

Walter
Hope Bessie had heard from Jack. Regards to Moir etc.

SEPTEMBER 6TH, 1945
[To parents]
Airport Hospital
Bangkok

Dear Mother and Father

Herewith the 5th. Was able to send off my first cable of 12 words yesterday. May be able to send another soon. Yesterday's was too rushed and I may not have filled out everything on it. Anyway, earlier letters I hope will have reached you sooner by air.

Yesterday morning three of us from here, one a Dutch doctor, were taken into Bangkok City in the Thai ambulance by the local little Thai doctor (he is M.O. sub-lieutenant in the Thai Air Force), and he very kindly showed us over the city, returning at 5 pm.

Most of the Thai officers and many others speak English. He told me "English is spoken everywhere; I will not die if I speak English!" First he introduced us to the main Bangkok Hospital and a Thai surgeon, young and pleasant, showed us around for 2 hours – a very nice place and fairly well equipped, though the Nips went off with their portable xray outfit. Some of the buildings are being used by us now for heavy sick who can't travel by air. We then saw the university grounds – closed 3 or 4 years since Nip occupation. Then several monuments. Then, by sheer good luck we got taken into the very heart of the big Royal Bangkok pagoda temple where the jade or emerald Buddha sits aloft. The massive doors of the inner chamber were specially opened for us by the man in charge – a Col. in the Thai army. The endless pieces of paintings (the whole wars? of Hammon's monkeys with the giants), The coloured wares of glass and stones, the inner golden pagoda, the bright coloured roofs with characteristic Siamese cupolas resembling head of certain bird -- I can't begin to describe it. We then walked about the Royal Palace grounds, passed our new C. in C. **[Commander in Chief]***, called at the Thai Dr's fiancée's house, went shopping (interesting silver metal inlay work "mello", peculiar to Siam), had coffee in a café and joined by 2 more Thai Air Force engineer young officers, another doctor's brother – and so back again – a full warm and tiring day without lunch, but what a treat after all this time!*

Now I'm satisfied and waiting for the trip home!

Love
Walter

SEPTEMBER 7th, 1945
[To parents]
Airport Hospital
Bangkok

Dear Mother and Father;

I think this my 6th. One is now quite used to seeing parties in transit passing through and being carried away overhead by plane. Our turn should not be much longer delayed now. There is very little to do now, just look after and dispose of any new sick in parties going off. We are now on a diet new for us, plenty of fried eggs, meats, fruit, bread, tin fish, etc. and a little goes a long way on a stomach used to rice and vegetable stew! Many get upset, especially from fats, and travelling by lorry, etc. I can't take much myself and get periods after, sometimes, of a bit of nausea and diarrhea. But one certainly doesn't mind getting used to good food again!

Good news – One of our senior Ex. P.O.W. Medical Lt. Col's was in just now, and says we are finished now, new people take over and I shall likely leave by plane for Rangoon tomorrow!! Advised even to have light packs ready this afternoon.

I looked over a few former Indian Troops yesterday who were for evacuation today. Most of the jobs here just now are treating the Java Dutch cook and orderly staff (they wait for ships to Java of course), and this has become sort of a district clinic for Thais! Opened up a large abscess on a Thai boy's hand under general anesthetic yesterday. His uncle came in the bright yellow robes of a Buddhist Priest.

One feels so ignorant about all the new drugs on the market, e.g. sulphathi-azol, s-quanidine, penicillin etc.

I set Sept. 16th as possible day for leaving Thailand – can hardly believe it may be tomorrow!

Heaps of love,
Walter

SEPTEMBER 8th, 1945
Bangkok to Rangoon

SEPTEMBER 9th, 1945
[To parents]
Rangoon Dist.
c/o Recovered P.W. Mail Centre,
Bombay, India Command

Dear Mother and Father;

Opportunity of sending off a chitti **[note]** *from here with all the facilities for sending mail and a few cables, one is a bit overwhelmed when opportunities for so long have been so rare. There seemed to be no restriction for the Japanese writing postcards home, but I wonder how many of their cards got to Japan. I know the few that we wrote were kept for months before being forwarded – probably too few Jap. interpreters to read them quickly.*

Arrived here and sent off a formal cable to you yesterday. It was a great thrill, and perhaps one can now realize something of what a bird sees and feels! Funny to recall what restrictions Capt. Jo. Gilchrist put upon going up long ago! At our time we were more than half as high again as Doda Beta! I suppose your monsoon weather is pretty well over by now – mid Sept. It is not over here, in fact we seem to have travelled back into it! I remember in the Japanese coolie camp just inside Burma last Oct. we had more rain than in Sept. but being storey ground **[ground level]** *there wasn't the frightful wind of other places along their railway and living with the Nips in their own hut was better protection from the weather than huts put up for coolies or others. It is very strange to be lying on a mattress again with sheets. I have used one of Jack Leech's good blankets since Jan. '43 and was asked to keep it safe for him. I still have it though it needs a bit of cleaning. The only thing of my own I saved was the thin grey flannelette sheet, which wore out to shreds – very sorry to lose it! For the first time I had oatmeal porridge and real bacon with the fried eggs for breakfast this a.m. Someone suggested a statue should be put up to the Thailand duck – duck's eggs which we could get from time to time have literally been a life saver. My old egg prejudice has gone!! Dutch officers introduced me to hot omelettes (with sugar or jam if available): Another life saver was the little "urad ki dal" - small and dark green* **[lentils]**.

Well, so much chat for this time.

Love
Walter

INDIAN POSTS AND TELEGRAPHS DEPARTMENT.

TO

Anderson

news wonderful thanks love

Marion

Walter's sister Marion cabled him September 13, 1945: "News wonderful thanks love Marion".

SEPTEMBER 14th, 1945
[To parents]
Rangoon

Capt. W.G. Anderson, I.M.S. (MZ23691)
c/o Recovered P.O.W. Mail Central,
Bombay, India Command

Dear Father and Mother

Anxious to get recent word from you, but that will likely be when I arrive in India. Our departure from here depends on many things, so hardly worth risking sending Indian mail on here I should think. It is nice to see papers and magazines again and try to fill up the gaps in our knowledge of events. It is amazing how in some camps hidden radios were kept going most of the time – frightfully risky thing to do of course! The Nips used to do sudden search raids of huts and kits etc, many unexpected, but again many times one of the Koreans would tip off our people and of course word would go rapidly round to be prepared! What annoyed me was that being more or less free for so long up in coolie camps, I had to give up certain articles not allowed to be held in P.O.W. camps only in April of this year. I had kept Rs 229 **[rupees]** *in notes and Rs 5 in change all the time till this April – had coins taken, and then destroyed the notes rather than let the Nips get it! Interesting to see how we will treat the Nips now, but myself I don't want to see anymore! Andy Taylor will have had a lot of experience by now.*

Well love.
Walter

SEPTEMBER 15th, 1945
INDIAN POSTS AND TELEGRAPHS DEPARTMENT
CANADIAN MISSION, DHAR, INDIA

ARRIVED SAFELY BRITISH HANDS HOPE BE HOME SOON WRITING ADDRESS LETTERS AND TELEGRAMS TO C/O RECOVERED P.W. MAILCENTER BOMBAY INDIA COMMAND
WALTER

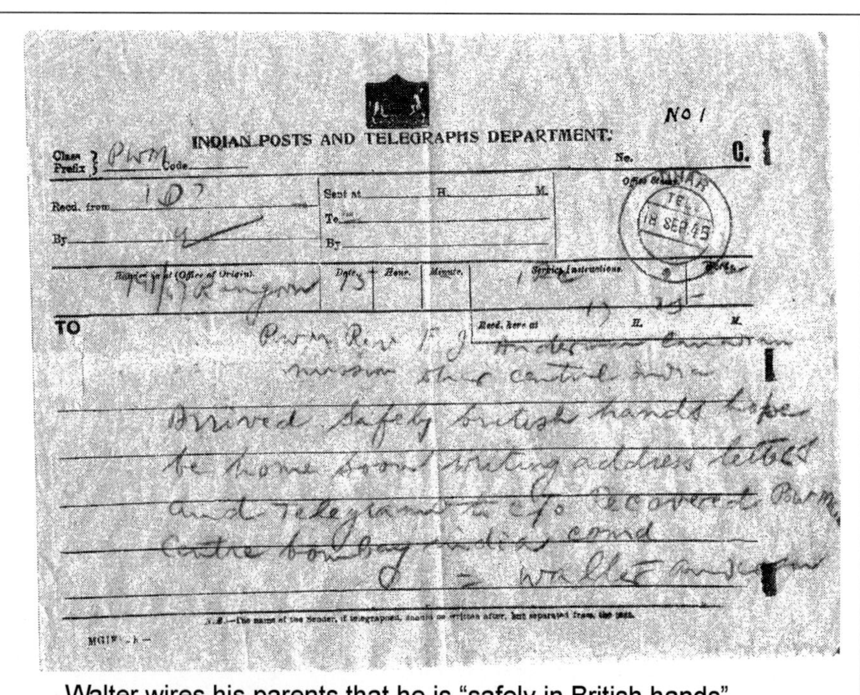

NO 1

INDIAN POSTS AND TELEGRAPHS DEPARTMENT.

Class Prefix } PWM Code No. C.

Recd. from 1 D 7 Sent at H. M.
By To
By

Office stamp: DHAR TEL 18 SEP 45

Number (Office of Origin). Rangoon | Date 15 | Hour | Minute | Service Instructions | Words

TO Recd. here at H. M.

Arrived safely british hands hope be home soon writing address letters and telegrams to c/o recovered ... centre bombay india comd = Walter

N.B.—The name of the Sender, if telegraphed, should be written after, but separated from, the text.

MGIPC—

Walter wires his parents that he is "safely in British hands".

SEPTEMBER 15th, 1945
[From parents]
United Church of Canada Mission
Dhar, Central India
Rev. F.J. Anderson
Secretary – Treasurer

My dear Walter

Our hearts are full of praise and thanksgiving to God for your wonderful deliverance and present safety and well being. Your 3rd P.O.W. card reached us July 1944 and since then we have been torn between hope and despair of hearing from you in view of the terrible P.O.W. camp horrors made known by the Press and Radio. When V.J.. [Victory in Japan] came we were on the alert to receive a cable but realized that every released P.O.W. could not cable immediately. When your three Air mail letters came on the 11th we could scarcely believe our eyes but held our breath till we knew they were not of ancient date and then to crown our joy we learned that you were not only living and safe but absolutely well also. I could scarcely listen as Mother read for the song in my heart that "this my son was dead and is alive again, was lost and is found", oh what a relief and joy your letters brought.

We telegraphed the glad tidings to all our Mission Stations and sent a cable to Dr. Armstrong. Already reply cables have come from Marion and the MacKay's on behalf of missionaries on furlough. Two more letters have come from you but not the cable referred to. We can now patiently wait a few more days or even weeks if necessary for your return but we do long to see you soon.

Bessie Leech had a cable from Jack on the 10th, I believe, from Melbourne, Australia.

Am told that I cannot cable to Bangkok as we wished to do, but this may get through to you before you leave Bangkok. All well here, wire us where and when to meet you. Shall we bring you supplies of anything – clothing etc.?

Love
Father and Mother

SEPTEMBER 15, 1945
[To Dr. Armstrong],
Rangoon.

Dear Dr. Armstrong:

Just a note while one has early opportunity of breaking silence after so long. It is hard to describe one's feelings of being in a free world again, and a bit difficult to begin picking up all the old threads. It will be a month tomorrow since our particular group was last surrounded by Japanese sentries – news of our freedom reaching us on August 16th evening. You may well imagine we could scarcely believe it, but we lost no time in hoisting a Union Jack and Dutch flag for the N.E.I. people, and sang "The King" as best we could with lumps in our throats. This was at a camp in Thailand, or Siam, some distance North-East of Bangkok.

After the fall of Singapore, I was in a P.O.W. camp on the island until the end of June, 1943, when I came up into Thailand on an all Medical party for various labour camps working on the Thai-Burma Railroad. I spent five months as doctor in a Java Dutch camp, then spent the whole of 1944 in native coolie camps (Tamils, Malays, Chinese, Javanese, and fortunately for me also a few Hindustani people) on the Burma-Siam boundary. I lived five months in a hut with Chinese, and over six months in the Japanese hut. It was pretty dense forest along the railway. One had to learn a bit of Malay to speak to people. That was the lingua franca. Odd bits of news filtered through from native overseers, etc., who got a few days leave in Bangkok or Kanburi. In April of this year I was returned to a regular P.O.W. camp in Thailand, and was looking after a ward in the camp hospital when the end came. We flew here to Rangoon from Bangkok a few days ago, and I expect to be going on to India soon.

The whole three and a half years I only received mail on three occasions, and was only able to send three post-cards out.

Walter G. Anderson

First Word Is Received from Dr. Anderson

The following letter from Capt. W. G. Anderson, prisoner of war, to Dr. A. E. Armstrong, is the first to be received since his release:

September 15, 1945, Rangoon.

Dear Dr. Armstrong:

Just a note while one has early opportunity of breaking silence after so long. It is hard to describe one's feelings of being in a free world again, and a bit difficult to begin picking up all the old threads. It will be a month tomorrow since our particular group was last surrounded by Japanese sentries—news of our freedom reaching us on August 16th evening. You may well imagine we could scarcely believe it, but we lost no time in hoisting a Union Jack and a Dutch flag for the N.E.I. people, and sang "The King" as best we could with lumps in our throats. This was at a camp in Thailand, or Siam, some distance North-East of Bangkok.

After the fall of Singapore, I was in a P.O.W. camp on the island until the end of June, 1943, when I came up into Thailand on an all medical party for various labour camps working on the Thai-Burma Railroad. I spent five months as doctor in a Java Dutch camp, then spent the whole of 1944 in native coolie camps (Tamils, Malays, Chinese, Javanese, and fortunately for me also a few Hindustani people) on the Burma-Siam boundary. I lived five months in a hut with Chinese, and over six months in the Japanese hut. It was pretty dense forest along the railway. One had to learn a bit of Malay to speak to people. That was the *lingua franca.* Odd bits of news filtered through from native overseers, etc., who got a few days leave in Bangkok or Kanburi. In April of this year I was returned to a regular P.O.W. camp in Thailand, and was looking after a ward in the camp hospital when the end came. We flew here to Rangoon from Bangkok a few days ago, and I expect to be going on to India soon.

The whole three and a half years I only received mail on three occasions, and was only able to send three postcards out.

WALTER G. ANDERSON.

Walter's letter to Dr. Armstrong reprinted in a Toronto newspaper.

SEPTEMBER 17, 1945

Jnr. Comdr.,
To: Rev. F.J. Anderson
U.C.C. MISSION,
DHAR, (C.I.)
PLEASED TO INFORM YOU YOUR SON LIEUT
WG ANDERSON IMS HAS BEEN REPORTED RECOVERED

CASUALTIES

INDIAN POSTS AND TELEGRAPHS DEPARTMENT.

The cable to Walter's parents announcing his recovery.

[The following letter was received by families of former POWs clearly an effort on the part of military authorities to be a support during the initial weeks as the men adjusted to life in freedom.]

No. 113819/P.W.2.
GENERAL HEADQUARTERS, INDIA,
Adjutant General's Branch,
New Delhi, 1945

Dear

Many Officers and men who have escaped or been repatriated from enemy prisoners of war camps have spoken of the problems which they have found on getting back home after spending some years as prisoners of war. They find it wonderful to get back home, to be free again and to be with their wives and families and friends once more, but they have also found that it takes quite a time to get properly into the way

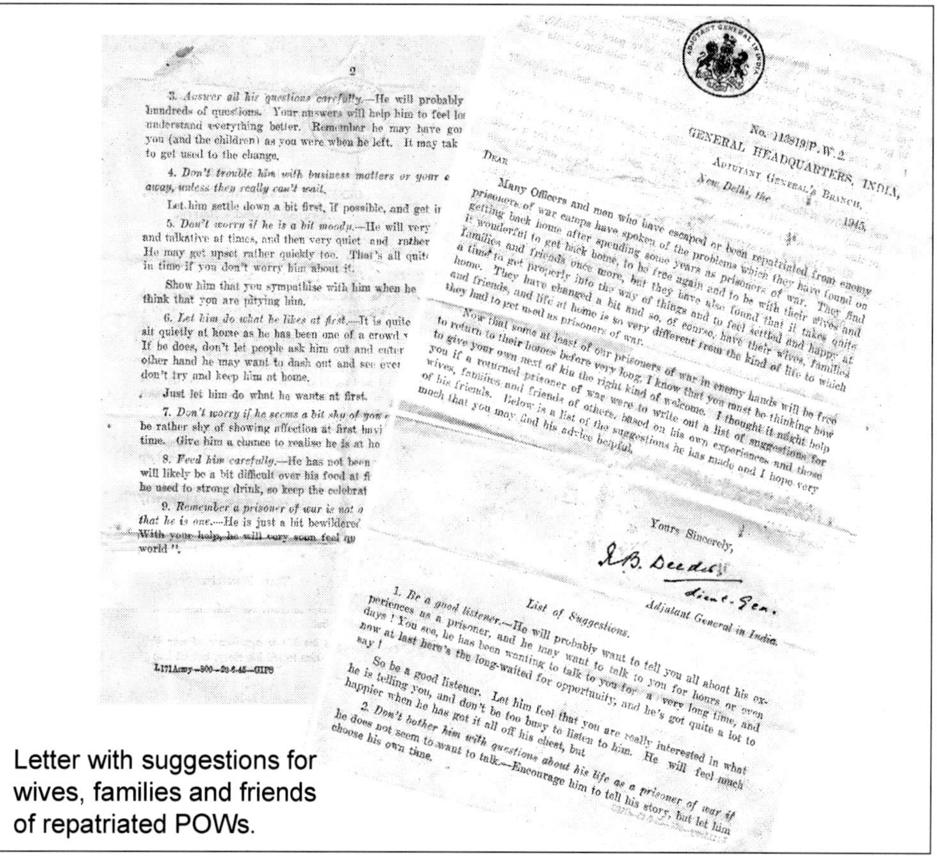

2

3. *Answer all his questions carefully.*—He will probably hundreds of questions. Your answers will help him to feel lo understand everything better. Remember he may have go you (and the children) as you were when he left. It may tak to get used to the change.

4. *Don't trouble him with business matters or your away, unless they really can't wait.*

Let him settle down a bit first, if possible, and get i

5. *Don't worry if he is a bit moody.*—He will very and talkative at times, and then very quiet and rather He may get upset rather quickly too. That's all quit in time if you don't worry him about it.

Show him that you sympathise with him when he think that you are pitying him.

6. *Let him do what he likes at first.*—It is quite sit quietly at home as he has been one of a crowd If he does, don't let people ask him out and enter other hand he may want to dash out and see eve don't try and keep him at home.

Just let him do what he wants at first.

7. *Don't worry if he seems a bit shy of you* be rather shy of showing affection at first havi time. Give him a chance to realise he is at ho

8. *Feed him carefully.*—He has not been will likely be a bit difficult over his food at f he used to strong drink, so keep the celebrat

9. *Remember a prisoner of war is not a that he is one.*—He is just a bit bewildered With your help, he will very soon feel qu world".

L171Army—500—29-6-45—GIPS

No. 112819/P.W. 2

GENERAL HEADQUARTERS, INDIA,

ADJUTANT GENERAL'S BRANCH,

New Delhi, the 1945.

DEAR

Many Officers and men who have escaped or been repatriated from enemy prisoners of war camps have spoken of the problems which they have found on getting back home after spending some years as prisoners of war. They find it wonderful to get back home, to be free again and to be with their wives and families and friends once more, but they have also found that it takes quite a time to get properly into the way of things and to feel settled and happy at home. They have changed a bit and so, of course, have their wives, families and friends, and life at home is so very different from the kind of life to which they had to get used as prisoners of war.

Now that some at least of our prisoners of war in enemy hands will be free to return to their homes before very long, I know that you must be thinking how to give your own next of kin the right kind of welcome. I thought it might help you if a returned prisoner of war were to write out a list of suggestions for wives, families and friends of others, based on his own experiences and those of his friends. Below is a list of the suggestions he has made and I hope very much that you may find his advice helpful.

Yours Sincerely,

R.B. Deedes

Lieut.-Gen.

Adjutant General in India.

List of Suggestions.

1. *Be a good listener.*—He will probably want to tell you all about his experiences as a prisoner, and he may want to talk to you for hours or even days! You see, he has been wanting to talk to you for a very long time, and now at last here's the long-waited for opportunity, and he's got quite a lot to say!

So be a good listener. Let him feel that you are really interested in what he is telling you, and don't be too busy to listen to him. He will feel much happier when he has got it all off his chest, but

2. *Don't bother him with questions about his life as a prisoner of war if he does not seem to want to talk.*—Encourage him to tell his story, but let him choose his own time.

Letter with suggestions for wives, families and friends of repatriated POWs.

of things and to feel settled and happy at home. They have changed a bit and so, of course, have their wives, families and friends, and life at home is so very different from the kind of life to which they had to get used to as a prisoner of war.

Now that some at least of our prisoners of war in enemy hands will be free to return to their homes before very long, I know that you must be thinking how to give your own next of kin the right kind of welcome. I thought it might help you if a returned prisoner of war were to write out a list of suggestions for wives, families and friends of others, based on his own experiences and those of his friends. Below is a list of the suggestions he has made and I hope very much that you may find his advice helpful.

Yours Sincerely,
Lieut. Gen.
Adjutant General in India

List of Suggestions

1. *Be a good listener.* -- He will probably want to tell you all about his experiences as a prisoner, and he may want to talk to you for hours or even days! You see, he has been wanting to talk to you for a very long time, and now at last here's the long-awaited for opportunity, and he's got quite a lot to say! So be a good listener. Let him feel that you are really interested in what he is telling you, and don't be too busy to listen to him. He will feel much happier when he has got it all off his chest, but
2. *Don't bother him with question about his life as a prisoner of war* if he does not seem to want to talk. – Encourage him to tell his story, but let him choose his own time.
3. *Answer all his questions carefully.* – He will probably want to ask you hundreds of questions. Your answers will help him to feel less strange, and to understand everything better. Remember he may have gone on thinking of you (and the children) as you were when he left. It may take him a little while to get used to the change.
4. *Don't trouble him with business matters or your own matters straight away, unless they really can't wait.* Let him settle down a bit first, if possible, and get into the way of things.
5. *Don't worry if he is a bit moody.* – He will very likely be very cheerful and talkative at times, and then very quiet and rather depressed for a spell. He may get upset rather quickly too. That's all quite natural, and will pass in time if you don't worry him about it. Show him that you sympathize with him when he needs it but don't let him think that you are pitying him.
6. *Let him do what he likes at first.* – It is quite likely that he will want to sit quietly at home as he has been one of a crowd with no privacy for so long. If he does, don't let people ask him out and entertain him too much. On the other hand he may want to dash out and see everyone. If so, let him go and don't try and keep him at home. Just let him do what he wants at first.

7. *Don't worry if he seems a bit shy of you and his family at first.* – He may be rather shy of showing affection at first having been starved of it for a long time. Give him a chance to realize he is at home with those who love him.
8. *Feed him carefully.* – He has not been used to good regular meals, so he will likely be a bit difficult over his food at first. Don't worry if he is. Nor is he used to strong drink, so keep the celebrations as quiet as you can!
9. *Remember a prisoner of war is not a sick man unless the doctor has said that he is one.* – He is just a bit bewildered and strange at first, that's all, With your help he will very soon feel quite "at home" and "on top of the world".

L171Army-800-29-6-45-GIPS

The following are some of the enthusiastic telegrams sent to Walter's parents in Dhar, India during September 1945:

"ALL RATLAM FRIENDS REJOICE WITH YOU" – Ratlam, India

"RASALPURA STAFF AND BOYS REJOICE WITH YOU IN GOOD NEWS" – Mhow, India, Mr & Mrs. F.S. Beckwith

"WONDERFUL NEWS REJOICING WITH YOU" – Ratlam, India, Rev. & Mrs. T. Buchanan

"ALL KHANVA FRIENDS REJOICE WITH YOU" – Mehidpuri, India, Miss F. Clearihue

"FIRST CHRONICLES SIXTEEN THIRTY TWO PSALMS FIVE ELEVEN PROVERBS FIVE EIGHTEEN HIS RICHEST BLESSING" – Banswara, India, Rev. & Mrs. H. Irwin

"HEARTS FULL GRATITUDE JOY SYMPATHY" – Indore, India, Bryce, Wilkie, Higgins, Grant

"VERY HAPPY TO HEAR YOUR GOOD NEWS" – Indore, India, Nicholson

"NEWS WONDERFUL THANKS LOVE" – Toronto, Ontario, Marion **[Walter's sister]**

"GREETINGS REJOICING GREATLY LOVE" – Toronto, Ontario, Mullin family

"COLLEGE STREET UNITED CHURCH FRIENDS REJOICE IN THE NEWS OF WALTERS SAFETY AND HOPE WE WILL BE WITH YOU SOON" – Toronto, Ontario, Session and Congregation

"REJOICING GLORIOUS NEWS WALTERS SAFETY LOVE" –Toronto, Ontario, Waters family

"FORMER COLLEAGUES SEND WARM FELICITATIONS" MacKay

SEPTEMBER 17th, 1945
[To parents]

MZ23691 Capt. W.G. Anderson I.M.S.
c/o Recovered P.O.W. Mail Centre,
Bombay, India Command

Dear Father and Mother;

This may possibly be my last from Rangoon. It is typically Sept. weather here, warm and sticky and perhaps more rain than in Sept. in C. I. makes one sleepy. A week ago Sunday night I wanted to go out to a "proper" service but it poured cats and dogs. Last night I did go and the rain came on in torrents while there, and it was a long wet walk home. It was a sort of thanksgiving service for Ex P.O.W. – combined C of E **[Church of England]** *and C of S* **[Church of Scotland]** *– held in Judson College chapel – a very fine hall, but echoes and acoustics very bad. Rev. Alcock (padre from my last camp at Pratchai) happened to come in and sat next to me. He is a fine little man and did very good work – poor fellow rec'd letters after peace signed, that his wife had died 10 months previous of food poisoning in England, and a brother died in Germany, and his mother had been very ill!*

It is nice to be in a proper building again – even one's own voice sounds different. Ever since coming up into Siam in July '43 and have lived in bamboo huts with "atap" roofing and sleeping on a platform off the ground built of bamboo split. One thing most of us have learned – is there anything you cannot do with bamboo?

Some of us were even called bamboo doctors by the Nips because we came back to soldier camps after being with coolies etc.!

The Nips just didn't care about coolies and said it was our job of course we must be inferior; curious reasoning!

It will be nice to hear from you again – nothing since last Dec. yet. Have been taking Nepracine since my last go of Malaria and it does give me a jaundice complexion.

I noticed the other day the Methodists have a large girl's High School here – damaged a bit too – but they certainly put up the big schools over the East! I met a Canadian from near Winnipeg who told me of the early days when he was working as P.O.W. at Tavoy, where there had been a Baptist Mission Station.

The Burmese Christians got in special food to our Americans and Canadians in the Camp.

I've seen a new 1 pice **[Indian currency]** *coin – very curious with a large hole in it. Managed to pick up a few stamps. Now I must prepare to be ready when word comes to move off.*

Kindest regards to all
Love
Walter

SEPTEMBER 19th, 1945
[From Father]

United Church of Canada Mission
Dhar, Central India

My dear Walter

Welcome back to India and home to Dhar.

The greatest thrill of our lives was occasioned by your first three Air letters from Bangkok received together on Sept. 11th. Mother, with steadier nerves, read while I could scarcely listen for the hymn of Doxology in head and heart. It was glorious news that you were alive and well and we lost no time in passing on the glad tidings to your friends in India and the Board of Overseas Missions in Toronto for broadcasting to your friends in Canada. Already replies have come from Marion, the Mullins, MacKays and College Street United Church. Then came two more air letters from Bangkok and last evening your cable from Rangoon.

Missionary Captured at Singapore to Return to India

The Board of Overseas Missions received on September 13th the following cablegram from Rev. and Mrs. F. J. Anderson of our Central India Mission:

"Glad tidings Walter writing from Bangkok, September fourth, declares himself absolutely well; expects arrive India soon."

This refers to Dr. Walter G. Anderson, who was born in India, and after his education in Canada returned in 1937 to become a medical missionary. In 1942, he became a medical officer in the Indian Army and was taken prisoner when his regiment was captured at the fall of Singapore. He was the only United Church missionary who was a prisoner of war. Only two messages reached his parents during more than three years. It is, therefore, a matter of great gratitude that he declares his health to be good.

Friends will rejoice with the parents and with his sister, Marion, in this country, that Dr. Walter Anderson is shortly to rejoin his family at Dhar in India. It is anticipated that the Andersons will reach Canada in the spring of 1946.

This clipping from the United Church Observer reports that the Board of Overseas Missions' is informed that medical Missionary Dr. Walter G. Anderson, prisoner of war since 1942, has sent word that he is well, and will rejoin his family in Dhar shortly. The news item confirms unequivocally that he was the only United Church missionary who was a prisoner of war.

Mother is writing you at length today and anything I might write would only be to duplicate her news items. She may forget to say that Moir and his family sailed for Canada in July.

Oh, we do rejoice at your safety and good health in spite of all your dreadful experiences during the past 3½ years. Now we wait for your telegram from Calcutta or Madras or Bombay. Where and when can we meet you? What can we bring to you? The car is ready to bring you home from Mhow or Ratlam. Special ration of petrol given us by Supt. of Police, Dhar for the purpose. Thanks be to God for answered prayers.

Love
Father

SEPTEMBER 19th, 1945
[From Mother]

Dear dear Walterji

You see, I too, don't know how to get started! There seems so much to be said, that I must be restricted and restrained! Your 1st from Prachai, then Bangkok on 2nd, and same town, all came together– and amounted almost to a shock! The last word from you, dear one, had been written, (we figured) about two years ago! We knew that as time passed it was reasonable to expect resistance to grow weaker, and added to this all that has transpired, as given in papers and over the air, in those and other parts; we certainly were not looking for letters when they came – last week Tues. Sept.11th. I think we are now beginning to realize that it is not all a wonderful dream, from which we might awake; thanks to many friends who have kept us reminded by letters and telegrams and cables. You won't have time to read Shakespeare when you get home Walter! Do get here as soon as you can – it's a good hill station. Fresh and cool after rains – I'm wearing a sweater as I sit to write, this morning. It's so fresh and green just now.

Your later letters from Bangkok, 3 have come, and only yesterday the cable you had mentioned came from Rangoon – and a second one identical to first. They were both dated "15th". Hope you had the "thrill" at flying that part at least.

We sent out to our Stations, most of them, the glad good news of first message. To say that all "rejoice" with us is putting it very mildly. I have so many letters, telegrams, and only four cables from Toronto! (MacKays – for all colleagues) Marion, Mullins, and College Street Church Session and Congregation.

Since you mention the possibility of being in Bangalore – I have written to Mr. Wilcox at the 'Clarence High School'. Now don't you think I am being composed to get my mind to work even this far, in all the excitement of this joyous news – the greatest joy in years and years! Anxiety and sorrow have told on my memory at least. I must hasten to let you know something of Marion's circumstances. Since May '43 she has been entirely on her own. At first she was on City Relief – before we knew it! Then she gradually got her feet – is Technician in the Toronto Hospital for T.B. at Weston, over a year now. Mrs. Beckwith was travelling in connection with Guides, or something, and was in Peterborough, and met Dr. and Mrs. Scott.

They together suggested that a woman, patient of Dr. Scott's be asked to board Ann and baby Randall. This woman, Mrs. McCurrach has two or three other children. Ann 5 yrs. and Randall (now two years old) are there, and getting best of good care. Marion visits them once a month. Some of your funds have been sent to help and devoted to paying the board for Ann. Marion pays for Randall, and we send sums for extras like new glasses, dental examinations, etc. etc. Now this may suffice for the present. Marion's cable said – "glorious news thanks love Marion".

Now can I give you an idea of who is where in our Mission, specially (Daniel wants his Salaams sent to you.) At the W.M.S. bungalow live Una and Arthur Dobson, and Helen, 3 yrs, and George Montgomery one year, nearly. Miss M – is still on furlough. Una has the School work and I the Evangelist for W.M.S. Ratlam – Bessie has heard from Jack – one day before your messages on 10th. He was on his way to Australia. Buchanans, Misses Gruchy, McLeod and Dr. Jean Whittier comprise the staff. Bessie has just now resigned and is giving herself to getting ready to go to England with Jack.

Auntie Whittier must be mentioned – she has been a comforter to us. Neemuch – Mrs. H.H.Smith, Rev. Kenneth Yohan-Masin, and Miss McHarrie.

Sitamao – Miss F. Steveson. Mandleshwar – Mr. Clarke, Miss Morson, and Dr. Sundhar Gaikwad. (her mother has died this summer) Rasalpura – Mr. Beckwith, and of course Capt. Gray, for the trainees. Indore – Dr. Bill Taylor (Col. Prin. acting) Mr. Bryce, Cliff Grant – Seminary, Miss Gardner, and new lady – Miss Bessie Mewhort, Dr. Smith and Miss Hilliard. The latter is at Vellore for an op – and Dr. Catherine Whittier is with her. No American Dr. at Miraj these days: Dr. Goheen on furlough. Banswara – Dr. Merle Patterson (new Dr. who studied here in Dhar) (she followed you at St. Mich's – Toronto), Miss Bucholtz, and Mr. and Mrs. Irwin and two daughters.

Dr. Catherine Whittier is waiting for passage home. Kharua – Misses Clearihue and Patterson and Rev. Hilda Johnson. Moir has departed! – couldn't see his family go without him. (We all hope he gets a nice big church with good salary in Can.!) Ujjain – Miss Munns and Rev. Mr. Wishard (Indian). Men missionaries are as plentiful as hen's teeth!

Dot Pearson is at Madras Christian College, Miss Florence Taylor (nurse specialist is at Vellore, S.I.) A very large party went home last July from here and W. China, bills paid by Father were over a hundred thousand rupees – to American Express. Dr. and Mrs. Quinn still in Canada – Capt. Toombs just now back in Mission work, the only man in Presbyterian Mission. Dr. Buchanan died in Feb. at Indore Nursing home.

Dr. Waters had an operation this past year – on stomach. Mrs. Waters is still an invalid in bed for 18 out of 24 hours, ever since Pneumonia – three years ago. Dr. Waters getting quite well now. Donnie Armstrong, John Colwell, Gordon Buchanan all safely home from German Prison camps. Billie Colwell and Gordon Davidson killed in action and Douglas Donald missing. Alex Mullin now in Italy, John on staff Camp Borden, Bob home from Italy, after leg injury, now in Forestry Dept. and doing well. David in 2nd year University. Mrs. Mullin badly afflicted with Asthma. Dr. Cochrane died July 13th – heart attack, while on holidays. Dr. J. W. Wilson died, perhaps, ere you left? Rev. Mr. Gowans at College Street Church; much liked. Mrs. McGill had stroke so partial invalid. Mrs. Dr. Nugent died in July, after a fall. Arthur Davidson home some time – nervous trouble. Mr. Davidson and Dr. Taylor retired – at home. Taylors bought house in Richmond Hill Village. Vera B. – got Kaiser-Hind before going home (as Civil Matron in Mhow (Ind.Mil.Hosp.). A plane roaring overhead – we seem to be on a route.

Mrs. Lewis writes from Dohad. David is in Eastern service. Arthur Dobson was 2 yrs at Simla, and nearly one year in Burma – latter engagement + Chaplain. He is now in charge of Dhar Station work. Father has plenty with Secretary and

Treasurer. Now I have given you enough to keep you thinking for at least a week. I must leave the rest for when you get home.

Do let us know in good time so we can make the train, in good time. Taking, almost for granted that you would be incapable of travelling alone, we were going to have Arthur D. meet you at a distance. Your nice sightseeing tour through Bangkok doesn't sound as though you needed help. So much more than anything we could dream of!!! The Toombs lately returned from a holiday in S.I. **[South India]** *and travelled with a returned P.O.W. from Singapore – Col. Christonsen – on his way from Madras to Mhow. He knew you in '42 in Changi. His reports were painful – they have not told us all yet. He suffered. Dr. Mullet has been from Hong Kong to Canada and now back to his work in China. Now I must let this go. Heaps of love, just aching to see you home.*

Ever yours
Mother

[written by hand at the bottom of the page]
Father and Sam busy – today's job is the agenda for Council – Oct. 23rd open in Indore – you and father and I are to be at Seminary with Cliff. **[Walter did manage to attend.]** *Meetings there too.*

SEPTEMBER 21st, 1945
[To parents]
MZ 23691 Capt. W. G. Anderson IMS/IAMC
c/o Recovered P.O.W. Mail Centre,
Bombay, India Command

Dear Mother and Father

I thought my last letter of the 17th was the last from Rangoon, but possibly this may be. It certainly has been wet and sticky here lately, but at the moment it looks like a short welcome break, of course here I think everything remains fresh looking and green all year. The same in Siam, though not quite so much rain there thank goodness. In certain circumstances their rain and mud was at least not encouraging!

I wonder if Bessie has heard yet from Jack Leech. He was supposed to have gone to Japan, but often what the Nips told us was far from the correct thing, so Jack could have really been sent anywhere in the Pacific area. He and I slept side by side Mar. '42 to Jan. '43 **[in POW barracks]**.

In a place like this one meets acquaintances of the lost 3½ years, who have been scattered about all over the place, and now as people come through, it is very interesting to meet up again and draw comparisons.

I forgot to say I made early enquiries in 1942 of David Angus, and found out then that he was with the civilian internees in the jail in Singapore – not being related of course I could never be allowed to visit him – I don't suppose he knew I was in Singapore. Jack Leech had met him often before. I hope he is all right still.

A Capt. Thomas who lives in Thailand who became a friend of mine has gone on to India earlier and said he would drop you a line from there to say I was coming!

Must do a spot of washing while the sun is out!

Love
Walter
P.S. I've written a note to Marion, the Mullins, and Dr. Armstrong.

SEPTEMBER 23rd, 1945
[From Father]
United Church of Canada Mission
Dhar, Central India
Rev. F. J. Anderson
Secretary – Treasurer

Dear Walter

Since your hop from Bangkok to Rangoon we feel cheated at not receiving a Daily Air letter but the one that you sent on the 9th Sept. from Rangoon gave us cause for further thanksgiving that you were a long stage nearer home. We have been speculating whether you would journey to Calcutta by air or come by ship to either Calcutta or Madras. And, if by ship we wonder if you are now on your way or waiting till all hospital cases are forwarded first.

Rangoon will probably not be so nice a tarrying place as Bangkok but you will be well cared for no doubt. We got word from Simla and Delhi that you were a recovered P.O.W so the fact has been registered at Government G.H.J. Yesterday I received the usual preliminary notification from Simla re: your salary cheque for Sept. The cheque will no doubt be here in a day or two. I shall keep the cash handy for your immediate needs. Should you need funds somewhere I shall try to send. If you arrive first in Bombay you can of course draw on your own personal account with the American Express Co.

Quite a bunch of cables, telegrams and letters have come in congratulating us and you on your safety and I hope there will be letters direct to you from our C. I. staff to the address given in your cable from Rangoon.

Mr. Beckwith is in charge at Rasalpura. His wife has not yet returned from Canada. Mrs. Bryce, Mrs. Grant and Mrs. Clark are also still in Canada but hope to be here soon. Graham, who was to return this fall and relieve the Buchanans at Ratlam, is reported to be ill and may not return for another year. Am not sure how that will affect the Buchanans. A. A. Scott and wife may not be back before next May or June.

Should you land at Madras, look up Dorothy Pearson who is teaching at the Women's Christian College. If you land at Calcutta you can get funds if needed by calling on Mrs. Emily Rees, Treasurer C.M.S. She handles lots of West China Mission funds for me, paying passage and maintenance of our W. C. missionaries as they come and go. Dr. and Mrs. Sparling are in Calcutta now awaiting a permit and plane to take them on to West China. Have had lots of sunshine recently but rain again for the past three days.

All well, we three are to be with Grant at the seminary for Council time (Oct.23 to ?)

Love and all good wishes
Father

SEPTEMBER 26th, 1945
[To Parents]
MZ23691 Capt. W. G. Anderson IMS/IAMC
c/o Recovered P.O.W. Mail Centre,
Bombay, India Command
Rangoon

Dear Father and Mother:

Perhaps this is my last letter from here! But all's well that ends well! How it can rain in this place, and here is the end nearly of Sept. When we were uncomfortable in the rain in our bamboo and atap huts (and once really settled into a well built hut with properly laid roof, and sides of matting, it was not too bad at all). We often used to wonder how uncomfortable our own chaps were fighting their way through in the probably heavier rain in northern Burma.

A very unusual thing is a fat little Dashound dog which one officer has here, which belonged to his wife in Singapore. His wife I understand was drowned trying to get away, during the war, and he has kept the dog ever since, bringing it up into Thailand and feeding it on rice and what not these years. Brought by plane then onto here.

When one is sitting waiting there is not much to say! I don't want to buy stuff here simply to carry on to India. (One has to carry one's own of course and no point in loading up now.) Most of my Medical friends, those of us up in the coolie camps, are leaving here for the U.K. at any moment, so I'm hoping not to tarry on too long after. Manage to put in time by doing odd jobs. Food is excellent and I think we are all well used to a normal diet by now!

Love to all
Walter

This is a watercolour in which the author, Ann Smith, has painted her image of the Burmese jungle described in her Uncle Walter's letters.

SEPTEMBER 28th, 1945
Went on board S.S. EKma

SEPTEMBER 29th, 1945
Sailed from Rangoon

RECORD OF ILLNESS

MALARIA :- SEP. '43 to end (27th) AUG. '45 (24 MO)
19 times remembered.
During March - June '44, Aug. - July '45, attacks every 18-21 days (worst periods)
1st slide examined Apr. '45 = B.T. & all subsequent B.T.

OEDEMATOUS BERI-BERI :- JULY '43; JAN. to MARCH '44; JUNE to AUG. '45; APR '45;

ENTERITIS :- SEP. '42; AUG '43; OCT. '43; JAN. '44; MAR. '44; MAR. '45.

W. G. Anderson
Capt. [illegible]

Characteristically, Walter maintained a meticulous record of his illnesses during his incarceration (Malaria 19 times, Beriberi 4 long periods, Enteritis 6 times) and it too was saved, along with all the other records.

OCTOBER 2nd, 1945
[To Parents]
c/o Recovered P.O.W. Mail Centre
Bombay, India Command
Madras

Dear Father and Mother –

Arrived by ship yesterday. Sent a reply paid wire this a.m. just to join up lines of communication!

Reply address for wire stated, Mail address as above. Expect to leave here for Poona probably in a couple of days, and where I get settled up will soon come on to Dhar, unless I hear in Bombay to the contrary! Love and hope to see you soon – writing –

Walter

OCTOBER 4TH, 1945
[Telegram to parents]
INDIAN POSTS AND TELEGRAPHS DEPARTMENT
ANDERSON MISSION DHAR

GREETINGS ARRIVED YESTERDAY
WELL HOPE SAME ADDRESS
MACKAYS GARDENS MADRAS
WALTER

OCTOBER 5th,1945
Left Madras for Poona and Bombay

OCTOBER 5TH, 1945
[Telegram from parents]
DHAR, INDIA
CAPT W. G. ANDERSON
MACKAYS GARDENS,
MADRAS, C.I.

WELCOME GREETINGS
ALL WELL HERE LETTERS RECEIVED
WIRE NEEDS AND TIME OF ARRIVAL.
ANDERSONS

OCTOBER 6th, 1945
[From Father]
United Church of Canada Mission
Dhar, Central India
Rev. F. J. Anderson
Secretary – Treasurer

Dear Walter

Your telegram and post card from Madras received. We sent the prepaid reply wire and a letter or two to Madras but doubt whether any of them would reach you in time. You keep hopping about from place to place so rapidly that we are almost dizzy trying to locate you and then, like the flea, when we think we have covered you with a letter, you are somewhere else!

But every hop brings you nearer home and that is the one big thing we have looked forward to for years. From day of arrival in Dhar next week Dhar will be your G.H.Q. **[general headquarters]**

We are not allowed – see how we suffer restrictions – to kill a fatted calf in honour of your homecoming but we may get some 'baku **[goat]** *' more or less tender for the occasion. Glad your diet now includes whatever you want or can obtain.*

$1-A-Day For POWs Maltreated By Foe

Ottawa, Oct. 10—(CP)—Canadians who were imprisoned by the Japanese and by certain German organziations during the Second World War will be paid $1 a day for each day of that imprisonment the Government announced today.

Prime Minister St. Laurent said in a statement these "mal-treatment," awards "cover Canadians who were held in Japanese operated internment or prison camps or in the hands of certain German organizations such as the Gestapo which were declared by the Nuremberg tribunal to be 'criminal organizations.'"

Roughly 1,600 veterans of the Hong Kong military expedition of 1941 would be among the recipients. A man in prison four years, as many of them were, would draw roughly $1,400.

The awards do not affect the great majority of Canadian prisoners-of-war who fell into German hands.

The awards will be made out of proceeds of German reparations and out of Japanese reparations and assets seized in Canada early in the war. About $10,000,000 is available, $7,000,000 from Germany and $3,000,000 from Japan.

The Hong Kong army group—remnants of the two-battalion detachment sent to the Pacific island in 1941—is believed to make up the only large single group to benefit from today's announcement of the $1-a-day awards.

However, numerous other Canadians would be affected, priests and other civilians caught in the Far East, airmen shot down in warfare with the Japanese, some Canadians caught by the Germans and put in camps such as Belsen and Buchenwald.

News report announcing that former POWs would be awarded $1 a day -- for Walter that would have been just short of $1300.

Mother wants you to call at Lawrence and Mays, Bombay for glasses she has under order from them. They are overdue and she needs them badly. Find out when they will be ready and whether the work is being done in Bombay or did both have to send away for the required glass or frame.

If you need money you can draw on your own account with the American Express Co. Bombay. Ask for mail at American Express Co. (one letter from mother there for you).

Floods have damaged the B.B. & C.I. Railway so better come via Khandwa. Am not sure when the trains arrive Mhow from Khandwa but believe they arrive about 8:30 a.m. and 7:30 p.m. Wire us so that we may meet you with car in Mhow for either train. Just in case of delay give us a little extra time! Beckwith is in Smillies place at Rasalpura.

Barnes POW got home to Dhar this week. Also Yumathun son of Gukdu of Dhar. Hop along son, we long to welcome you.

Lovingly,
Father
[written around the edge:] *Can you get a soldier's ration card for supplies in Mhow? It might be useful.*

OCTOBER 7th, 1945
[From Father]
United Church of Canada Mission
Dhar, C.I.
Rev. F. J. Anderson,
Secretary – Treasurer

Dear Walter Ji

Welcome to Poona, then via Bombay, Khanadwa, Mhow and Dhar.

We hope you received our telegram in Madras and as learned that we are still in Dhar waiting your arrival, your letters from Bangkok came through in good time and relieved our minds of a great burden of anxiety. The cable has not come yet. Then we received your cable and letters from Rangoon. We sent a reply cable to Rangoon but it may not have reached you.

It was a delight to get your successive messages marking out steady progress homewards and today, according to yesterday's post card, we can imagine that you have already reached Poona or will be then in a day or two. So this is an attempt to catch up and inform you that all is well with us and Marion etc. etc.

In Bombay you will probably find letters at the "Recovered POW Mail Centre", and one at least at both the American Express Co. and The Inter-Mission Business Office, 240 Hornley Road (Nausain Bldg). Please call for them if you go to Bombay. Funds are available in your own personal account with the American Express Co. and I have some of your cash in hand here. Your salary has been coming to me regularly from Simla, including salary for September which money I have in cash! If we know in time we shall meet you with our car at Mhow Station. Not sure when trains arrive there from Khandwa but probably about 8:30 A.M. and 7:30 P.M. Mr. Beckwith is in charge at Rasalpura.

We confidently expect you home this week and Dhar will be your G.H.Q. till we sail (all of us) for Canada next Spring! Glad you will be in time for Commissions and Council at Indore beginning Oct. 23rd; you are to be with us at the Seminary – Grant in charge there. J. T. Taylor in Canada.

Lovingly,
Father
PS. Two POW Dhar men arrived Dhar last week Barnes & Yunathar Subhdeo ??

OCTOBER 10th, 1945
Arrive Mhow, India

OCTOBER 11th, 1945
Arrive Dhar **[HOME]**

Home at last! Walter with his parents.

INDIAN POSTS AND TELEGRAPHS DEPARTMENT.

TO Anderson Mission
Arriving Mhow seven-fifteen this evening
Water

Walter's cable announcing his arrival in Mhow. The signature has Walter's name misspelled "Water".

[From Walter to his sister]

Indian Military Hospital
Mhow, C. I.
5th, Feb. 1946

Dear Marion

Many thanks for your air mail of Jan. 7th with birthday greetings which was sent on to me here and received on the 28th, just the day before. Good Timing!

I was posted to the I.M.H., Mhow on Jan. 9th, when my POW leave expired. It is lucky to be right here in C.I. so close. Rasalpura is within easy reach of the hospital by bicycle, so I am living with Mrs. Beckwith and cycle into Mhow each morning and afternoon. I have to take my turn as Orderly Medical Officer on duty and stay down at the hospital all night. This comes about every three or four days. But now patients are few and there is not much to do. I have charge of the surgical ward but have only about 18 patients. Anyway it is nice to get into the atmosphere *of a real hospital again, even for a short time. I am being released on Feb. 15th, ie. In another ten days. That is the anniversary of being taken POW in Singapore four years ago, so I can celebrate it this time by being quite free and honourably released from the Army. I get then 56 days release leave, plus one day for every month overseas, which in my case was 44 months, so I should get a total of 100 days leave on military pay, and then whatever benefits they give for five years service. I have just recently been charged "Rent" by the Military Accounts people for the period from the day the Japanese War ended up to my landing back in India! That is I am charged rent by our own government for living another 2 weeks as we did in a bamboo hut in a Jap POW camp on a Jap rice diet! – rent for working a week in the Bangkok Airport hospital, and rent for waiting in a transit camp in a tent in Rangoon. It is incredibly astonishing! I'm writing to enquire if they really mean it.*

Will return to Dhar on 15th and will have to help soon in breaking up house. It is a very unpleasant job and Mother is dreading it terribly. It is hard to pull up your roots and move away for good when you have had everything arranged about you in your own home for years. They are neither as well as they might be either. Where they move in to Ratlam in March or April we will have to be just "camping" there. Furniture and stuff has to be sold off and may be difficult to get rid of just now. It is going to be a tiring and worrying job. Must close for now.

Love
Walter

News clipping reports that Japanese prisoners of war were put to work clearing the railway along the Kwai river, urgently needed for transporting rice from the districts.

Japs Clear Siam "Death Valley" Railway

More than 5,000 Jap prisoners of war have been put to work clea ring the "death valley" railway in Siam, the building of which cost the lives of thousands of Allied prisoners of war and civilians slave-driven by the Japs. The r ailway is now urgently required for the transport of rice from outlying districts. The picture shows Japs working as coolies, on the line near Bangkok, under the supervision of British and Dutch ex-prisoners.

[Here we have inserted some letters from POW friends who kept in touch with Walter long after the war.]

From Lim Djin Pin
Kanchanaburi, Siam.
3rd, February, '46

Dr. W. G. Anderson
Dhar, Central India

My Dear Dr. Anderson,

You can rest assured how excited I was when your letter reached me, dated 14th December, enclosed in my letter from S'pore and there is no greater bliss to hear from you that you are reunited to your beloved parents. All this while, I had the vision that some day that your letter will reach me but not till the 2nd of February. I had decided to write to you first, somewhere in December, but then mail to India was forbidden to civilians.

Immediately after the declaration of surrender, I had been restless to find your whereabouts and the first camp that I went was Tamuang where I met Maj. Nardell, who was kind to me and the first thing he did after inquiring about my condition was to send me to the Dental surgeon without my asking him. He told me that it was of little chance of meeting you in the camp somewhere in Bangkok for by that time you would be likely flying home. The next place I went was Ranchanaburi camp, expecting to meet Capt. Cowans but he left for Bangkok the day before, only to find two English doctors, Capt. Wallace and Capt. Lenose, who were exerting every inch of their energies treating P.O.W. patients. Then somewhere in the month of October, Capt. Dawson came to TFMFTU from Bangkok with a small band of Dutch soldiers in a jeep and gleamed with delight to see me safe and sound. He told me his mission was to arrest The Maniac Dai Ichi Major, the 2nd Lt. supposed to be of royal-blood, and Chin, the great surgeon, in reality a 1st grade dresser, of the Dai Ni Hospital. I told Capt. Dawson that Chin had absconded on the 5th of Sept. and informing him as well that the appropriate man who can give the correct detail of Chin's residence in Province Wellesly.

After the day I left Dai Ichi for Seremban in Malaya, I was allowed to see my uncle through my threat of absconding unless I see my uncle which the Japs readily granted. My uncle insisted upon me to continue my study under Japanese teaching which I objected on the thought that it will bring unnecessary trouble to my uncle with the Japs and on the second that I would be compelled to become Japs puppet soldier which was compulsory to every able body in Jap's occupied Malaya. On my return to Siam, I brought books for you and Maj. Nardell, and cigars for Capt. Cowan and Capt. Young, but on the way I was given to understand from my friends on the same duty as mine that you all had been moved up. Needless to say about the unpleasant journey, but I should congratulate myself to have escaped the same fate of my friends, who had to cover a good distance on foot at every bombed area and the worst of all was the big bridge of Suratani, which is the longest bridge on the way south of Chimpong.

I hope you still remember Chimpong, the last main station to Nonpradock, was completely reduced to ashes, and nothing you will see but twisted irons and deep craters infested with big fishes.

Reaching Kanchanaburi I was transferred to the main butai in Banpong, the chief of all butais of Siam-Burma Railway under a Maj. General Cadachi, as a typist recording the labourers. The life there was monotonous among those monkey-faces and we were just like birds in a cage. We were let off once a week for 4 hours to Banpong and as the time was critical to the Japs, we were more or less imprisoned in the camp for more than a month. But you know me better than anybody else, that nothing could stop me to satisfied my always hungry stomach by acquiring food from outside, in spite of the ever-patrolling God sent soldiers.

Then the fall of the 50 years old aggrandizement of Japan had been declared, I got myself attached to the TFMFTU as a dresser. The hospital is situated in the Old P.O.W. camp in Kanchanaburi having the capacity of accommodating more than 1000 patients. There is another FMFTU in Tamuang having half the capacity of accommodation.

The patients, here, are leading a genuine hospital life, surpassing thousand times that Japan could offer to their ill fated labourers. Gifts from the Red Cross are distributed weekly to the patients, and on their discharge one suit is given to everyone.

As I write to you this letter, we are having Small-pox epidemic since the last three months in Thailand with a good number of coolies subjected to this disease, but all pulled through very well. In spite of the long establishment of this Hospital and after discharging thousands of patients, fresh lots of patients pouring in daily composing 98% of Tamils with the complaints of pneumonia and V.D. greatly all these labourers are no longer in up-country since the last two and a half months. They are centred in four big camps in the area of Kanchanaburi and Tamuang. The biggest is the Tamamarn Camp, the old camp beside the concrete bridge about 2 miles from Dai Ni Hospital, accommodating about 9000 labourers. The reason for the labourers ill-health is, they are possessed with ill-founded idea that after through series of hardships under the Japs, that now they have absolute right drowning themselves on the form of pleasure in the contemptible Thai rice-wine resulting their soft landing in a British Hospital.

In regards your stamps, I will try to get for you in my next letter as I haven't the time now.

Please give my regards to your parents, Maj. Nardell, Capt. Cowan and others whom I know.

We are on the next chapter of life and may God bless you.

Yours sincerely,
P.D. Pin
P.S. In the TFMFTU the dressers are supplied with uniforms and every Jap has to salute us. Believe me! I am well compensated.

Ten Hong Lee
19 Chin Hin Street,
Singapore.
March 2, 1946

To: Capt. W. G. Anderson
Dhar, Central India

Dear Capt. W. G. Anderson

I am very glad to hear that you have returned to your home in India. There must be a great joy with your people there.

I have come back from Siam only two week ago after serving the British Military Unit there for five months.

I still remember your kindness to me while in Siam and I hope I may meet you again in future.

With kind regards,

Yours sincerely,
Ten Hong Lee
C.P.O. Adnan bin Raji
C/O Local Forces Record Office,
Beach Road, Singapore.

15th April 1946

TO: Doctor W. G. Anderson
Central Mission Hospital.
Ratlam, Central India
INDIA

Dear Doctor,

I have received your letter dated 22nd, March 1946 on the 12th, April 1946 with many thanks.

I am very happy to hear from you, that you had returned to your Former Job, and I hope that you will be happy that you are going to have a good Practice in your professional job.

So what about my promise to you to come to Singapore to start your own business; I think you still remembered about this matter that we were always discussed at Piah Tunju in Burma and Thailand Border.

I still unable to forget how I enjoyed myself in the real jungle live, but you know how we suffered. I shall be much thankful, if you could let me know about Mr. Wallace. I have given my statement to Security officer in Singapore about of what had happened to me while I was in Thailand and Burma.

I have nothing more to pen at present except sending my best wishes to you and families. I am keeping very well with all of my families. Hoping to hear from you soon.

KAWAN KAWAN SEMUA-NYA ADA BAIK

Yours faithfully.
Adnan bin Raji

Sender
Lieut. J. B. Leech,
Upper Norwood,
London, SE 19
May 12, 1946

Capt. W.G. Anderson,
c/o Mission Hospital,
Ratlam, C.I.

Dear Walter,

Just another month and I hope to have this cast off. My, what a relief it will be. Have you ever tried to write in a cast? If not you must compliment me.

Bessie is in London and the children are at school. I was advised to vegetate a while longer in the country, but am due back in hospital in early June for removal of cast – Xray – and further examinations.

The papers seem to paint a bad picture of England and shortage, but it is luxury after Changi etc. What is happening in India, and what do you feel about the prospects of European Christian work in the future? It seems as if it will be the best part of 12 months before!

Bessie is quite well, we have a daily mail which keeps us closely in touch. Ian has fallen for a young girl and has already gone to **[??]**, *he certainly is starting young. Patricia started in school on our arrival and has been moved up into a higher grade.*

Give your folks our love and kind regards and we hope to see you again soon in Canada.

Yours as always,
Jack

From Lim Djin Pin
TFMFTU
c/o S.E. A.C.
Siam
May 30th, 1946

Dear Sir,

Received your letter on the 20th of May and am certainly glad to learn that you got yourself attached in your pre-war's post again. The present number of Malayan labourers is around 5,000 and majority of labourers, consisting about 4,000 are stationed in Tamakarn Camp, which is beside the concrete bridge of the doomed railway-line. The other two camps, which I had given you a description in my last letter; the one that is in Kaorin is no longer in existence and had been moved up to Tamuang in the old P.O.W.s camp and the other, midway between Kanburi and Tamuang , is at the point of closing. It is consisting about 100 labourers only. I presume that the Military Administration had done a pretty good work in executing the evacuation of more than 28,000 labourers to Malaya in this complicated world.

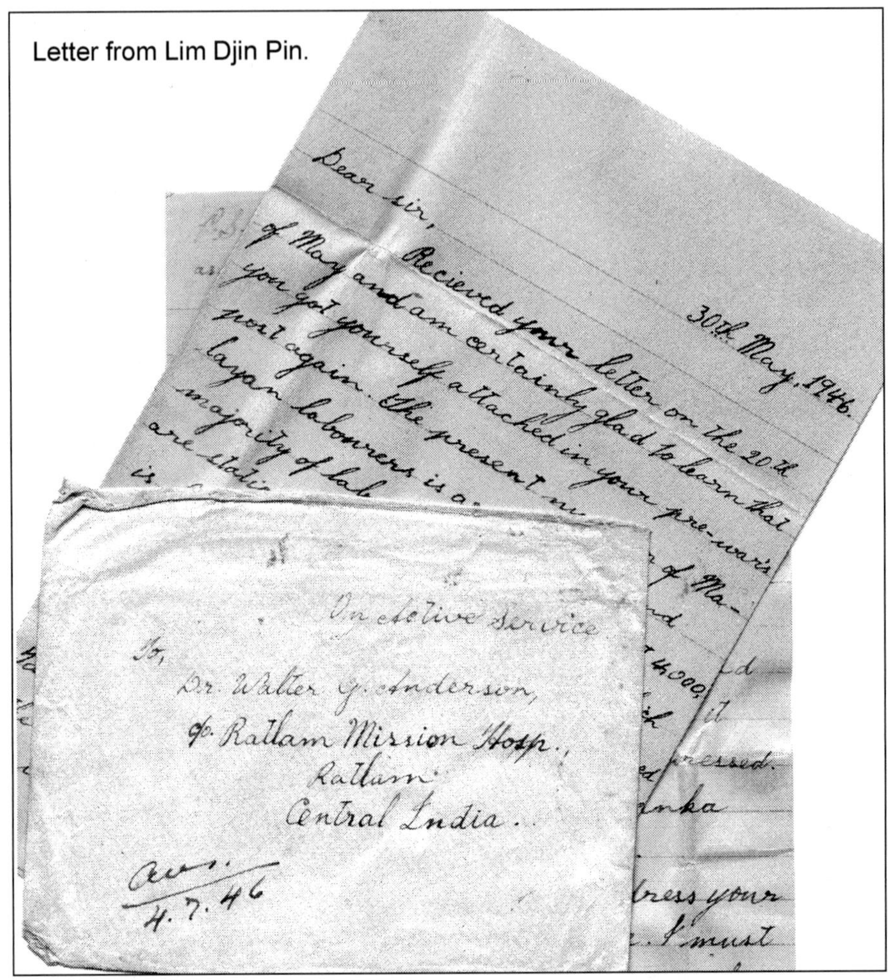
30th May, 1946.

Dear sir,

Recieved your letter on the 20th of May and am certainly glad to learn that you got yourself attached in your pre-war's post again. The present nu... of Ma- layan labourers is a... majority of lab... are statio... is ...

On Active Service

To,

Dr. Walter G. Anderson,

c/o Ratlam Mission Hosp.,

Ratlam

Central India.

Ans. 4.7.46

Letter from Lim Djin Pin.

Do you still remember the two boys, who served us in Timonta? Well, one of them, the taller boy was admitted to my ward four months ago with the complaint of lobar Pneumonia pretty badly. He got through splendidly and told me his friend is with him in his camp. I also met those pompous Perak's women in the hospital, they kept asking of you and appreciated your work greatly. The big-voiced Perak's so called Dai Cooli-toe and S.K. were in Tamakarn and most probably by now had left for Malaya. I am in the lurch about the ill-fated labourers of 800 strong of Timonta. I am wondering how many of them are alive to-day. I nearly forget to mention that the Perak's women are having the good fortune of acquiring new husbands like we used to have meat in Ranburi. I hope you will be able to re-collect the English speaking Chinese lad, Su coolie-toe of K.L., who was very badly emanciated with

Malaria then, who made good of his escape after being found of stealing a carton of cigarettes. He is really a good chap and handsome in his bearing. At present he is working in Tamakarn as a clerk and was with me in Banpong before the surrender. The jaga, who was taken ill with Malaria, is at present working in the Hospital as the chief of jagas. Gregory had left for S'pore 8 days ago.

I am attached to a surgical ward, we are doing minor operations such as fistula, Phimosis and opening of abcess. The major operations are being done in Bangkok or sent to Malaya. My jungle surgical practice had been a great help to my knowledge. As all Malayans had to give accounts of cruelties witnessed in the Jap's regime, I had to give mine narrating of the cold and slow murder of five Chinese in black and white. I was brought for interrogation and had to repeat "I solemnly swear that my statement is nothing but the truth". Where upon, I had to identify my victims. There were about 30 Japs filed in twos, and I had simply to walk round them and had to tap them on the shoulder if I were to recognize them. Their features were sunken and some of them making themselves unrecognizable with spectacles on. I failed to recognize them at first. I asked the Major in charge of the investigation to have the permission to be allowed to identify without their spectacles which he readily complied. Bhy jove! I got my two men in the lots. I am hoping that my star with favour to find the ring-leader whose present existence remains obscured.

Two days ago, I received a letter from my mother pleading for my return to Banka Island by May. She stated that my younger brother has to continue his study by all means either in S'pore or Shanghai. It was a pathetic letter and I shall certainly leave Thailand for her. She is a good mother and it would melt me to see her depressed. I will be leaving for Banka shortly in the month of July.

By the way, please address your letter to my uncle in S'pore. I must put aside my pen now and my best regards to you.

Yours sincerely,
Lim Djin Pin

P.S. Regarding your stamps, I'll send to you as soon as I am in S'pore.

[Walter determined that he was entitled to a number of medals. He faced a surprising amount of red tape trying to actually obtain them. Examples of his telegraphic exchange with the military bureaucracy follow.]

AUGUST 29, 1952
DELHI TELE 41/613
No 06888/11/MPRS (0)
MILY TRUNK 318
Army Headquarters
Adjutant General's Branch
Medical Directorate
DHQPO NEW DELHI - 11

To- Dr. W. G. Anderson,
(Ex MZ – 23691 Capt. AMC)
U.C. Canada Mission Hospital,
RATLAM (MADHYA BHARAT)

Subject: - CAMPAIGN STARS AND MEDALS

Reference your application dated 24 Aug. 1952

Please complete the attached AFB – 2068 (Claim for Defence Medal), AFB-2070 (Claim for Campaign Stars) and IAFZ – 3014 (Claim for India Service Medal) and return to this HQ for verification and further action.

DIRECTOR OF MEDICAL SERVICES
DELHI TELE 41/613
No 06888/11/MPRS (0)
MIL TRUNK 318
ARMY HEADQUARTERS

SEPTEMBER 8, 1952
Adjutant General's Branch
Medical Directorate
DHQPO NEW DELHI – 11

To: Dr W G Anderson
(Ex MZ-23691 Capt AMC)
Ic United Church of Canada Mission Hospital,
RATLAM, MADHYA BHARAT

Subject:- CAMPAIGN STARS AND MEDALS

Reference your application dt 3 Sep 1952

You are entitled to the following Stars/Medal. These have been claimed from the Medal Section, Calcutta, and will be sent to you on receipt.

1939-45 Star

Burma Star

War Medal

You are NOT eligible for the award of Pacific Star/ and Defence Medal.

DIRECTOR OF MEDICAL SERVICES

DELHI TELEPHONE 41/613
No 06888/11MPRS (0)
MILITARY TRUNK 318
ARMY HEADQUARTERS

OCTOBER 23, 1953
ADJUTANT GENERAL'S BRANCH
DHQPO NEW DELHI- 11

To-
Dr W G Anderson
(Ex MZ-23691 Capt AMC)
1/c U.C.C. Mission Hospital
RATLAM, (M.B.)

Subject:- CAMPAIGN STARS/MEDALS

Ref. Your letter of 18 Oct. 53

The Campaign Stars/Medals admissible to you have been requisitioned from Ministry of Defence, Medal Section, CALCUTTA and are still awaited. These will be sent to you on receipt.

DIRECTOR OF MEDICAL SERVICES

[Pencilled notation, 23 years later] *Not yet received 17.8.76!! WGA*

[Walter never did receive his medals, and in preparation for this book, I had to purchase them in order to be able to include a photo for everyone to see what they looked like.]

Dr. Walter G. Anderson, civilian
November, 1948.

EPILOGUE

The story of Dr. Walter Gilray Anderson is far from being told in its entirety. I hope someday that I or one of the family members will be able to complete the story of his life as a Medical Missionary in Central India spanning from 1937 to 1976.

When Walter returned to his home in India, he and his parents travelled to Canada for a holiday before returning to his duties in India. There are many stories that have been told by various fellow missionaries and many articles written in The United Church Observer about him and written by him; one being an article about the mail delivery during the war. So many letters were written back and forth even after his parents retired in 1947 which document the many situations that Walter encountered.

Home on furlough with his parents, his niece Ann and nephew Randy, 1946.

His friendship with Dr. Robert McClure continued even after retirement for both of them. Walter also wrote articles for the India Torch touching on many subjects regarding the mission work.

Walter's mother started him collecting stamps when he was seven years old and he continued to study and collect them his entire life. He told an amusing story: his mother once thought she was doing the right thing and started to trim all the serrated edges off them which was not the right thing to do. She also made little bundles of stamps and tied them together with thread.

Walter wrote articles for various philately magazines; he found flaws in stamps and reported them. We believe he was the person who found the mistake in the stamp of Coastal Vessels of September 24, 1975 with the flag blowing one direction and the smoke from a ship blowing the opposite way. One time he was visiting a friend and the friend asked if Walter had seen a certain article in a pamphlet and he turned to a page to show Walter and then Walter pointed to the name of the author of the article, himself. He continued his love of stamp collecting and also constantly signed up for courses at Glendon College on Bayview Avenue in Toronto. He was interested in nature, architecture, the constellations and so many other topics. He continued to attend classes well into his 90's. He always rode the subway and streetcars in Toronto and collected transfers from every location he could.

Another collection he enjoyed was rocks. He would put a piece of paper with each one explaining where he had found them. Once he found a nice black stone in the shape of a heart so had the jeweller set it in gold and gave it to his sister as a gift. He loved the opera and Shakespeare plays which he had read during his POW days, thanks to a friendly Coolie who found the complete set for him.

Walter enjoyed travelling and managed to visit Australia, Alaska, Russia, China and many other places around the world including the many Provinces of Canada and many parts of the United States. He always took lots of photographs of the scenery and architecture and he would quite often be asked to show his slides of his trips at his church.

Interest, fellowship, kindness and concern were "his thing" and he was always ready to help. Walter had a phenomenal passion and curiosity for life. He would never refer to himself as "I", he always would refer to "one" does this or one sees that. He never praised or bragged about himself or his accomplishments. He was thought of by his friends and patients as "another Mother Theresa". One Indian family stated in a letter that if Dr. Anderson entered their home, their home would be holy.

His concern for the growth of the Indian Christian church was vital. He took his place in the Hindi speaking congregation and frequently was the preacher in the English speaking church.

Walter had his many rituals that stayed with him over the years. I am sure due to the fact he was far more aware of how fast diseases could spread, he would tell us that several hands had most likely touched the fruit we had bought for consumption, and so each piece was washed with soap and water very carefully before eating even the ones that the peel was not edible.

He believed in eating very slowly and never overate. He sure did enjoy his piece of pie at each dinner and even when we had a different dessert he would always mention that he liked his pie. Walter didn't mind helping out with the clean-up of the dishes but it was an extra long process with double washing and rinsing with extra hot water.

There was nothing that could compare to Indian cotton, so he found it very difficult to give up on old shirts and pyjamas even when they had worn through. He would ask me to repair them till there just wasn't any hope for them.

In approximately 1974, we purchased some land to build a cottage and Walter was home on furlough and came along to help us clear the land. He was sitting on the ground and holding a bowsaw to cut a large limb up, he stopped while half way through and looked up at me and said "If this was a leg one was amputating, one would not be allowed to stop, otherwise the saw would freeze into the leg".

He had many stories of situations during his medical years as a missionary. Walter once told a friend that during the war while using a latrine he had to lean on another person for support and that person moved the wrong way and he fell into the latrine. He said one laughs now about it but back then it was not funny. The latrines were narrow and approximately 3 – 4 feet deep.

I have tried to touch on all different subjects to show what an interesting life Walter lead. His influence will be felt for a long time and his voice will long be heard in the hearts of his people, his relatives and his friends. He is survived by his niece Ann L. Smith, the writer, and nephew John R. Goodchild and their families and his many relatives throughout Canada and the United States. That was our compassionate, bright spirited and gentle Dr. Walter G. Anderson, and we do hope you found his story interesting.

Along with his late sister Marion, who sadly passed away during the last stages of preparing this book, we thank our many friends for helping us with the deciphering of Walter's handwriting and for sharing the many stories he told them.

Ann Louise Smith

In honour of

Her Majesty Queen Elizabeth II
and
His Royal Highness The Prince Philip, Duke of Edinburgh

The Commonwealth High Commissioners in India
request the pleasure of the company of

Dr. W. G. Anderson

at a Reception on Wednesday, 25th January, 1961
from 12 noon to 1.0. p. m.
at 2, King George's Avenue, New Delhi.

R.S.V.P.
The Comptroller to the
U. K. High Commissioner.
2, King George's Avenue.
New Delhi. 2.

Lounge Suits or
National Dress

An exciting moment in Walter's life, after his return to his missionary work in India, was the opportunity in 1961 to exchange a few words, a handshake and a smile with Her Majesty, Queen Elizabeth II and His Royal Highness The Prince Philip, Duke of Edinburgh.

Walter G. Anderson, retired missionary doctor, in 1976 (wearing a tie with the Anderson tartan).

APPENDICES

For Your
Tomorrow
Canadians and the Burma Campaign
1941 – 1945
Robert H.
Farquharson

Robert H. Farquharson

These are some excerpts based on first-hand interviews with Walter G. Anderson. recorded in Robert Farquharson's book "For Your Tomorrow", reprinted with the generous permission of the author.

As Anderson remembers it, his group was concentrated into Raffles Square in central Singapore. Through February 14 and 15th they heard the incessant sounds of battle; when they awoke on the 16th there was only a frightening silence. Soon the Japanese troops entered the square and ordered the British to pile arms and stand back. Dr. Anderson managed to snatch a towel from the ruins of Raffles Department Store to add to the meager store of medical supplies in his zealously guarded Red Cross pannier. Then they were marched away to Changi prison camp. Over the gate of the camp there was a defiant sign in Latin: QUI ULTIMA RIDET OPTIMA RIDET (He who laughs last, laughs best). Anderson treasured the memory of that sign in the years that followed.

Five soldiers escaped and were recaptured. The Japanese executed them on the spot and then required that all prisoners sign an undertaking not to escape. Their own officers warned that to sign was treason. The Japanese responded by making all the prisoners sit packed together under the hot sun on one third rations until they did. For three days this stand-off continued until at last the senior British officer declared that they could sign, since any promise given under such duress need not be honoured.

After a short stay at Changi the prisoners were taken away to work on the railway. Anderson still recalls the horror of that trip. "We were crowded into metal box cars and with the sun beating down, it was like being in an oven. There was scarcely room to stand and absolutely no thought of lying down or even squatting. We were given a handful of boiled rice once a day and there were no sanitary facilities. By the end of the second day urine and feces were floating around our feet. You can imagine the stench." After three days on the train they were transferred to a launch and taken up the river to a camp housing Dutch prisoners. He was the only medical man in the camp.

The route of the Bangkok-to-Burma railway had been surveyed years earlier by the British but had been rejected because of the high hills, deep gorges and pestilent swamps. The Japanese looked again and decided that with prisoner – and slave – labour it could be done. Work began in October 1942 with a projected finish date of December 1943. Midway through a "speedo" order came from Tokyo and the line was actually completed three months ahead of schedule, a phenomenal record for rail laying, even in ideal conditions. In the end 60,000 prisoners and 279,000 slaves from Malaya, Burma and Siam toiled around the clock in 12 and 14 hour shifts under sharp eye of Korean guards who were even more brutal than their Japanese masters. For the prisoners conditions were unbelievably primitive and punishing. They lived in hastily built jungle lean-to's and ate the same meal every day, boiled rice with weevils and maggots as protein enrichment and sometimes a wee bit of salt fish or spinach or a token taste of stewed pumpkin. For the indentured workers from Malaya and Burma conditions were more deplorable. They were fed even less than the prisoners and sickness was everywhere. The usual jungle maladies of malaria, dysentery, and beriberi, intensified by malnutrition and exhaustion, were rampant but never an excuse for missing a shift at work. Even shivering, sweating, feverish malaria victims who could not get up off the sleeping shelf were beaten to their feet and sent out to break rock. Those who could not stand were required to sit in a row and pull rails into position.

Dr. Anderson protested that the "hospital" patients at least should be excused from work but the only response was to be beaten on the side of the head with a scabbarded sword. His pleas for medicines and medical supplies were scorned, though vaccine was forthcoming when cholera appeared, for the threat of cholera sent shivers of terror through the Japanese tent. His one medical success was in the treatment of the suppurating jungle sores that plagued most of the prisoners. A Dutch prisoner had presented with an ugly open carbuncle on the back of his neck. Anderson stole some kitchen scraps, rotted them in a length of bamboo and grew his own private colony of maggots. Discarding the hairy black maggots, he tweezered out the white ones, since they ate only morbid flesh, and planted them in the enflamed opening. Next day, the wound was a healthy pink.

Once the railway was finished the POWs were withdrawn, but the Malayans, Burmese and Siamese were kept on to maintain it. Anderson was kept on as well, but now he was allowed to sleep in the tent with Japanese officers. "We can't speak," his diary records, "but I am treated respectfully and there is no interference with my work." Also he now ate Nip food, "rather tasteless, but much better than coolie food, white rice, miso soup. Miso fried with onions was very good and most tasty of all (one spoonful enough for a bowl of rice)". Somehow he got hold of a copy of Shakespeare plays. He read it through twice, memorized long passages, and commented in his diary: "What a boon in this Burma jungle in the monsoon rain." The Japanese soldier in charge of the cookhouse had a Roman Catholic wife back in Japan and he surreptitiously gave Dr. Anderson a bit of Khaki cloth to patch his shirt and a pair of wooden clogs to replace his worn out Malayan running shoes. The clogs didn't last long, for the white ants ate them at night. As his captivity stretched on, Dr. Anderson saw in the repeated bombing of the railway bridges signs that the sway of war was turning against his captors. On one occasion they suffered a raid by nine Liberator bombers and he cursed and blessed the RAF as he ran around a tree trying to escape the strafing.

His afternoons were fairly free and he once wandered off, following the overgrown remnants of a fence. It led him to a row of small crosses bearing English names, the last and lost resting place for a few of the railway's many victims. He tried to clear it, but he didn't dare let the Japanese know what he was doing.

When the war ended, Anderson was called to Rangoon to testify about "good and bad Japs." His one happy memory of that time is of being able to testify positively about a Japanese sergeant interpreter who had treated them well. The man had once hummed a Negro spiritual, "Lord, I want to be a Christian," when he noticed Dr. Anderson alone with him in the area.

Walter Anderson is a gentle man and one who tries to live his Christian faith. Pressed about the brutality and torture he experienced, he diffidently tells of being forced to go down into a six foot deep grease pit near the kitchen and scoop out the filth with his bare hands while the Japanese stood round the rim and laughed at him. Bitterness is not in him, but it is easy to see that the memories are strong. With a two inch stub of a pencil he made a calendar and kept a "diary", a few scrappy notes hidden in a length of bamboo. Today he still treasures an aluminum mess tin **[see illustrations on opposite page]** that a British sergeant had etched for him. On it is the crest of the Indian Medical Corps and a few significant dates, "Singapore 5.2.1942; Prisoner of War 15.2.1942; Changi 17.2 1942; Selarang Incident 2/5.9.1942."

Prisoners who were so sick or incapacitated that they were absolutely unable to work and yet refused to die, were sent back to a "base hospital" at Chungkai, 100 KM. North west of Bangkok. Eventually the camp held 700 patients, a good many of whom owed their lives to the ministrations of Major Jacob Markowitz.

[…the story focuses on Markowitz for a page or two, and then continues...]

Dr. Anderson is reticent to tell of the horrors of the railway camps, and Dr. Markowitz does not dwell on them either . Less charitable accounts of life on the Bangkok-to-Burma railway tell sickening tales of camps flooded with rain and latrine filth, of Japanese and Korean guards who are inhumanly brutal , of starving men shaking with malaria and weak with dysentery whipped out to build a railway. For the least infraction of discipline, even for not bowing promptly or to a properly respectful angle when a Japanese soldier passed, prisoners were forced to stand all day under the searing sun holding a heavy rock above their heads, or were beaten senseless with a club. For good reason the project is called the Death Railway.

Right: Several views of the mess tin mentioned above.

THAILAND
BURMA

THAILAND
BURMA THREE PAGODA PASS
KANBURI
TAMUANG

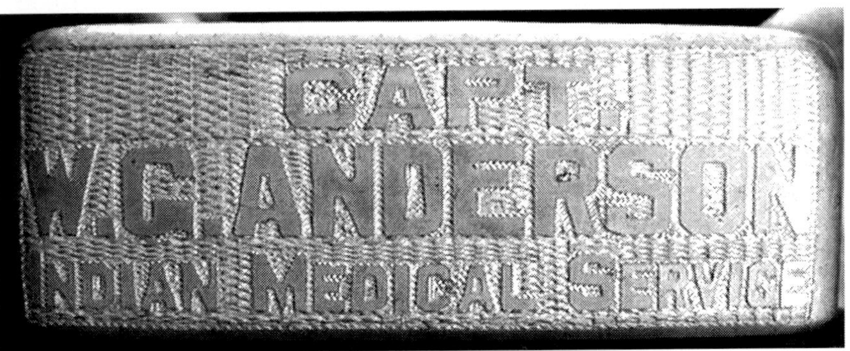
CAPT.
W.G. ANDERSON
MEDICAL SERVICE

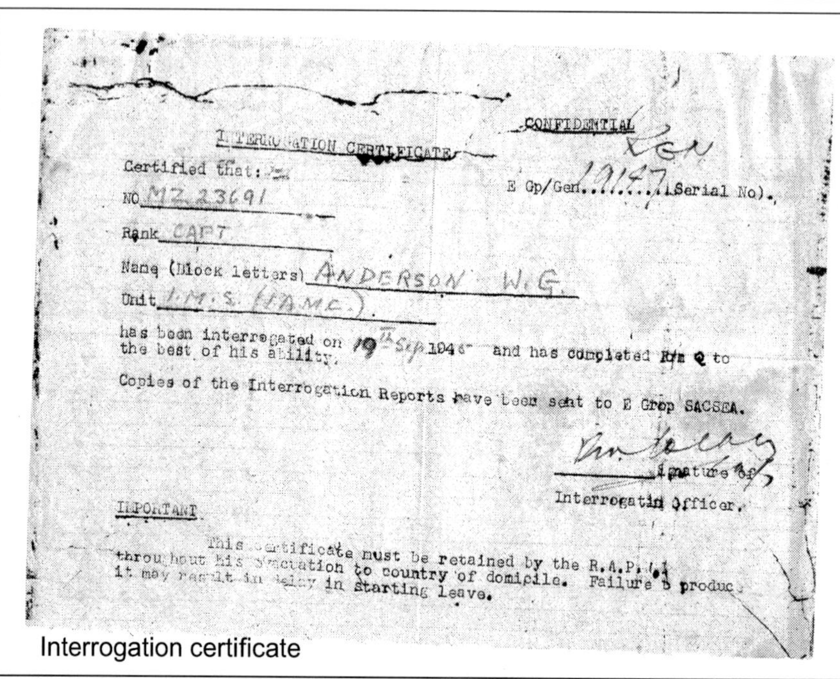

CONFIDENTIAL

INTERROGATION CERTIFICATE

Certified that:

E Gp/Gen. 19147 (Serial No).

NO MZ 23691

Rank CAPT

Name (Block letters) ANDERSON W.G.

Unit I.M.S. (I.A.M.C.)

has been interrogated on 19th Sep 1945 and has completed R/m Q to the best of his ability.

Copies of the Interrogation Reports have been sent to E Grop SACSEA.

Signature of Interrogating Officer.

IMPORTANT

This certificate must be retained by the R.A.P.W.I. throughout his evacuation to country of domicile. Failure to produce it may result in delay in starting leave.

Interrogation certificate

TEL:5

CONFIDENTIAL

HQ MHOW AREA, MHOW CI
No.122 11 A- 14 Feb 46

~~Major~~ Capt W.G.ANDERSON, IAMC
Indian Mily Hospital,
MHOW CI

Subject:- WAR CRIMES

Ref telephone conversation of today.

1. The following message has been received from HQ Central Command, Agra:-

"SUBJECT 4 CRIMINALS (.) MAJOR W.G.ANDERSON (MZ-23691) IAMC AT PRESENT ON LEAVE IN INDIA WAS WITNESS OF WAR CRIME COMMITTED BY JAPAN AGAINST SOME 150000 COOLIES ON BURMA-SIAM RAILWAY (.) ADDRESS CARE OF REV F.J.ANDERSON, DHAR CENTRAL INDIA (.) HE SHOULD BE INSTRUCTED TO REPORT TO THIS HQ FOR ANDERSON STATEMENT (.) FULLEST DETAILED INFORMATION REQUIRED TO ASSIST APPREHENSION OF THOSE RESPONSIBLE FOR MALTREATMENT AND STARVATION COOLIES (.) WIRE ETA"

2. In view of the information you gave on the telephone, it has been confirmed with Central Command that you need not proceed to AGRA at present.

3. You are requested, however, to send a written statement direct to Central Command showing what you have already done in this matter and any further information which may be of assistance.

4. On receipt of this statement, you will be advised whether any further interview is necessary.

5. As you are proceeding on release tomorrow, please ~~in where~~ also advise Central Command where you may be contacted.

Capt
SC

Copy to:-

HQ CENTRAL Command - ref your A1606 of 13 Feb 46 and telephone conversation today DAAG-Staff Capt 'A'.

DPH/Sim

Request for war crimes report.

Report on War Crimes

And related documentation

Walter was interrogated upon his release, and later asked to bear witness to his experiences during his imprisonment.

CONFIDENTIAL
INTERROGATION CERTIFICATE
Certified that:-
E Gp/Gen 19147 Serial No.
No. MZ 23691
Rank – Capt.
Name (Block letters) ANDERSON, W. G.
Unit I.M.S. (I.A.M.C.
Has been interrogated on 19th Sept. 1945 and has completed Form Q to the best of his ability.
Copies of the Interrogation Reports have been sent to E Group SAC-SEA
__________Signature of Interrogation Officer.

IMPORTANT

This certificate must be retained by the R.A.P. throughout his evacuation to country of domicile. Failure to produce it may result in delay in starting leave.

Tel: CONFIDENTIAL
Capt. W.G. Anderson, IAMC
HQ Mhow Area, Mhow, CI
Indian Mily Hospital
No. 122 11 A – 14th Feb. '46
MHOW, C.I.

Subject:- WAR CRIMES

Ref. telephone conversation of today.

1. The following message has been received from HQ Central Command, Agra:-

"SUBJECT 4 CRIMINALS (.) MAJOR W.G.ANDERSON (MZ-23691) IMAC AT PRESENT ON LEAVE IN INDIA WAS WITNESS OF WAR CRIME COMMITTED BY JAPAN AGAINST SOME 150,000 COOLIES ON BURMA-SIAM RAILWAY (.) ADDRESS CARE OF REV F.J.ANDERSON, DHAR CENTRAL INDIA (.) HE SHOULD BE INSTRUCTED TO REPORT TO THIS HQ FOR ANDERSON STATEMENT (.) FULLEST DETAILED INFORMATION REQUIRED TO ASSIST APPREHENSION OF THOSE RESPONSIBLE FOR MALTREATMENT AND STARVATION COOLIES (.) WIRE ETA"

2. In view of the information you gave on the telephone, it has been confirmed with Central Command that you need not proceed to AGRA at present.

3. You are requested, however, to send a written statement direct to Central Command showing what you have already done in this matter and any further information which may be of assistance.

4. On receipt of this statement, you will be advised whether any further interview is necessary.

5. As you are proceeding on release tomorrow, please also advise Central Command where you may be contacted.

Signature
Capt. SC
Copy to:-
HQ CENTRAL Command – ref your A1606 of 13 Feb. '46 and telephone conversation today DAAG-staff Capt 'A".

Captain Anderson's handwritten pages describing atrocities and crimes committed by his Japanese captors, aspects of his incarceration which he was reluctant to talk about with his family and friends.

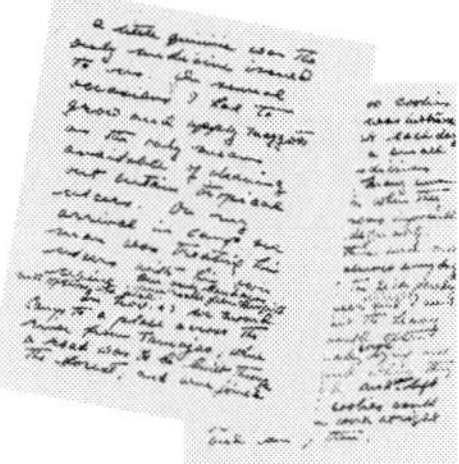

These small jottings attached to the report, as well as marginal notes within the document, are indications of the precision with which its author searched his memory for an accurate recollection.

CONFIDENTIAL

Indian Military Hospital
Mhow, Central India
H.Q. Central Command
15th, February 1946
Agra

SUBJECT: WAR CRIMES

Ref. Your A1606 of Feb.13/46 to H.Q. Mhow area, Mhow, C.I. and their No. 122 – 11.A – of Feb. 14/46 in reply (para.3)

1.. I am requested to send a written statement direct to Central Command showing what I have already done in this matter, and any further information which may be of assistance.

2. In Rangoon on 19th Sept. '45 I completed Form Q (Atrocity Sheet), for which I received and still have a signed Interrogation Certificate from the Interrogation Officer. This is numbered R.G.M. E Gp/Gen 19147 (Serial No.), and states that copies of the Interrogation Reports have been sent to E Group SACSEA.

3. In substance, the three statements I made on Form Q were as follows:- Sent from Changi POW Camp, Singapore 25.6.43 on K Force (30 MO 200 Med. Orderlies) to Siam-Burma Ry. Labour Camps.

1) Dutch P.O.W.: On 25 July '43 I was sent by the Japanese as M.O. to a small Dutch camp working on embankments for the future "Station" of Takanum, in Siam, on the new Siam-Burma railroad. This was a rush job. Great pressure was brought to bear on the Dutch troops. They were up before daylight and returned to camp so late it was difficult to see to do medical treatments. Often there were extra night shifts, and one would frequently be called out to the line to attend someone too ill to carry on work. The Camp, sited by the Japanese, was the filthiest I ever went into. The tents were unfit for use, so that many men with soaking wet day clothing (it was the monsoon season) came home to find wet clothing and bedding. Most men slept on the ground. No men were allowed to be kept in

camp for sanitation duties. There were many sick. Some of these were often driven to work if the Japanese considered there were not enough others on the job. There were nine deaths in Aug. '43 (about 150 men in camp), including one suicide. One man named Vogel was hit on the head by a Jap with a shovel, about Aug. 6th,'43, and died three days later with clinical signs of intracranial hemorrhage. The Japanese were amused at the diagnosis. I reported this case, etc. at the first opportunity, to Lt. Col. Williamson R.A., O.C., of the No. 2 Base P.O.W. camp at Takanum. Other Witnesses: - Capt. H. Jonker N.E.I.F. Camp O.C. and Capt. J. Heck N.E.I.F. (Veterinary Surgeon) –Japanese; - Lt. Aoto Military Engineers – Camp Commanders and directly responsible for conditions.

[Side note, difficult to decipher, may have errors] A boy named Kroen refused to work. He was tied to a tree all day in a loin cloth, beaten and burned with cigarette ends, died later at "Schwine" (Aoto's batman at Tamajoo)? Twice kicked Oliver on unloading train at Takanum 25.9.43 --- **[another side note]** ---Schwine on 2.9.43 hit Westhoff ?? on the head with solid bamboo for not loading train quicker. Stories of the "Bull" - …in charge of cookhouse? In Jan. '44 the Dutch were moved back down the line and this Japanese "Aoto-tai" group went on into Burma, alledgedly to Akyab. I was then transferred as M.O. to the Coolie Camp, and left with some of them on a three day march to Timonta.

2) Coolies: I was in coolie camps from Jan. '44 to March '45, being one of an all-medical party ("K" Force) sent up from Singapore to look after these people and others on railroad construction work.

a) Camp near Timonta Ry. "Station" in Siam, Jan. '44 to May '44. Majority of the 500 to 600 coolies were Tamils and Telugus, but there were also many Malays, and some Chinese – all from Malaya. Work from dawn to about an hour before sunset was on road construction parallel to the railway. Food was very poor, often only rice and dried spinach. Sweet potatoes, pumpkin and vegetable marrow were, however, given when available, also sometimes salt fish. The Indians often risked being absent from work to go off to buy extra food from Siamese villages. The Malays, being much less energetic, subsisted on the ration and developed a high percentage of beri-beri. The numbers of sick were high, some days nearly 50% remaining in camp. Deaths in Camp were 83. The Japanese clearly showed they had no use for the sick. For a period no mid-day meal was allowed to all remaining in camp. This did not deter some who chose to remain rather than put up with certain?… the Japanese in charge of parties. This particular area of forest yielded an extremely high incidence of Malaria. The Medical supplies given us were totally inadequate. Frequently after coolies had gone to work all the sick were ordered out of the huts; and the less sick-looking ones were sent off to work with reduced pay. On the work there were the usual Japanese style slappings and beatings but in our camp none serious. However, one fatality was caused (first Sunday in May '44) where some Indian Tamil boys were digging a ditch. A Japanese soldier accused one boy of playing instead of working and pushed him into the ditch. The boy was dead when brought to me by the father. Previously, this same man's (the father) brother had died of dysentery, but in his misery attempted suicide by cutting into his trachea. The Japanese promised they would report the soldier to their own H.Q. We were extremely fortunate in not having Cholera in this camp which was plentiful in other places. During Allied Air raids along the railway line coolies in this camp were slapped if they ran into the forest to hide instead of sitting in the rat trenches around the huts. (Note- In fairness I should add that in March '44 we were permitted to do our thing which I did not hear of being done in any other coolie camp – we raised a sum of money among ourselves, I made out a list of simple medical requirements, such as cotton, wool, scalpel, syringe and a few simple drugs, and Mr. Lim Djin Pin, the group Chinese dresser, was granted 10 days leave in Bangkok to make our purchases. He was able to bring back most of the articles, in spite of coming under Allied air machine-gunning along the way. Without those, especially the cotton, and wool, I do not know how we would have managed). Unfortunately, I do not know the actual names or unit of these Japanese, my dealings with them being as far as possible through a young Chinese dresser who shared the medical work with me and who could speak some Japanese. At the time I could speak no Malay. In June '44 this unit moved to

Mandalay, where at least the former camp adjutant is known to have died. Their H.Q. (Bu-Tai) in Siam had been at KonKoita.

b) Camp at "Three Pagoda Pass", kilometer 306, just inside Burma – June '44 to December '44.

This was run by Civil-Military personnel. The food was poor but the man in charge, Hanchow Hiono, happened to be of the more decent sort and all the coolies stated that at least they were treated better than in other camps. Only for a case of theft were two coolies tied up tightly to a tree for a day and night and then expelled from the camp. Slappings or beatings at work, which was railroad maintenance, were only on a very minor scale. Camps of this section of the line were controlled by Lt. Col. Konasawa at Nike, the unit being known as the Konasawa Butai. Many of the sick could be evacuated to coolie hospitals. I worked alone in this camp, living in the Japanese hut.

c) "Dai-ni coolie base hospital camp at Kanburi, Siam

I was here from 20th Dec. '44 to 6th April '45. During this period our scattered medical party ("K" Force and a second party "L" Force), were gradually being collected prior to being returned to a P.O.W. camp. In charge was a Japanese Major, head of "Hombu", who controlled the medical work of all the coolie camps up the railway line. We called him "Poppy". The coolie patients were fairly well treated, the light sick being taken for walks to the river to bathe, and bring back bits of firewood. They were only fed two poor meals a day, though there was a canteen for those who had money. While I was there two despondent coolies committed suicide the same night – one lying on the railway track and the other hanging himself in the latrine trench whom we saw and reported. Such things were not infrequent.

We ourselves were treated here very much as P.O.W. – servants to the hospital camp. We were not allowed to speak to the coolies. Working parties (British, Australian and Dutch) with no M.O.'s in charge, dug latrines and graves, built bamboo huts, carried bamboo and bags of rice, etc. One Japanese named Scumado was noted for bashing both men and M.O. in charge on his working parties. The men had long distances to walk to work on stoney roads without adequate footwear, many barefooted. The food ration was unnecessarily bad. One Dutch M.O. was bashed by the Jap. Serg. Maj. for privately treating a coolie boy.

Many statements have been made about our treatment here from "Poppy" and his staff by others longer in the camp than myself: e.g. Maj. R. Crawford, J.V.E., O.C. "K" Force, Lt. Col. Benson, RAMC, O.C. "L" Force.

3). Personal: Early in Aug. '43 I was taken from my Dutch camp at Takanum to nurse a Japanese soldier cholera case, in a Jap. Camp some 4 kilometres away, for nearly a week. I was made to give my own individual mosquito net to the cholera patient, and had to live in a segregated tent with a proven Jap. Cholera carrier. I was also general chore boy to the whole group of Jap. contacts. This risk of infection, with so much cholera about at that time, was quite unnecessary. The Japanese camp … at Bangan, between Takanum and Brankasi, commanded by 2/Lt. Shemidzer of the military engineers and the Jap. Doctor in medical charge was 2/Lt. Ida. I was alone in this camp.

Illustrating the attitude taken by Lt. Aoto, commanding the Dutch camp mentioned in Para. (1); once in Oct. '43 when I asked him for permission to send six more Dutch sick to a P.O.W. hospital, knowing that we were to move camp and these men would be unable to work for a long time, I was struck on the head with a sheathed sword. These are small things of little consequences, but they show how little time and regard the Japanese have for the sick.

4. The above statements re: coolies and Dutch, where I was M.O., I have also made to Maj. R. Crawford, Johore Volunteer Engineers, O.C. of "K" Force (Address: 25 Kingsford Ave., Muirend, Glasgow), who in Aug. '45 was compiling information re: treatment of coolies, etc., witnessed by members of his Force. Witnesses to (2) (a) are:-

1. Lt.Col. G. Walls, Jr. RAOC, Colville Terrace, Crossgate, Fife, Scotland

2. Mr. Lim Djin Pin (Chinese dresser), 66 Bras Basa Rd., Singapore
3. Mr. Adanan Bin Raji (Malay overseer of coolies) of 14 Burma Rd., Singapore

5. As from 16th Feb. '46 I shall be on release leave in India – address: c/o Rev. F.J. Anderson, Dhar, C.I. – where I may be contacted if any further interview is necessary.

Signed W.G. Anderson Capt. I.M.S./ I.A.M.C.

[Attached on a separate piece of paper was the following.]

A little quinine was the only medicine issued to us. On several occasions I had to grow and apply maggots as the only means available of cleansing out certain tropical ulcers. On my arrival in camp one man was treating his ulcers with his own urine. Our only bandages were made from mosquitoe nets of those who had died.

In Nov. '43 we moved camp to a place across the river from Tamajao, where a road was to be built through the forest, and were joined by some 200 – 300 coolies from Malaya. I was instructed to attend their sick each day, only at 5 PM and a small assortment of medicines were provided. Many were in poor condition when they arrived and it was impossible to treat them adequately. During Dec. '43 there were one or two deaths almost every day. Each day after the sick parade, a Chinese overseer (now dead) and I went around to visit the heavy sick and would often discover the dead, some lying out on the ground where they had crawled and were left till the other coolies could return from work at night and bury them.

INDIAN POST AND TELEGRAPHS DEPARTMENT
From AGRA
TO: Capt. W. G. Anderson
c/o Rev. F.J. Anderson Dhar, C.I.
A1770 (.) Your statement of 15th Feb. read (.) GHQ confirm sworn statement rec'd (.) Please report DJAG Central Command Agra earliest (.) Advise estimated time arrival (.) 211430FF
Centcom
Col. Kerin -- DJAG

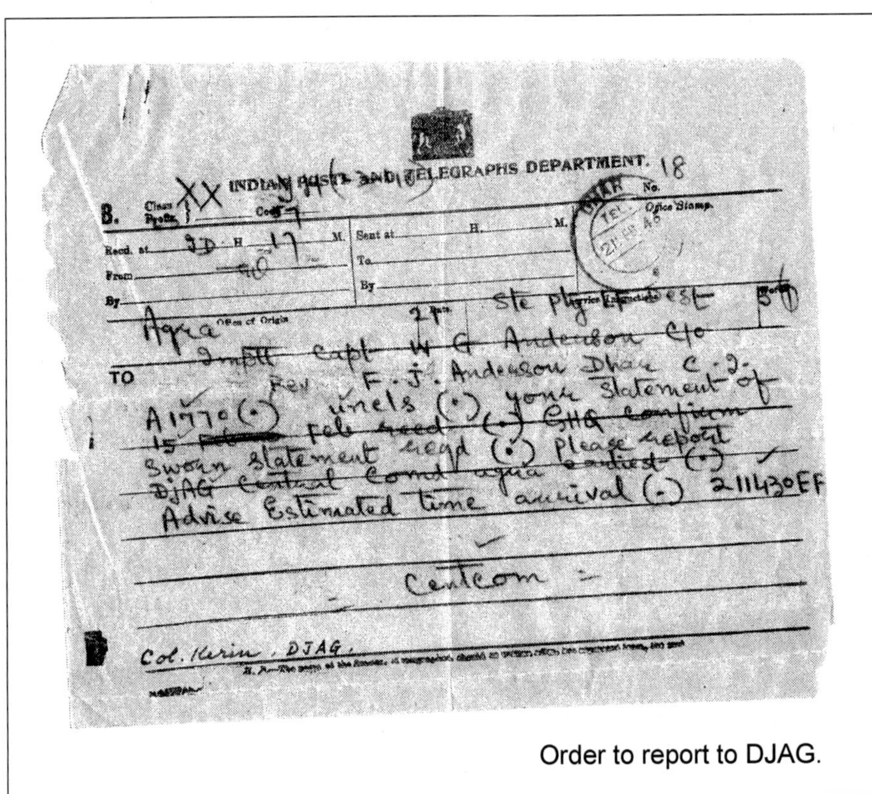
INDIAN POSTS AND TELEGRAPHS DEPARTMENT. 18
No.
Office Stamp
Recd. at
From
By
Sent at H. M.
To
By
Agra Office of Origin
TO Capt W G Anderson c/o Rev F. J. Anderson Dhar C.I.
A1770 (.) your statement of 15 Feb read (.) GHQ confirm sworn statement recd (.) Please report DJAG Central Comd Agra earliest (.) Advise Estimated time arrival (.) 211430FF
Centcom
Col. Kerin, DJAG.

Order to report to DJAG.

A Sampling of What Some Friends and Fellow Missionaries Wrote to Honour Their Friend and Colleague

Comments from Missionary Rev. Muriel Stephenson

Dr. Walter Anderson was the doctor at Ratlam Christian Hospital, on the Christian compound in Ratlam, M.P. India for several years after Dr. Bob McClure retired and returned to Canada. I was a Missionary in the field of Education and Evangelism and had the privilege to know Dr. Walter as a missionary colleague. We had many social evenings in our homes with other Canadian missionaries as well as Indian colleagues and friends. Dr. Walter was always a very good host and conversationalist. He was up to date on world news and items of interest. He had a quiet demeanor, was very approachable and was very kind and gentle in nature. Dr. Anderson had a good rapport with everyone – Christian and non-Christian alike. Having been born in India he was very fluent in the Hindi language. With his deep faith in God he was able to minister to patients with God's grace, love and wisdom which in itself helped to bring healing. We praise God for his great service in the medical field in India. I am grateful to God for the joy that was mine in being associated with Dr. Anderson in Ratlam, India for quite a number of years.

Rev. Muriel Stephenson

Comments from Missionary Rev. Earl Leard

Many times when I would be going through Ratlam and needed a place to stay overnight, I always stayed with Walter. Walter returned to his native land, India, to live out his faith and to serve the people he loved. India was important to him and he became important to the people. Walter will be remembered with respect and affection by those privileged to know him and work with him, and by his many Indian friends, from the Maharajah of Ratlam and his family, to the lowliest villagers. He was at ease in his gracious ways with all members of the community. On their behalf, it is my privilege to say Thanks be to God! For this cultivated, gentle, humble and perceptive man of God who dedicated his life to the people of India.

Grace, peace and joy to his family and closest friends as they celebrate his remarkable life.

Yes, indeed, Thanks be to God!

Rev. Earl Leard

Comments From Missionary Rev. Fred Cline

My wife and I knew and respected Walter Anderson during our years in India. In fact we lived together in Banswara for some time. We always admired his great command of the Hindi language, of course, since he grew up learning and speaking it as a child. Many of us encouraged him to marry, and he had many opportunities, but somehow it never worked out. Walter was a quiet man, the very opposite to the boisterous Dr. Robert McClure, who took over the hospital from him in Ratlam. Dr. Anderson often spoke to us about the terrible experiences during the Second World War in the Japanese prisoner of war camps. Many of the men never made it through, but Walter was a survivor. Having lived in India most of his life he took on the Hindu approach of not taking a life. I remember him telling me how in medical school he couldn't face killing a frog for dissection and would have his fellow students do it. Walter was a kindly man who gave himself fully to the medical work. He had a great love of travelling to see new places and went on several trips with us to Israel and Europe. He lived out his Christian life in service to others. Not one to talk much about his faith but showing it through service to others. We are grateful to have known him and our lives are richer because of it, as are the lives of countless Indian folk.

Fran and Fred Cline

John H. Talman:

The Bridge on The River Kwai

The man who introduced Bob McClure to the Rotary Club was Dr. Walter G. Anderson, who was in charge of the Ratlam Mission Hospital in India. In 1954, Dr. Anderson went on a furlough and Bob ran that hospital until 1967.

Dr. Anderson is now about 90 years old, with very young ideas, and lives in Toronto. We are both members of the Toronto Stamp Collectors Club which usually meets at the Military Institute once a month during most of the year. Sadly, for us, he is no longer a Rotarian. I am writing this to hopefully coincide with our Remembrance Day Program and the memory of those who served in the wars. Here is a brief outline of Dr. Anderson's service.

My friend Dr. Walter Anderson was the Mission Doctor at Ratlam starting in 1937. This was soon interrupted by the events of the Second World War. He joined the Indian Army Medical Corps and was posted to Singapore in time to be taken prisoner by the Japanese. He was originally sent to a Dutch P.O.W. Camp but after a year was sent, as part of a Medical Reinforcement Group, to one of the infamous camps along the River Kwai. His responsibility was to keep the forced labour (Prisoners of War and Native Labour) workers healthy enough to keep working. At one point he asked the commanding Lieutenant if he could send more prisoners to hospital. Tapping the Doctor on the head with his sword, the officer stated that, if too many men went to hospital, the Doctor would have to get out and do the manual work. The NCO would visit the Sick Bay daily and with a flick of his switch would say this one or that one must get up and go out to work. Dr. Anderson recalls one small prisoner being pushed into a pit and rupturing a spleen and eventually dying in the poor conditions of the Camp.

After the rail line was built he spent time in native labour camps where he was the only white person. At the end of the war he was in such a camp in Thailand. He had been a prisoner for three years and six months.

Later, he was to visit Japan. He found much in common with the people, but there were very few young people in the streets. It was at this point in time that he found forgiveness.

Written by John H. Talman for the Rotary Club of Toronto in 1997.

Glossary of Illnesses & Diseases during WW II

Beriberi

A severe form of Vitamin B deficiency which has been widespread, particularly in the Orient. During the war years a lot of rice was the main food distributed among the POW's. It was the process of conversion from brown rice to white that removed the Vitamin B (Thiamine). Symptons were weakness, numbness and derangements in nervous and cardiac functions.

Conjunctivitis

Also known as "Pink Eye", increase of blood in a part or an area, hemorrhage or injury. Infections beneath the upper lid and cannot be exposed to view unless the lid is turned out.

Dysentery

An inflammatory disease of the large intestines which generally results in diarrhea, cramps and fever. Dysentery is usually caused by toxins in spoiled food or a virus in water.

Enteritis

This is an acute inflammation mainly of the lining of the small bowel, but not throughout the entire intestinal tract. It is due to irritants contained in food, such as unripe fruit, or formed in the digestive tract as a result of indigestion.

Malaria

Malaria is transmitted by several species of mosquitoes. It causes fever, chills, headaches, nausea, generalized aches and pains. Different strains and species of Malaria produce different symptoms. Treated with anti-malarial drugs but the disease can recur over and over.

Neuritis

Neuritis means inflammation of a nerve. There are many different causes such as diabetes, arthritis of the spine, alcoholic excess and vitamin deficiency, drug toxicity, and a variety of other infections. Neuritis can cause partial paralysis in the hands and feet. Heat to painful muscles and pain killing drugs are used along with bed rest. Physiotherapy is needed after the acute stage is over to restore functions in paralyzed muscles.

Pellagra

This disease is produced by a lack of Vitamin B3, called niacin, a vitamin which the body requires from outside sources because it cannot produce it by itself. This disease is prominent in countries where corn or rice are the basic food.

Pemphigus

The lesions of this disease consist of discrete blisters which occur on normal appearing skin, enlarge and finally break, leaving stretched sacs. This disease is of unknown cause and is almost invariably fatal unless treated with a cortisone drug.

Dengue

This is similar to Malaria, fever, headaches, severe pain, red rash, dizziness, bleeding nose and loss of appetite.

The following are articles written by Dr. Walter G. Anderson after his return to Canada in 1976.

Summary of PoW Period Under The Japanese in Singapore and Siam,

3 ½ years: February 15th, 1942 to August 16th, 1945

15th March 1941: Lieutenant in the Indian Medical Service (Indian Army Medical Corps.) – joining at Poona, India. In September 1937 I had gone out to India from Toronto to engage in medical work under the United Church of Canada Overseas Missions Board. My parents and grandparents were Canadian born, and my parents engaged in Canadian Mission work in India for 47 years where I was born. I returned later to Canada for education and training.

After serving with the Indian Military Hospitals at Sangor and Jubbulpore I was posted overseas to Malaya with routine reinforcements arriving in Singapore on 5th Feb. 1942 and attached to the U.I.B.C. On 15th Feb. 1942 Singapore fell to the Japanese and all troops became PoW.

Feb. 1942 to May 1943 – served as M.O. [Medical Officer] to various 11th Indian Division British Groups within the main PoW camp at Changi, Singapore Island. Apart from a mild attack of Enteritis and the new effects of a total rice diet, I was fortunate in not having any other health disturbances during this period. Acute dysentery, diphtheria and deficiency diseases were common in the camp, and we had all undergone a short punishment period of acute concentration known as the Selerang Incident.

In June 1943 to Jan. 1944 I was taken from duty up into Thailand with the Medical. Party 'K' Force as M.O. to a camp of Dutch PoW's from Java who were working on construction of the Siam-Burma railroad in the Thailand Jungle. Here I first contracted Malaria, which was to recur for the next 6 years. Pressure from the Japanese; mental and physical was the greatest of the whole PoW period, and since the railroad had to be completed by schedule (all hand labour) to carry their war supplies and troops into Burma. Malaria, dysentery, tropical ulcers, malnutrition and exhaustion without any medical supplies from the Japanese, caused many deaths, and it was made worse by the monsoon weather in the tropic jungle which created appalling conditions in the camp.

January 1944 to March 1945 – I was M.O. with various Malayan native conscript labour camps doing railroad maintenance for the Japanese. Part of this time I lived with Japanese in Burma and consequently had better food. Malaria kept recurring. Harrassment was not so great once the railway and jungle roads were completed.

March 1945 to 16th August 1945 – Final period in large allied PoW camps at Taiwan and in eastern Thailand, at Prachi near Sraburi when war ended.

With cessation of hostilities, evacuation was by air from Bangkok to Rangoon, and thence by ship to India. After some leave and service at Mhow Indian Military Hospital, I was released from the Indian Army on Feb. 15th, 1946, and returned to former services with the Canadian Mission. Malarial attacks recurred until 1949.

Dr. W. G. Anderson

Mail Delivery Problems from India to P.O.W. in Japanese Occupied S.E. Asia

Mail delivery to Prisoners of War in Japanese occupied Singapore and Thailand during W.W. II was difficult, to say the least. Forwarding of mail to military prisoners who, in Japanese traditional thinking, should not exist, seemed to be a matter of no importance, and it took months to arrange for handling, censoring and delivery of mail to large P.O.W. camps. Meanwhile, P.O.W. from Singapore were being dispersed all over the S.E. Asia region to work on Japanese military projects, most notably building the jungle railway line alongside the Kay Noi river in Thailand and over the border Three Pagodas Pass into Burma.

There were also mail forwarding problems in India. Mail service to Malaya was no longer possible and for a time letters were returned to sender. Much later there came to be a P.O.W. mail service through the Japanese Red Cross in Tokyo, however reliable it might be.

Later on in the War, when communications between Japan and its distant war areas were being damaged severely by the Allied war effort in the Pacific, P.O.W. mail service virtually ceased and letters from India addressed to Thailand etc., were again returned to sender.

At the War's end, with so many Recovered Allied Prisoners of War and Internees (RAPWI) returning by sea for various destinations, there was naturally some confusion in mail delivery to individuals, and letters whose addressees could not be traced were sent to the D.L.O. For instance, from the RAPWI Mail Centre in Bombay, some mail was sent by air to Army Post in Columbo to connect there with a repatriation ship going to the west. Mail for an addressee found to be 'Not on Board" was returned to the D.L.O. Bombay.

On the Japanese side, there were at least three occasions when P.O.W. could send mail messages out: twice from Changi in Singapore and once at least from camps in Thailand. These were cards with several printed messages, such as "I am well and working for pay" and "I am sick and in hospital" etc. Only two of these messages could be retained and the rest struck out.

Fortunately for the addressee in India, the sender of the P.O.W. covers illustrated, on all three occasions, Japanese cards were safely delivered, the last one, however, being in July 1944, more than a year before the war ended.

The following are a few examples of covers illustrating some of the problems encountered. These are addressed to and eventually were received by the same fortunate individual and are therefore in relative sequence through the Singapore-Thailand war period.

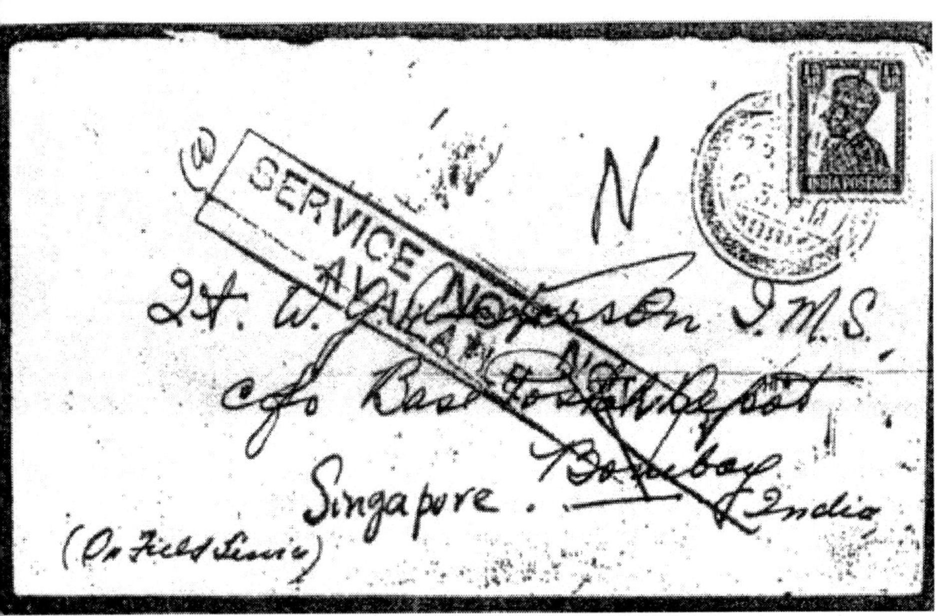

COVER I: Posted 23 January 1942 from Dhar, Central India, to Base Postal Depot, Bombay, for forwarding 'On Field Service'. Inland postage rate was 1a.3ps. At the Base, the addressee's destination was found to be Singapore, which was entered in red ink. On 30th August 1942 the letter was returned to sender through the Dead Letter Offices in Bombay and Nagpur and was stamped across in no uncertain way that for Singapore, 'SERVICE NOT NOW AVAILABLE'. It was finally received by the addressee in September 1945, after the war. Singapore fell to the Japanese on 15th February 1942. The Japanese surrender was exactly three and a half years later, on 15th August 1945.

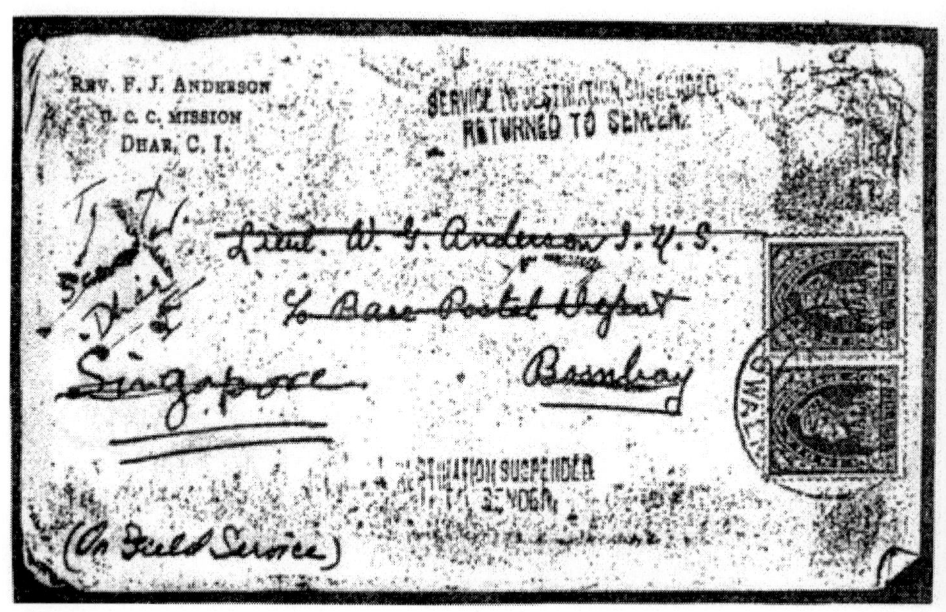

COVER II: Mailed to Base Postal Depot, Bombay, on 29th January 1942 and returned 16th July 1942 stamped 'SERVICE TO DESTINATION SUSPENDED/RETURNED TO SENDER'. Interestingly this letter was mailed in Gwalior State territory and bears five KGVI 3ps. over-printed Gwalior stamps, three being on the back.

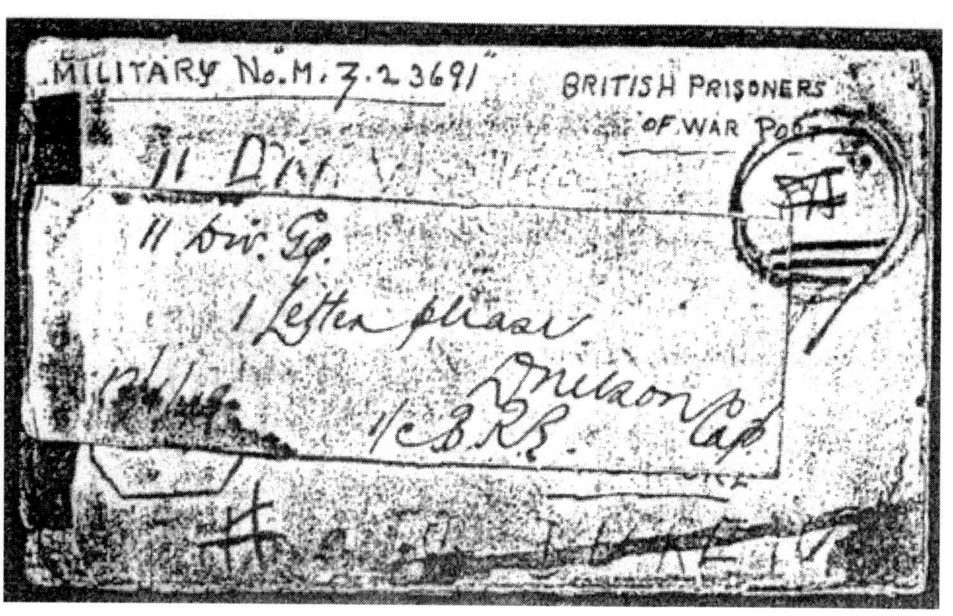

COVER IIA: This cover illustrates one early process of identifying mail for forwarding to a P.O.W. area, and postage not required. The letter was posted in Indore on 31st October 1942 and addressed 'Serving Last at Singapore'. It passed Censor DHP/9 and was sent to the Bureau of Records for checking. Somewhere along the way a loose flap of instruction or request was attached and tied with a heavy blue pencil circle. Two small red corner area markings were stroked out with blue, and !! Div added (Eleventh Indian Division). This unit was correct and the letter was eventually received by the addressee in Changi P.O.W. Camp, Singapore, on 18th April 1943. The route taken is not indicated. The letter is rather soiled since it was carried about for the rest of the war period under some extraordinary circumstances.

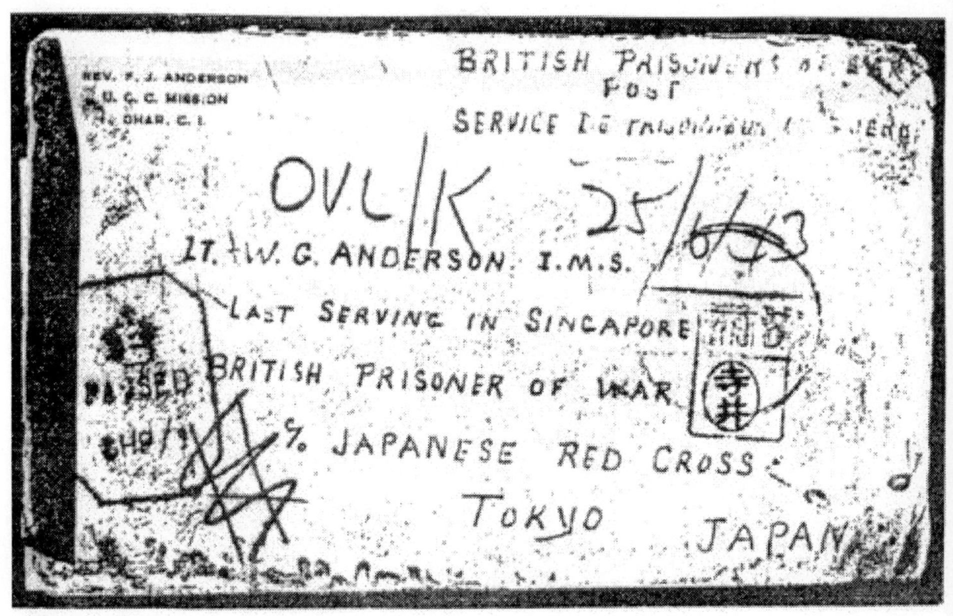

COVER III: Mailed 25th December 1942, stampless P.O.W. mail, c/o Japanese Red Cross, Tokyo, and bears three Japanese markings of which the small oval is a personal official seal. This letter was received by addressee on 27th December 1944, in Thailand.

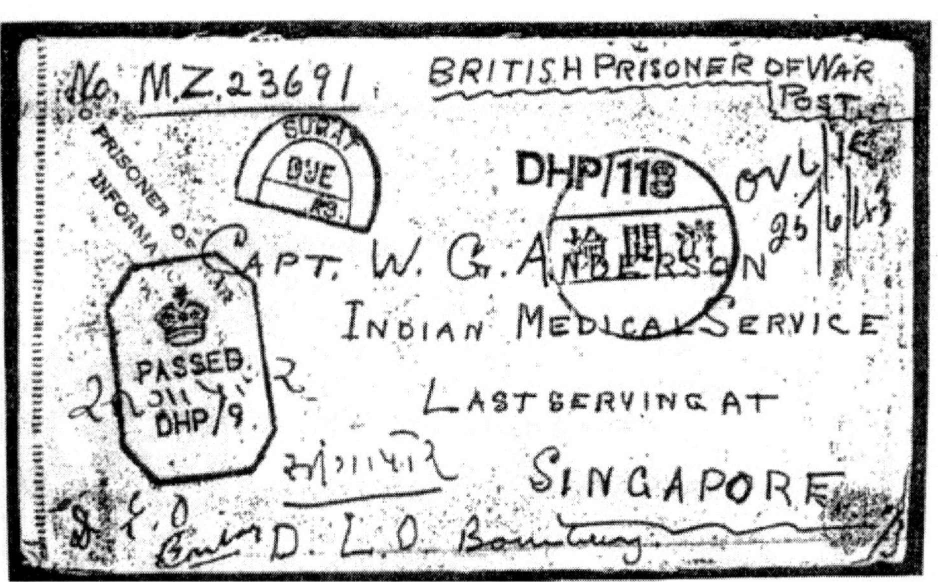

COVER IV: Posted at Mount Abu 17th June 1943. There are five Surat P.O. stampings on the back and a Surat/Due on the front. Being addressed to Singapore, the letter must have perplexed this P.O. since destination was rewritten in Hindi and the letter sent to D.L.O. Bombay. However, after censoring, it was forwarded c/o Prisoner of War Information Bureau, Tokyo, and finally received by addressee on 27th December 1944 in Thailand, where undelivered mail had accumulated.

Soon after the fall of Singapore, a long list of all P.O.W. was compiled and the Japanese ordered that thereafter no changes in military rank could be made. Somehow the Japanese lost this list and ordered a new one to be made! Consequently officers with time promotion due were able to appear promoted on the new list and eventually a copy was made available to Allied Command. This cover indicates that the addressee was thus duly promoted to Captain!

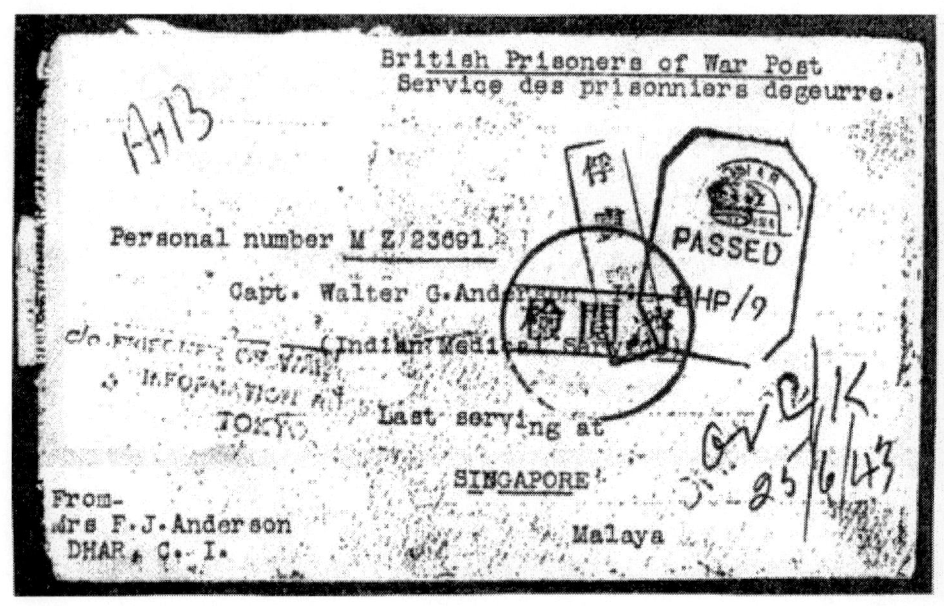

COVER V: Mailed at Dhar, C.I., on 29th September 1943 and received in Thailand also on 27th December 1944. It bears a different type of Japanese handstamp.

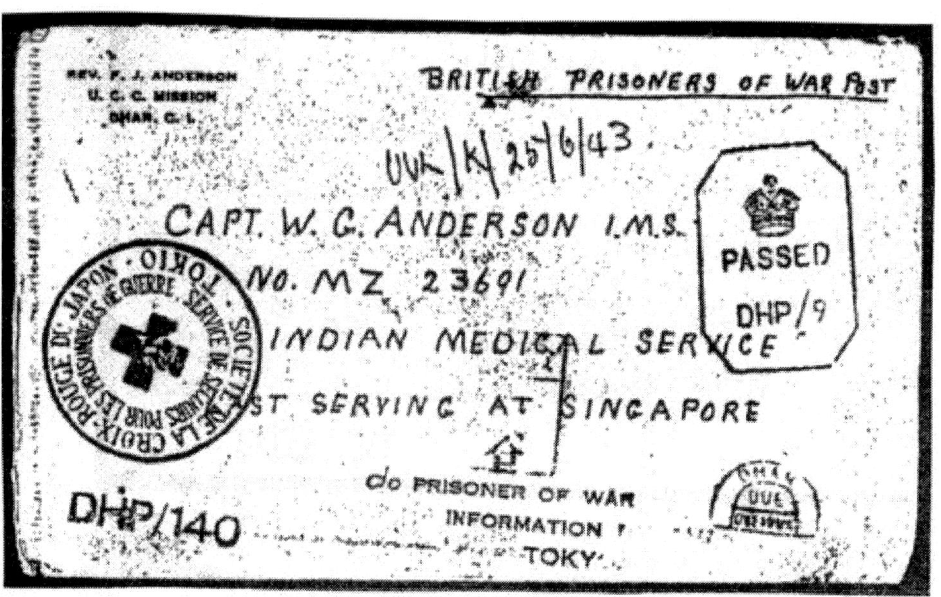

COVER VI: Mail on 14th November 1943, with Dhar Due One Anna. It bears a large red circular handstamp of the Japanese Red Cross Society, Service to Help Prisoners of War, Tokyo – in French. Received by addressee on 2nd September 1945, soon after the war's end.

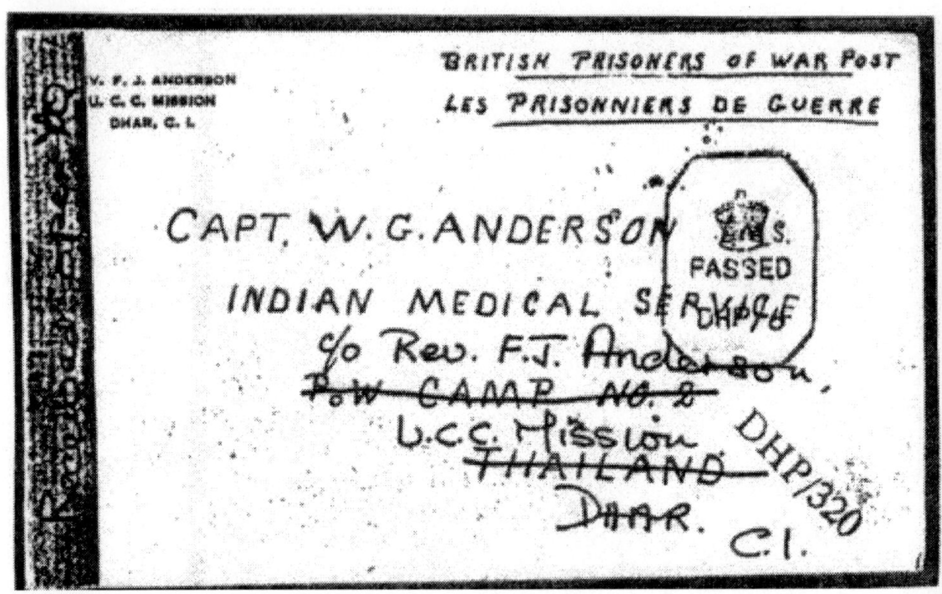

COVER VII: Posted in Dhar on 15th April 1945 and addressed to P.O.W. Camp No.2, Thailand, but returned to sender. Received by addressee on 5th December 1945, after the war. One double circle stamp on the back is 305/4 Dec. 45. This '305' office stamp appears on the back of a number of covers at this time.

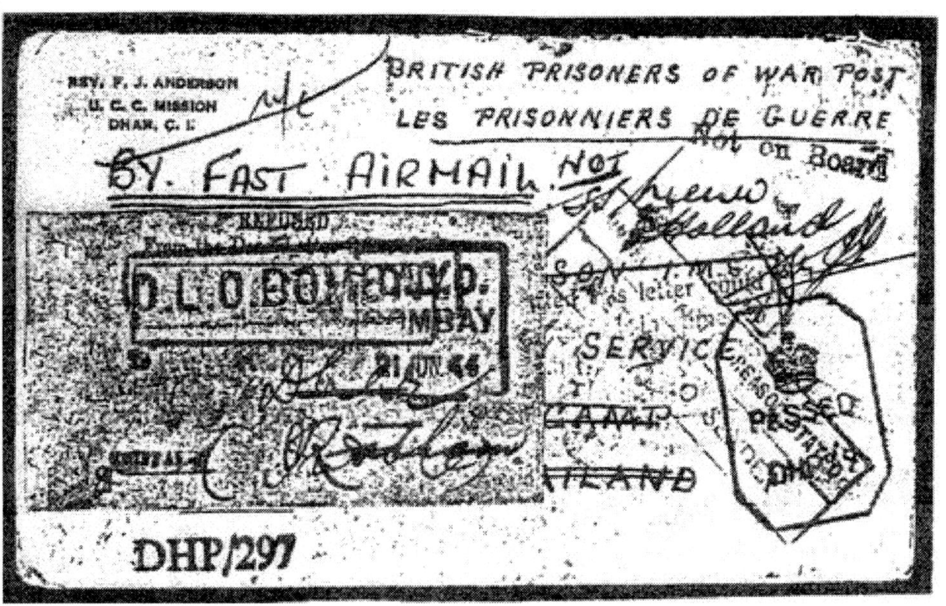

COVER VIII: Mailed 7th August 1945, just a week before the Japanese surrender, and addressed to Thailand. With the war soon ended, and as arrangements could be made, Allied Recovered Prisoners of War and Internees (RAPWI) began returning from the war area to Europe and India, this letter was sent by Fast Air Mail to RAPWI Army Post, Colombo, c/o the repatriation ship S.S. Niew Holland. Since the addressee was 'Not On Board", it was handstamped 'It is regretted this letter could not be forwarded in time to connect with…(illegible)' and 'Undelivered for reasons stated/Return to sender', and was sent to D.L.O. Bombay. On 21st June 1946, the letter was returned to Dhar, from where it was forwarded through Indore to Ratlam, where addressee finally received it on 26th June 1946!

COVER IX: Letter of 19th September 1945 from Dhar, one month after war ended, addressed directly to Recovered P.O.W. Mail Centre, Bombay, and requiring one and a half annas postage rate. With the continuing problem of trying to locate individuals, and unaware that this addressee had returned by a ship from Rangoon to Madras, the letter was sent by air to connect with a ship through RAPWI, Army Post, Colombo. Not being on board, the letter was stamped 'No Record of Repatriation of Addressee' and was returned to D.L.O. Bombay on 10th March 1946. It was forwarded to sender in Dhar and received on 14th March 1946.

(Illustrations are all reduced to 80% of originals.)

First published in the INDIA POST, the quarterly of the India Study Circle for Philately, October/November 1988.

Acknowledgments

My sincere thanks to my dear departed Mum (Marion L. Anderson/Goodchild) for all her work on deciphering my Uncle Walter's writings. Her brother's writings were very small with lots of abbreviations to allow more space since it was so difficult to get another notebook.

Also, our appreciation goes out to Mum's friend Stan Quinn, from the Retirement Home in Brooklin, Ontario, who constantly encouraged me to write this book and was a tremendous help in deciphering Walter's writings.

I can't thank my very good friend Wayne Ireland enough. He helped with maps and proofreading and above all was beyond patient with me through the stress of reading through stacks and stacks of papers, sorting, sometimes misplacing papers and photos and notes. He kept me calm and on track through the long hours I spent working well into the night to complete one or another section of this volume.

I am grateful as well to Dean Owen, who said he would be glad to help in any way he could, as he has a broad range of knowledge and many connections with military people. He was in the army for ten years, and is a historian, tutorial advisor for many books of military history, has worked with groups in Canada, USA and the UK. He has also consulted on many movies, supplying them with paraphernalia from his large collection of military articles. He has written a book on military slang terminology which I'm sure would be very interesting to read. Dean was so kind to take time in his very busy schedule to look up information for me, and advise me where I could find certain materials on the internet. Thank you so much, Dean.

My many thanks to Bill and Sarina Bayer who were good friends of my Uncle Walter and who are volunteers and travel back to India periodically. They know a lot of the terminology from India and kindly shared their knowledge with me along with the help of another missionary named Lillias Brown. Sarina was born in India and was adopted by Dr. Mina MacKenzie who worked in India as a medical doctor from 1904 – 1940. She is the president of the Dr. Mina MacKenzie Memorial Trust Fund. She adopted 40 children while working in India. The Bayers are always happy to find folks who will adopt a child and send funds to help with their education, which my Mum has done for several years now.

I must not forget to thank Andrea Percy who suggested Kaca Henley to help me with the book as my editor and to her partner, Charles Cooper who had so many wonderful suggestions and guided me to various locations on the Internet for information.

My sincere thanks to Robert H. Farquharson for allowing me to include his article about Walter from his book "For Your Tomorrow". And, also my appreciation goes out to John H. Talman for his permission to quote what he wrote about Walter for the Rotarian's Remembrance Day program in 1997.

I can't find the right words to express how grateful I am to Kaca Henley for guiding me along the way and building my confidence to complete this project. It has been a lot more work than we first realized and I appreciate all the long hours spent. Thank you so much Kaca.

Thanks to all my close friends who put up with my constant chatter about what I was working on at the time.

I wanted our relatives to see all the material that had been stored for so many years; letters, documents, photos and mostly the journal or diary that he took time to write during his terrible ordeal. Having a book in one's possession will be a much nicer way to share this history with future members of our own family and friends.

Ann Louise Smith
Lindsay, Ontario, Autumn 2008

I drew this sketch of my Uncle Walter, with his benign smile and gentle gaze, as he looked in his later years, and this is how I remember him best.

Ann L. Smith
23 Park Cres. R.R. 1
Lindsay Ontario
K9V 4R1